Manifest Destinies and Indigenous Peoples

Edited by David Maybury-Lewis, Theodore Macdonald,
and Biorn Maybury-Lewis

Published by Harvard University David Rockefeller Center for Latin
American Studies

Distributed by Harvard University Press
Cambridge, Massachusetts
London, England
2009

Library of Congress Cataloging-In-Publication Data

Manifest destinies and indigenous peoples / edited by David Maybury-Lewis,
   Theodore Macdonald, and Biorn Maybury-Lewis.

   p. ; cm.

   Papers presented at an interdisciplinary seminar on May 5–6, 2006 at Harvard
University, David Rockefeller Center for Latin American Studies.
   Includes bibliographical references and index.
   ISBN: 978-0-674-03313-9

1. Messianism, Political—History. 2. America—Territorial expansion—19th
century. 3. Nationalism—History—19th century. 4. Indigenous peoples—
America—History. I. Maybury-Lewis, David. II. Macdonald, Theodore. III.
Maybury-Lewis, Biorn. IV. David Rockefeller Center for Latin American Studies.

JC314 .M36 2009
320.12/01812

Contents

About the Contributors

José Bengoa is a Professor at the Departments of Anthropology and History at the Universidad Academia de Humanismo Cristiano of Santiago, Chile. He specializes in the culture and history of the indigenous people of Chile. Among his many books on that subject are: *Historia del pueblo mapuche,* 7th ed. 2008; *Historia de los antiguos mapuches del sur,* 2nd ed. 2007; *Historia de un conflicto,* 3rd. ed. 2007; and *La emergencia indígena en América Latina,* 2nd ed. 2007. In the more general realm of cultural commentary he has contributed many articles and books, the latest being *La comunidad reclamada* (2nd ed. 2008). He has been a visiting professor at, among others, University of Indiana, University of Paris, Leiden University, and the Universidad Complutense of Madrid. Outside the academy, he was a member of the Human Rights Subcommittee and the Working Group on Minorities of the United Nations. In 2008 he was elected independent member of the UN Consulting Committee for Human Rights.

Claudia N. Briones is Professor of Anthropology at the University of Buenos Aires, and Researcher of the National Council for Scientific and Technological Research (CONICET), Argentina. Her primary research areas are indigenous movements, rights and policy; differentiated citizenships and national formations of alterity in Argentina; kinship, knowledge and politics of the Mapuche people. Her most recent publications include *La Alteridad del Cuarto Mundo. Una deconstrucción antropológica de la diferencia* (1998), *Contemporary Perspectives on the Native Peoples of Pampa, Patagonia, and Tierra del Fuego: Living on the Edge* (co-edited with J. Lanata, 2002), *Metacultura del estado-nación y estado de la metacultura* (2005), and *Cartografías Argentinas. Políticas indigenistas y formaciones provinciales de alteridad* (editor, 2005).

J. Edward Chamberlin was born in Vancouver, and educated at the universities of British Columbia, Oxford, and Toronto. Since 1970, he has been on the faculty of the University of Toronto, where he is now University Professor of English and Comparative Literature. He has lectured widely on literary, historical, and cultural issues; and he was an advisor to the Mackenzie Valley Pipeline Inquiry and the Alaska Native Claims Commission, Senior Research Associate with the Royal Commission on Aboriginal Peoples, and has worked on native land claims in Canada, the United States, Africa and Australia. His books include *The Harrowing of Eden: White Attitudes*

Towards Native Americans (1975), *Ripe Was the Drowsy Hour: The Age of Oscar Wilde* (1977), *Come Back To Me My Language: Poetry and the West Indies* (1993), *If This Is Your Land, Where Are Your Stories? Finding Common Ground* (2003), and *Horse: How the Horse Has Shaped Civilizations* (2006).

Walter Delrio teaches Anthropology and History at the University of Buenos Aires. He is Researcher of the National Council for Scientific and Technological Research (CONICET), Argentina. His primary research areas are ethnohistory and historical anthropology of South American indigenous peoples with focus on white-Mapuche relationships both in Chile and Argentina. He authored *Memorias de Expropiación. Sometimiento e Incorporación Indígena en la Patagonia* (Editorial de la Universidad de Quilmes, 2005). He is coordinator of the Red de Investigadores sobre el Genocidio y la Política Indígena del Estado Argentino.

Theodore Macdonald is a Fellow at Harvard University's Committee on Human Rights Studies, and a Lecturer in Anthropology and Social Studies. From 1979 until 1992 he was Projects Director for Cultural Survival, and then served as Associate Director of the Program on Nonviolent Sanctions and Cultural Survival at Harvard's Weatherhead Center for International Affairs until 2004. His research focuses on indigenous rights, particularly land and natural resource disputes in Latin America.

David Maybury-Lewis (1929–2007) was Professor of Anthropology at Harvard University. His life and work are remembered in the Afterword in this volume.

Biorn Maybury-Lewis, a political scientist with a Ph.D. and M.Phil. from Columbia, MA from Johns Hopkins (SAIS), and AB from Harvard, has been working on Latin American issues for more than thirty years. He specializes in the political sociology of developing areas and has extensive research experience in the interior of Brazil, most recently in the Amazon region. He has written a book on the Brazilian rural workers union movement's emergence under the military regime, *The Politics of the Possible: The Brazilian Rural Workers' Trade Union Movement, 1964–1985,* as well as articles on Brazil's agrarian reform debate, human rights issues, and rural social movements. Recently, he has conducted research and written on the rubber tappers of Acre, in the Brazilian-Bolivian-Peruvian frontier region, and the riverine peasantries of central Amazonia. He has taught at universities in Florida and Massachusetts as well as at five universities in the Brazilian federal university system. He has consulted to numerous international organizations on human rights and educational issues. He has represented Cultural Survival on visits to the Caiapô, Shavante, and Sherente Indians of Central Brazil. During the past ten years, as a senior college administrator in Massachusetts and Florida, he co-founded one undergraduate and two graduate degree-granting programs. He is presently dean of academic affairs at the New England Institute of Art in Brookline, Massachusetts.

Roger L. Nichols is Professor of History and Affiliate Professor in American Indian Studies at the University of Arizona. His scholarship focuses mainly on the invasion and occupation of North America, and the experiences of indigenous and immigrant groups in the United States, and to a lesser degree in Canada. President of the Pacific Coast Branch, American Historical Association, his recent publications include *The American Indian: Past and Present* (Oklahoma, 2008); *American Indians in US History* (Oklahoma, 2003); *Natives and Strangers* (with Dinnerstein & Reimers, Oxford, 2003); and *Indians in the United States and Canada: A Comparative History* (Nebraska, 1998).

João Pacheco de Oliveira is Professor and Curator of Ethnology at the National Museum/Brazil; and Professor at the Post-Graduate Program in Social Anthropology (PPGAS/UFRJ/Brazil). He did extensive fieldwork among the Ticuna Indians in Amazonia. This research produced the book *O Nosso Governo: Os Ticuna e o Regime Tutelar* (Marco Zero/CNPq: São Paulo, 1988). During the last ten years he has researched the history of the process of "territorialization" of Indian peoples within the Brazilian nation. This second interest resulted in three books: *Ensaios em Antropologia Histórica* (Ed.UFRJ: Rio de Janeiro, 1999); *O reconhecimento étnico em Exame – dois estudos sobre os Caxixós* (Contracapa: Rio de Janeiro, 2003) in collaboration with Ana Flávia Moreira Santos; *A Viagem da Volta: Etnicidade, política e reelaboração cultural do nordeste indígena* (Contracapa: Rio de Janeiro. 2004) 2ª. ed. He also published *Storia, Política e Religione tra i Ticuna* (Bulzoni Editore: Roma, 2005); *Hacia una Antropologia del Indigenismo* (CAAAP: Lima and Contracapa: Rio de Janeiro, 2006); and many articles in Brazil, U.S., France, Belgium, Portugal and Colombia. He has been Visiting Professor to various universities in Brazil (Unicamp/SP, UFBA/Bahia, UFPE/Pernambuco), and abroad (Università La Sapienza/ Italy, Universidad Nacional de La Plata/Argentina; and École des Hautes en Sciences Sociales/France). He was President of the Brazilian Anthropological Association-ABA (1994/1996).

Anders Stephanson teaches, among other things, the history of U.S. foreign relations at Columbia University. His two central concerns here have been the nature of the Cold War as a period and the self-conception of the United States in the world. He hopes one day to finish a historiography of what is quaintly known as diplomatic history as it has evolved since the 1930s.

Richard White is Margaret Byrne Professor of American History at Stanford University. He is a historian of the North American West and is recently most interested in shifting spatial relationships over time and the creation of modern spaces. He is at work on a book on transcontinental railroads in western North America during the nineteenth century, of which a preliminary version of one chapter appeared as "Information, Markets, and Corruption: Transcontinental Railroads in the Gilded Age," *Journal of American History,* 90 (1) (June 2003).

1

Introduction

Theodore Macdonald

How was frontier expansion rationalized in the Americas of the late nineteenth century? As the new claimants fleshed out expanded national maps, how did they represent their advances? How, more specifically, did the recently de-colonized peoples of European descent explain the subsequent subjugation, marginalization, or elimination of the original inhabitants? Were there any salient pan-American patterns to this push and its justifications?

Harvard University's David Rockefeller Center for Latin American Studies approached these broad questions at an interdisciplinary seminar on April 7–8, 2006. The convener, David Maybury-Lewis, had suggested that Manifest Destiny, as one widely known mandate, could be a concept worth testing. Did this powerful concept have its nationalist, or rather nationalizing equivalent in other countries of the Americas as they too expanded their frontiers onto the lands of indigenous peoples in the late nineteenth century?

The participants demonstrated that Manifest Destiny is, as Anders Stephanson argues in this volume, "a unique American [U.S.] trope." Nevertheless, the authors presented a set of frontier narratives that were similar nationalist rationalizations for expansion. What emerged from the conference were comparable historical accounts, as well as similar historicizing narratives: stories that the people who benefited from the expansion told (or sang—see Edward Chamberlin's chapter) about their territorial claims, and thus explained why it was acceptable to realize those claims. The comparisons are the theme of this book, and the rich and varied national stories are its content.

The chapters explore how, beginning in the nineteenth century, ex-colonials, who then became Chileans, Argentineans, or Americans, conceptualized indigenous peoples living in what were, for these non-indigenous protagonists, the frontier counties or regions. The emphasis in this book is on *ideas,* often rationalized as progress and expressed as public narratives, such as Manifest Destiny or the Conquest of the Desert in Argentina. There is no need to review the bloody record of nineteenth-century frontier practices that the ideas inspired in the United States. That is the stuff of Dee Brown's *Bury My Heart at Wounded Knee* and Cormac McCarthy's *Blood Meridian.* In Chile and Argentina there were similar notions of progress. These notions subsequently resulted in the near-erasure of indigenous peoples—experiences and ideas reviewed here by Claudia Briones, Walter Delrio, and José Bengoa. Canada provides a more beneficent panorama, as we see in the chapters by Roger Nichols and Edward Chamberlin, that is, until the provinces confederated and were less threatened by the United States. Brazil was to wait a while to expand into its interior. Yet João Pacheco's analysis of Brazil's romantic images and tales of Amazonian peoples clearly illustrates the power of nationalist images. What each country shared in the late nineteenth century was the production of narratives, each of which fed and historicized emerging sentiments of nationalism.

Most scholars of Latin American nationalism agree that ideas of homeland (*patria*) first appeared during the second half of the nineteenth (Miller 2006, Chasteen 2003, and Castro-Klaren), and spread and strengthened in the twentieth century. In the United States, sentiments of divine destiny appeared in John Winthrop's famous City on a Hill sermon (1630) and continue as American exceptionalism to the present (Stephanson 1996, and here). Most of the chapters here spill over into earlier and later periods. But what links most of them are, roughly, the years from about 1865–1889—the end of the Civil War in the United States to the demise of the monarchy in Brazil.

The general questions for the seminar arose from David Maybury-Lewis's thinking, musing, and teaching over the last 30 years. How, he asked, did American states interpret their treatment of those indigenous peoples who found themselves living on someone else's frontier, a political space not of their creation or even their imagination? Maybury-Lewis first considered the problem along lines developed by Gunnar Myrdal, which suggested an earlier title—*A New World Dilemma*—as a way to look at the high ideals and poor performance in response to what states regarded as the "Indian question." The idea was to explore the various notions of nationhood and the subsequent treatment of native peoples. For the contemporary period, many of these ideas were brought together in *The Politics of Ethnicity* (Maybury-Lewis 2002*).

The authors in the present book speak of an earlier period, when Argentina, Brazil, Chile, Canada, and the United States were focused on increasing space. Those people who then identified as "Americans" or called their home their *patria* claimed territories in which indigenous peoples lived, and saw these natives as economic and political obstacles. In several countries national expansion stories were crafted earlier, and for some they remain alive. But narratives of expansion and boundaries flowered at that time in each of the countries reviewed here. This book thus explores the perceptions that stirred or rationalized expansion, and emphasizes their impact on the native residents.

Nationalism

Nationalism, in general, is decried by most historians and social scientists (Berlin 1992, Gellner 1983, Hobsbawm 1990, Ignatieff 1995, Smith 2001). Ernest Gellner's tone is typical when he writes that nationalism "is not the awaking of nations to self-consciousness: it invents nations where they do not exist" (Gellner 1964:169). Such deconstructing sentiments are understandable in view of the horrors that ethnic nationalism and its exclusivity wrought on Europe, Asia, and Africa during the twentieth century. Meanwhile the sort of civic nationalism—centered on ideas of political legitimacy, social contract, and open citizenship rather than membership in an ethnic group—that characterizes the Americas has drawn less attention.

Civic nationalism is generally seen as more acceptable, or at least more benign than ethnic nationalism. That notion is, of course, easily challenged in the light of conquest and slavery in the Americas. However, it is beyond the scope of this book to fully consider whether ethnically neutral categories such as *American* or *patria* serve as discursive devices to mask differences in the Americas, where genuine race and ethnicity—indigenous, African, and European—have long existed and matter so much. Likewise, ethnic relations, however salient and critical, cannot be reviewed adequately here. What is of concern and focus here is the *cultural manner* in which civic nationalist notions have arisen in the Americas.

Imagined Communities

The emergence of nationalist sentiments has received considerable theoretical and analytical interest since the appearance of Benedict Anderson's *Imagined Communities* (1991), which has drawn much attention globally and in Latin America in particular. Briefly, Anderson, explaining his use of "invented," argues that "all communities larger than primordial villages of face-to-face contact (and perhaps even these) are imagined. Communities are to be distinguished, not by their falsity/genuineness, but by the style in which they are imagined" (1991: 6). He then suggests that these cultural forms and social constructions appear in two modern phenomena: print capitalism (particularly newspapers and other uses of a single vernacular), and local elites who are linked to the colonial powers, travel widely within the colonies, but are denied access to the colonizing metropole and the status obtained from it.

Anderson suggests the ways in which these self-contained colonial administrative units, shaped arbitrarily by London's or Madrid's commercial policies, allowed them to be perceived as "fatherlands." For Ibero-America this social creation occurred among some of the elites—the America-born Creoles who were denied the status of *peninsulares*, or "true" Spaniards. The Creoles' stories in the newspapers created "imagined communities among a specific assemblage of fellow-readers" (ibid: 62). Anderson then argues that print capitalism and its stories created nationalist identities that were used to justify independence. In addition, for populations isolated physically by geography and commercially by trade, these sentiments were more easily attached to the current patchwork of countries instead of larger political units of the short-lived Gran Colombia and the United Provinces of the Rio de la Plata.

Anderson posits that these local elites, drawing on modern technologies, created and reinforced unique nationalist images. In developing his theory of nationalist imaginings, he pays particular attention to the New World-born elites, or "Creole Pioneers" of Spanish America (ibid: 52–54), during the period just prior to the break with Spain. Though admittedly basing his hypothesis on a very limited number of secondary sources, he writes that these were "historically the first such states to emerge on the world stage and therefore inevitably provided the first real models of what such states should 'look like.'" Spanish America is thus presented as the prototypical imagined community.

These historical conclusions have been challenged by recent scholarship. There is no doubt that the North American experiment—from Tocqueville's town meetings to Jefferson's Constitution—exerted enormous influence on much of the rest of the world. However, numerous scholars strongly dispute Anderson's projection of South American revolutionaries' imaginings and his claim that these countries later served as models for others. The research, whose lack Anderson lamented in his 1991 edition, has occurred more recently in a conference convened by Sara Castro-Klaren and John Charles Chesteen (2003), the strong critique by Claudio

Lomnitz (2000), and a recent review by Nicola Miller (2006). But these scholars emphasize that current research does not support Anderson's argument. Nationalist imaginations, they demonstrate, did not create nations in Latin America at the time of independence. Nationalism emerged later, beginning in the late nineteenth century, as we suggest here. The historical accuracy of *Imagined Communities*, however, is not the point here. The value of Anderson's book for the study of the Americas, as with several of the chapters in this book, lies in its imaginative methods.

From Creole Communities to States

Miller (2006: 205) writes that although Anderson's Latin American history may have been off by about a century, "it would be hard to overstate his influence on the work of the 1990's." Fernando Unzueta (2003: 117) sums it up.

> While modern political doctrines and practices are still central to [Anderson's] approach to the rise of nations, his major insight consists of seeing nationalism a cultural system (instead of a political ideology) . . . From this constructivist perspective, as opposed to strictly materialist or essentialist orientations, the nation came to be seen as an "artifact" produced through a wide range of symbols, narratives, and discursive formations, including newspaper writing, history, and literature.

In brief, the cultural and symbolic manner in which Anderson creates his argument has been embraced by many scholars of Latin America.

By the late nineteenth century a variety of forces, both material (politics and commerce) and ideological, were at work to create distinct senses of nations. Edward Chamberlin's chapter here illustrates the link between political and geographic images through folk songs and poetry of western North America. For the more urbanized core Latin America, Doris Sommer (1991) has demonstrated that nationalizing narratives were often "foundational fictions" in which interest groups and political factions—often presented as individuals—courted, seduced, or married each other into a national fabric (see also Unzueta 2003: 117–122). For countries that emerged from the earlier centers of indigenous and colonial power—the viceroyalties of Peru and Mexico—Sommer argues that manuscripts, often novels, served as a popular means for exposing and sometimes overcoming the factionalism or the party politics that had made unity and nation-building so difficult in the early nineteenth century. For the peripheries

—Chile, Argentina, western United States and Canada, and non-coastal Brazil—new national stories served largely to justify and settle outline maps. They filled in the blank "unoccupied" spaces with "nationals," or at least demonstrated possession in some visible way.

Indigenous peoples did not play that role, and in many cases prevented it. Those of the frontier were not easily blended into a *patria*, as was done in Peru (Castro-Klaren 2003, Mariátegui 1971) and Mexico (Aguirre Bel-trán 1957). More often they were relocated (Chile, North America, Canada) or nearly eliminated altogether (Argentina). In none of these cases were indigenous peoples permitted their previous sovereignty. For the frontier regions or nations in the late nineteenth century, assertion of nationalism entailed a denial of independent status to indigenous peoples and their lands. Who remembered the Indians along the Columbia River? As Cham-berlin tells it, not even twentieth-century social critic Woody Guthrie:

> Well, the world has seven wonders that the travelers always tell,
> Some gardens and some towers, I guess you know them well;
> But now the greatest wonder in *Uncle Sam's fair land*,
> It's the King Colombia River and the big Grand Coulee Dam
> (emphasis added)

The "imagined communities" of the late nineteenth century and beyond were quite different from the Enlightenment-inspired images of the late eighteenth and early nineteenth centuries. By late in the century, nationalist sentiments had shifted from lofty notions of uniqueness and justifications for independence to more pragmatic goals like increased production, trade, and communication. The accompanying narratives were fashioned from idealized images that served to delimit physical boundaries and subsequently incorporate that space into new nations. The indigenous peoples, who had barely figured in the justifications for inde-pendence, now sat in the way.

From Polity to Territory

Argentina in 1870 was largely a fortress city from which farmers were moving cautiously onto the Pampas. Chile at that time was the city of San-tiago and lands to the north; the south was Mapuche Indian territory. The United States was reconstructing the South, while railroads carried settlers westward. Brazil remained a monarchy. And eastern Canada had only con-federated in 1867. Variety, more than anything else, seemed to character-ize the Americas. What did they have in common? And what, of real interest, can cross-national comparisons tell us of nationalist imagery as it affected indigenous peoples? Let us consider the following events.

- Beginning in 1869, a combined civil and military plan to incorporate Chile's south central Araucania, or "Chile *Indígena*" as José Bengoa calls it here, moved smoothly ahead until troops met with the unwilling Mapuche leader, *lonco* Quilín. Military actions were then delayed when the troops were sent north to fight the War of the Pacific (1870–1884). But the army returned, better armed and flush with victory over Peru and Bolivia, and launched an aggressive final campaign. Most historians agree that this ended the 300 year-long War of Arauco, and thus mapped modern Chile.

- At about the same time, Argentine General Julio C. Roca led the "Conquest of the Desert" (1879–1884) against the Araucanian (Mapuche) Indians who, Briones and Delrio tell us, were regarded as foreigners from Chile. Roca thus ended indigenous control of the south and gave Argentina most of its current shape.

- Canadians, federated in 1867, were granted additional lands by England in 1870. Previously and publicly respectful of indigenous lands, Canadians thereafter moved more aggressively. As Nichols and Chamberlin describe here, Canada then worked to colonize the western region and thus to establish a living border in the face of a land-hungry United States to the south.

- On February 8, 1887, the United States passed the Dawes Act, by which Indian lands were to be divided into small parcels (40–160 acres per head of family). This, as White describes here, was said to permit the Indians' full integration into society and economy unencumbered by primitive communal tribal lands. It also allowed the United States to settle all lands west of the Mississippi with "Americans."

By contrast, Brazil at the time was still focused on its long coastal region, where indigenous populations were all but eliminated by this time. Those of the vast interior Amazon Basin, however, inspired an artistic and literary movement called *Indianismo*. As João Pacheco de Oliveira notes here, artists used "native words and instruments as props . . . to celebrate the originality and destiny of the Brazilian nation which was being born." There was little other interest in the vast Amazonian region or the indigenous residents, except for the devastating but nonetheless short-lived Rubber Boom. But the romantic narrative inspired the region's first Brazilian explorer-engineer, General Cándido Rondón, to create Brazil's Indian Protection Service.

In each of these countries, save Brazil, there was a push, during a relatively short time, to clear the land of indigenous peoples and to settle what had been the interior or frontier before that time. These were not uncontested territories; Canada was still wary of the United States, while both Argentina and Chile coveted the southern Pampas. That sort of expansion, redrawing international boundaries at each others' expense, is as important and as decisive as capitalist expansion.

The expansion needed justification. The imagery of each country was that of taking possession of what was theirs by some right. Indigenous peoples were impediments at best. By 1895, when Brazil ended its monarchy, the boundary map of the Americas was, for the most part, established. And narratives had legitimated it.

Railroads

Nationalist imaginings was, of course, not the only story. Scanning the landscape with a more materialist lens, Richard White also demonstrates here that, paralleling the changes in Indian land laws, railroads west of the Mississippi created a complex and competitive patchwork of lands, rights of way, and relations with the indigenous inhabitants. These spanned in all direction after the Union Pacific Railroad laid the 1869 "golden spike" and linked the Atlantic to the Pacific oceans. But it was not until the 1887 Dawes Act that the large tracts of land paralleling the railways were finally opened for claims, and thus allowed for a more orderly penetration of the West by non-indigenous peoples. From then on, indigenous peoples would be confronted as groups if they presented themselves as obstacles, but not negotiated with as communally landed groups.

Railroads played a key role in Argentine development as well. The Conquest of the Desert allowed British engineers of the Central Argentine Railway to move south and lay what would eventually become over 40,000 miles of rails in Argentina, far more than in all of Europe (Goodwin 1977). Trains moved tons of beef and grains for export and facilitated the settlement of thousands of new immigrants from Spain and Italy. In Canada, an 1881 charter permitted the Canadian Pacific Railroad to grow westward and connect to the Pacific coast by 1885. Brazil, again by contrast, was busy with coffee and grains in the south and did not expand into the vast Amazonian interior until the mid-twentieth century. Yet while railroads, immigrants, settlements, and commerce may be the *real* stories of expansion in each county, they were not the stories the elites told to themselves.

The Narratives

Some general approaches to these narratives—from God's word to motifs in folk songs to heroic conquerors—are clearly illustrated in the chapters by Anders Stephanson, Edward Chamberlin, Claudia Briones, and Walter Delrio. The need for and use of similarly imagined communities runs through all of the other contributions as well. In the late nineteenth century the new American national narratives were very similar to the ones told at the time by European powers as they raced, with Social Darwinism on their side, to expand trading colonies in Africa and Asia into vast empires. But the Americas' stories spoke to a different sort of territorial predation—internal expansion of colonial inhabitants at the expense of indigenous populations. The United States expanded as part of some perceived higher order, or right, while Latin America and Canada took possession of what was "theirs" by some imperial or papal decree. In any case it was the beginning what is later to be known as internal colonialism in the multiethnic Americas. Hence both the romantic tales of Brazilian indigenous peoples and those of conquest in Chile and Argentina illustrate the clear use of narratives to render nationalist mapping understandable. While Brazil may have *acted* differently at the time, Brazilians *narrated* their nationalism through a similarly imagined Americas medium.

These stories are quite different from the early tales of initial contacts, conquests, or settlements along the shores that the Europeans first populated. The late nineteenth-century narratives, often equally grand, have a new tone and intent as they seek to differentiate the new national destinies from those of European monarchies. These narratives no longer spoke philosophically of or to indigenous peoples' issues. They no longer ask questions in terms of "Natural Law"—questions such as: Were indigenous peoples humans? Could they be enslaved? Could their lands be taken? Could a just war be waged against them? These were the older debates of distant theologians, jurists, political philosophers of the seventeenth and eighteenth centuries—Bartolomé de las Casas, Ginés de Sepúlveda, Giambattista Vico.

The new narratives, however lofty and philosophical the statements and writing of the likes of Argentine General Julio C. Roca and U.S. journalist John L. O'Sullivan, served immediate material needs—space. Likewise, the noble natives of Alonso de Ercilla's epic poem "La Araucana" (1589–90) were replaced by the gothic Indians who sometimes surrounded, infiltrated, and menaced the campsites of José Hernández's *Martín Fierro* (1872). So the new questions were not those of the early philosophers of natural rights who asked "Who are these people?" and "What are the standards of fairness?" The new ones asked "How do we deal with these impediments to our national progress?" Some new states, for example Argentina, simply denied any prior indigenous claims (Briones and Delrio), while other replaced protection of aboriginal land claims with relocation (Chamberlin, Nichols, White). Most narratives now spoke reflexively to questions like "who are we?" not "who are they?"

Thus, by the end of the nineteenth century the distant *Indies* had become our *Americas* in a full territorial and demographic sense. The descendants of Europeans had divided the continent into countries that they ran by themselves. Up until that time peninsular Europeans had focused their attention on the land, labor, and resources of the relatively dense indigenous populations of the Central Andes, Mesoamerica, and the coast of Brazil. Their English and French counterparts concentrated largely on their "core" areas—the eastern United States and Canada. By the late nineteenth century their interest expanded to include the new countries' interiors, hinterlands, peripheries, or frontiers. Each of these terms is, of course, a subjective labeling of social and physical space that was home for the indigenous residents. But for those who created countries from the often tiny American metropoles—Santiago, Buenos Aires, Rio de Janeiro, Ottawa, New York, and Washington—the public narratives spoke of destiny and rights. The patterns in these narratives, we suggest here, illustrate the ethos of the times. It was not the only story told at the time, but for indigenous peoples and their lands, it was the most significant. Each country had its own story, framed in its new national identity.

Manifest Destiny: Unique yet Prototypical

Anders Stephanson sets the tone for this book. He traces the idea of Manifest Destiny over time—from 1840 to post-9/11 United States—and illustrates what the other chapters contextualize in more specific time and space. The providential ideas form a meta-narrative as they explain a particular set of actions at a particular time in a particular place. Stephanson emphasizes that what makes Manifest Destiny unique is not its blend of "God, Providence and History," which appears in other colonialist and imperialist logic, but its efficacy. As with most of the nationalist narratives here, "public ideology expresses a certain normative way of doing things, even if one ends up doing something seemingly different." It is Manifest Destiny's historical efficacy that is interesting, not its "crude ideology."

While all nations may justify their actions as Providence, the United States is defined as "absolutely different" from the others, and has acted, and continues to act accordingly. In addition, the Manifest Destiny story is "a political trope [that] has had the advantage of being malleable and open to new content"—that illustrates most dramatically the power of a nationalist narrative to convince its speakers of themselves and their place in time and space.

Argentina

Claudia Briones and Walter Delrio present the Conquest of the Desert as a nationalist narrative for assertion of self as well as negation of indigenous peoples. For the Argentine state "[the Conquest] collapses into simple lines of reasoning the complex array of relations, practices, and significations that such a state venture set in place." For indigenous peoples it sets up a hierarchy of "alterity based on the negation of any indigenous contribution to the formation of Argentineness and Argentina itself."

Argentinian leaders argued that the Mapuche people who occupied the "desert" of the southern Pampas and northern Patagonia were not natives but foreigners who had wandered over the Andes from Chile. The Mapuche were said to have displaced the previous and thus "real" indigenous inhabitants, the nomadic Tehuelche. The latter, coincidentally, were no longer around, or at least not in sufficient numbers to lay claim to the lands that were now Argentina. The Conquest is thus painted as a recovery of lands usurped by foreigners.

Briones and Delrio then go on describe how the desert was subsequently and truly "desertified" by progressive relocation of indigenous peoples. Then the authors record the voices of those indigenous people who, according to the official narratives at least, should not exist. They, of course, do, and they tell the depressed and tragic tales that are all too common in the Americas.

Chile

José Bengoa points out that the Chilean army's late nineteenth-century Araucanian Campaign was seen as erasing an ethnic boundary, rather than clearing a desert. Lands conquered earlier were "Chile *Mestizo*." Boundaries were created by the Mapuche, who had held off the colonizers from 1598 until 1881, and this formed "Chile *Indígena*" from the Bio Bio River south to the Toltén River. The Mapuche Indians, Chileans argued, prevented *Mestizo* Chile from reaching, in a contiguous terrestrial manner, its "southern destiny"—the Straits of Magellan. Despite such highly dramatic rhetoric, early Chilean efforts to take possession of southern lands appear as half-hearted. Movements to open the lands were limited largely to a set of regular and unsuccessful summer military forays, played out as much like chivalric military rites as national necessities.

While the Mapuche had earlier been seen as the unconquerable and often revered defenders of their land, by the late nineteenth century that narrative had withered. Mapuche lands had been reduced to an east-west corridor between the Bío Bío and the Toltén rivers. Bengoa emphasizes that a corridor filled with "savages" was, at that time, seen to prevent Chile from realizing its potential among the modern ex-colonies that were attracting large numbers of immigrants. Likewise, the then-popular Social Darwinism, detailed by Chilean historian Diego Barras Arana in his *Historia General de Chile*, paints a picture of savage and retrograde existence south of the Central Valley. These were unacceptable images, justifying conquest.

When the battles were over, Chileans were startled by the large numbers of Mapuche who lived in the area. However much Chileans may have wanted the Mapuche to appear as a small blemish on a white nation, they were and remain a significant presence. Bengoa then shows how the Chilean narrative still lives uncomfortably with this now 1.2-million person national ethnic "imperfection" that seeks greater recognition and respect.

Brazil

João Pacheco de Oliveira argues that the true narrative of Brazil also begins in the nineteenth century, drawing heavily on the imagery of the Amazon. Until then the colony had been administered as two separate bodies—the seaboard and the Amazon. Brazilians lived along the seaboard, as had many native peoples. Deemed to be of no use as slaves by the Crown, these coastal indigenous peoples were cast aside, physically and symbolically, and replaced by African slave workers. The coastal natives were then portrayed as "primitive and technologically precarious," having perhaps undergone "an intense period of cultural decadence."

By contrast, the distant Amazon's indigenous inhabitants were displayed as inseparable from the landscape. Both the Amazon and its indigenous people were highly romanticized and both served to distinguish Brazil from its Portuguese roots. The Amazon and its indigenous peoples—both simple and both majestic—became parables of an independent Brazil. With independence and the need for unique national identity, the image of the "wild Indian" was projected as uniquely Brazilian, framed by the romantic movement of "Indianism." As the newly independent monarchy took shape, officials argued that it was the state's obligation to treat indigenous people with "comprehension and dignity."

Brazil thus moved away from earlier discussions of "just war" against indigenous peoples, to one based on two principles—a "refusal to use force" and "the recommendation that humane treatment lead the Indians to civilization and subsequent participation in the national society." Despite the horrors of the late nineteenth-century "rubber boom," this imagery persisted and guided the celebrated telegraph cable mission of General Cándido Rondón and the indigenous polices that developed from his work. The tension between this positive imagery, Rondón's legacy, and Brazil's twentieth-century needs for the Amazon's resources and space set the tenor for future narratives.

Contrasting Canada and the United States

Edward Chamberlin writes of Canada and the United States using two quite different sorts of stories, one official and one popular. The first details the legal, parliamentary, and scholarly discussion of indigenous issues within each country. He also extends his analysis well into the twentieth century, as debates whirred in professional and government circles. In Canada there was an enlightened debate over indigenous peoples, their land, and their rights, which contrasts noticeably with the issues and disputes below the Canada-United States border.

Until the late nineteenth century Canadians accepted, and often argued in support of, the strong relationship between indigenous peoples and the land. Government support assured that tenure was continuous. Consequently, the westward flow of settlers toward the Pacific was more of a meandering trickle though an archipelago of native communities than the sort of rush across lands already alienated from them, as in the United States.

In the second half of his essay, Chamberlin moistens the dry narrative with an interpretation of images played out in stories and folk songs, many of which illustrate changing perceptions of land and water, and links the metaphors to indigenous peoples. The stories and songs illustrate how the earlier, relatively benevolent behavior changed in the late nineteenth and twentieth centuries, as the west of both Canada and the United States developed, and debated that development. Water control, manifested through the construction of huge dams, becomes a leitmotif detached from indigenous users by the 1930s. The stories drift over indigenous peoples in both the United States and Canada. Indigenous peoples are either backstage or backdrops in these dramas.

Roger Nichols likewise emphasizes the radical differences in policies and practices between the two countries. Initially, left with a significantly smaller set of demographics and distinct geography, Canadians saw themselves as allies, not enemies, of indigenous peoples. There is no parallel to the early nineteenth-century "civilizational programs," or Chief Justice John Marshall's 1831 decision (*Cherokee vs. Georgia*) that denied sovereignty and created "domestic dependent nations" of indigenous peoples. In Canada, aside from two revolts (1869 and 1885), there were few confrontations. Nichols shows us that the situation was certainly not a factor of national character, but "simple demographics."

In addition, he points out that the westward flow of settlers was inhibited by the Hudson's Bay Company, which held huge land rights and provided significant income for English interests. Those who promoted transcontinental rails talked not so much of opening this land for homesteaders but of providing a means to transport goods from the eastern provinces to Asian markets. However, after Canada federated in 1867, settlers arrived in larger numbers and the country began to develop a sense of itself as a country.

Canadian scholars, we learn, spent few if any pages examining the national mission. Consequently, there was no explanatory narrative overriding the expansion of a federated Canada onto Indian lands. It was simply that, by the late nineteenth century, indigenous "allies" were no longer in the demographic and nationalist arguments supported their assimilation and displacement.

United States

Richard White divides U.S. expansionism into two phases—pre- and post-Civil War. The early expansionism was purely geographic and barely touched on indigenous peoples. Then, in the post-Civil War/pre-Spanish American War period (1865–1890), a "second Indian story" emerges. It is "largely a domestic story of the relations between Indians and the federal government and the evolution of federal Indian policy." The second era moves the United States into the ideological realm of expansionist justification detailed here by Stephanson and earlier by Albert Weinberg (1935). In these explanations the country flipped between a discussion of a persistent morality of expansion and the pragmatics of that expansion, now enabled by capitalism, particularly railroad companies.

White then rolls out a complex map of competing companies and rail systems that fanned out from the east-west Union Pacific route. Each adopted different strategies for the indigenous communities along projected routes. In some case companies acted benevolently—established and protecting relationships, declaring indigenous lands inviolable, and, along the way, preventing the entry of competitors. The reason was that, despite the formal end to treaties with indigenous nations, land and access routes rested to a surprisingly large extent with the indigenous populations, from whom they got, or did not get, permissions.

We see that as railroad companies' inviting and happy public tales became public narratives of expansion, in many cases they were wishful thinking, or qualified lies designed to attract future settlers. The stories also served to get political leaders to apply the pressure on Congress that was needed to open Indian lands. When these were opened, it was not, as many have assumed, a case of railroads simply taking possession of lands on either side of the track. They had to negotiate access with tribes, many of which were not interested. All that ended with the Dawes Act (1887), which made Indians freeholders of property and thus changed most of the lands in the West from communal holdings to individual and absolute (i.e., fee simple) property.

Conclusion

From these distinct and individual narratives, a broad pan-American pattern emerges. In less than one-half century and largely independent of one another, a set of ideas and images appeared that would permit, or at least justify, the subsequent occupation of frontiers, countries, and regions by people who were not indigenous, and who would do so at the natives' expense. The incorporation of these frontiers thus created, for most intents and purposes, the boundaries of the present countries in the Americas. While the expansion took place on the lands and homes of indigenous peoples, the old residents, with the exception of few well-known rebels such as Chief Joseph, Sitting Bull, and *lonko* Quilín, were seen largely as anonymous objects on a newly interpreted landscape.

The essays in this book illustrate the variety and the similarities of these nationalist ideas and experiences. In most cases, they were expressed in symbolic and cultural terms, rather than offered as simple materialist or essentialist claims. However different or contested that reality may be, it was a reality that, in territorial terms, "worked."

The frontier regions of Americas thus share unique expressions of nationalism—a vision of empty space, yet populated by indigenous peoples. In terms of state development the nationalist sentiments expressed by each

country seem to leap over, neglect, by-pass, and otherwise forget indigenous peoples *once they are subjugated and when national boundaries are
established*. What characterized this new nationalism, therefore, was not so
what leaders and writers imagined *into* their nations—e.g., old primor-
dialized symbols—but what was imagined *out* of the new landscape-
indigenous peoples.

The essays also illustrate that civic nationalism, often seen as inclusive
as, and more benign than, ethnic nationalism, can produce similarly
destructive human and cultural ends. The relationships and sentiments
are simply less obvious and indirect. As such the essays in this book suggest new ways to view nationalism as a theoretical concept, and frontier
expansion as a historical phenomenon.

A Look at Present Trends

The chapters here are not optimistic. Several suggest that after about 1889
the "Indian Problem" ended, or more respectfully, that the "Indian Question" in the Americas was answered with the Dawes Act, the Conquest of
the Desert, and the Araucanian Campaign. So some final words are in
order. Otherwise, the state signatories of the 2007 United Nations Declaration on the Rights of Indigenous Peoples can be seen as dancing with
wolves, the authors here can be charged with myopia, and the convener,
David Maybury-Lewis, can be said to have forgotten that he wrote force-
fully for decades about indigenous peoples' rights and founded the NGO
Cultural Survival to advocate on their behalf.

As we will see in the essays that follow, civic nationalism would not
prove to be benign during the violent territorial expansions onto the frontier lands occupied by indigenous peoples in the nineteenth century. Nor
did much subsequent assimilation take place there. Indigenous people
were more often led to tears, alcoholism, suicide, and other expressions of
passive desperation throughout the Americas. However, it was not all over
for indigenous peoples when the states filled in their national space.

Nationalism, as we have seen, is a social construction, and not some
static condition. New nationalist ideas subsequent to the period covered
in this book did turn toward the indigenous peoples. Peruvian writer José
Carlos Mariátegui, whose *Seven Interpretive Essays on Peruvian Reality*
(1928) included a chapter titled "The Problems of the Indian," popularized a new, uniquely Latin American nationalism in the 1930s and
beyond. He argued that the "problem" for Peru's Indians and for much of
Latin America as well sprang from an imbalanced, estate-based, land-
holding social order. This system was not only oppressive to indigenous

peoples, but had been hegemonically imposed by Spanish colonialism. A true Peruvian/Latin American nationalism must free itself of this externally imposed system and should define and create itself though what, as he saw it, is indigenous.

Mariátegui's approach to Latin America's future stressed a unique, alternative, socialist approach to land and people. Putting such ideas into practice in the highly factionalized and personalized politics of Peru proved problematic. Nevertheless, his widely read essays produced a shift in the argument away from what the state should do "with" or "for" indigenous peoples and toward the "problems for" and "questions by" them.

Mariátegui, in brief, took an ethnic question, framed it as Marxist analysis, relocated that in a distinct cultural and political geography, and then converted it all into a re-imagining of civic nationalism as an amalgam of indigenous roots in a struggle with capitalist economics. This pluralist and interactive view of Latin American politics, culture, and society was new.

Other indigenous peoples, their communities, their organizations, and their supporters have acted more as Mariátegui suggested, and have recently sought to alter the imposed landscape and to locate indigenous peoples within politics and civil society. In doing so, they demonstrate the plasticity of civic nationalism in Latin America.

The plasticity is most clearly illustrated in Latin America today by Hugo Chávez in Venezuela, Evo Morales in Bolivia, and Rafael Correa in Ecuador. Pulled by startlingly heavy and obvious doses of populism, these countries are now being drawn to uniquely Latin American aspirations—such as regional banks and trade groups, Latin American media, and transcontinental pipelines—largely to escape the economic and political hegemony of the United States. Each leader also draws publicly on indigenous symbolism. Others countries—Argentina, Brazil, Chile, Peru, and Uruguay—are moving in that direction, albeit with less noticeable national symbolism.

It's easy to challenge the sincerity and subsequent reality of such political imagery. Regardless, the opportunities for indigenous peoples to expand and advance their own politics of identity and de-stigmatization at such times have not been lost on them. Indigenous organizations have generally embraced such politics at these times although adding cautious criticism of the high-placed messengers.

The new sort of inclusive political and economic nationalism, largely in opposition to U.S. domination, presents an opportunity for indigenous organizations to alter the national economic and political landscape by placing themselves clearly and publicly within it, and to add to their increasing agency. The rise of ethnically based, indigenous political movements in the Americas has been under way since the 1970s. An outpouring of recent and largely supportive literature has highlighted the indigenous situation and produced a wellspring of support. Indigenous people parallel this by assuming an active and public voice in defining their situation and its remedies. Whatever happens in the future politics, indigenous peoples have located themselves on the national landscape in each country and are unlikely to let themselves or their unique identities be removed again.

References

Aguirre Beltrán, Gonzalo. 1956. *El proceso de aculturación*. Mexico, D.F.: Instituto Nacional Indigenista.

Anderson, Benedict. 1991. *Imagined Communities*. New York: Verso.

Barras Arana, Diego. 1886. *Historia general de Chile*. Santiago: Rafael Jover.

Bengoa, José. 2007. "Chile *Mestizo*, Chile *Indígena*" (this volume).

Berlin, Isaiah. 1992. "The Bent Twig: On the Rise of Nationalism." In Berlin, Isaiah, *The Crooked Timber of Humanity*. New York: Vintage.

Briones, Claudia and Walter Delrio. 2008. "The "Conquest of the Desert" as a Trope and Enactment of Argentina's Manifest Destiny" (this volume).

Brown, Dee. 2001. *Bury My Heart at Wounded Knee: An Indian History of the American West*. New York: Henry Holt.

Chamberlin, J. Edward. 2008. "Homeland and Frontier" (this volume).

Chasteen, John Charles. 2003. "Introduction." In Castro-Klarén, Sara and John Charles Chasteen, *Beyond Imagined Communities: Reading and Writing the Nation in Nineteenth-Century Latin America*. Baltimore: Johns Hopkins Press.

de Ercilla, Alonso. 2006. *La Araucana*. New York: Linkgua US.

Gellner, Ernest. 1983. *Nations and Nationalism*. Ithaca: Cornell University Press.

Goodwin, Paul B. Jr. 1977. "The Central Argentine Railways and the Economic Development of Argentina, 1854–1881." *The Hispanic American Historical Review* 57(4): 613–632.

Hernández, José. 2004. *Martín Fierro*. Madrid: Edimat Libros.

Hobsbawm, Eric. 1990. *Nations and Nationalism since 1780*. New York: Cambridge University Press.

Ignatieff, Michael. 1995. *Blood and Belonging: Journeys into the New Nationalism*. New York: Farrar, Straus and Giroux.

Lomnitz, Claudio. 2000. "Nationalism as a Practical System: Benedict Anderson's Theory of Nationalism from the Vantage Point of South America." In Centeno

M. A. and F. Lopez Alves (eds.). *The Other Mirror: Grand Theory through the Lens of Latin America*. Princeton: Princeton University Press.

Mariátegui, José Carlos. 2007 (1928). *Siete ensayos de interpretación de la realidad peruana*. New York: Linkgua US.

Maybury-Lewis, David (ed.). 2002. *The Politics of Ethnicity: Indigenous Peoples in Latin America States*. Cambridge, MA: DRCLAS/Harvard.

McCarthy, Cormac. 1992. *Blood Meridian: Or the Evening Redness in the West*. New York: Vintage.

Miller, Nicola. 2006. "The Historiography of Nationalism and National Identity in Latin America." *Nations and Nationalism,* 12(2): 201–221.

Myrdal, Gunnar. 1975. *An American Dilemma*: *The Negro Problem and Modern Democracy*. New York: Pantheon.

Nichols, Roger. 2008. "National Expansion and Native Peoples of the United States and Canada" (this volume).

Pacheco de Oliveira, João. 2008. "*Sertões, Sertanistas,* and Wild Indians" (this volume).

Smith, Anthony D. 2001. *Nationalism: Theory, Ideology, History.* New York: Polity Press.

Sommer, Doris. 1991. *Foundational Fictions.* Berkeley: University of California Press.

Stephanson, Anders. 1996. *Manifest Destiny: American Expansion and the Empire of Right.* New York: Hill and Wang.

———. 2008. "An American Story?" (this volume).

Unzueta, Fernando. 2003. "Scenes of Reading." In Castro-Klarén, Sara and John Charles Chasteen. *Beyond Imagined Communities: Reading and Writing the Nation in Nineteenth-Century Latin America*. Baltimore: Johns Hopkins Press.

Weinberg, Albert K. 1979. *Manifest Destiny: A Study of Nationalist Expansionism in American History.* New York: AMS Press.

White, Richard. 2008. "The American West and American Empire" (this volume).

2

An American Story? Second Thoughts on Manifest Destiny

Anders Stephanson

In one of the many metaphors that marked his analyses, George F. Kennan once likened the United States to a huge "prehistoric monster" with "a brain the size of a pin."[1] He wanted to convey that the United States, when provoked in the world, tends to react slowly but then to wield its enormous power without much reflection or nuance. His point, as so often, was both right and wrong.

He was wrong, certainly, about provocation and speed. Long before the early 1950s, when the disgruntled Kennan made the statement, the United States had been very quick indeed to take umbrage at injuries real and imagined and to act expeditiously and powerfully to redress them. Amerindians and Mexicans of the nineteenth century could readily testify to that. Kennan was right, however, that the governing concepts have not only been simple but simplistic. As a realist he believed that such lack of clarity was a recipe for disaster. He never recognized that the United States, precisely because of its massive power, did not have to be "right" to be successful. The intellectual grounds on which any given opponent is flattened matter less than the fact of the flattening.[2] Official and public opinion has been "wrong" factually and conceptually about lots of events, but being wrong has not prevented results of the most favorable kind. One might well think, for instance, that the spirit of Manifest Destiny in which the United States went to war against Mexico in the 1840s was mistaken, along with the specific allegations of Mexican wrong-doing. If so, it was an error that added vast territories by chopping off the northern half of that unfortunate neighbor to the southwest.[3] One has every reason, then, to take U.S. "errors" seriously.

My own interest in such errors happens to stem from one instance (probably *the* instance) when error actually generated a monumental defeat, namely, Vietnam. Getting things wrong in almost every way really did have disastrous effects. All manner of lessons were and are said to have been learnt from this. Certainly, the U.S. Army officer corps is still indelibly marked, negatively, by the experience, which is one reason there was but feeble enthusiasm in 2003 for the Iraqi operation.[4] One aspect of Vietnam and Iraq alike is the manner in which they were "produced" as places and events, how they were conceived in such a way as to warrant the kind of actions that followed. In turn, this has to do with the deeper problem of what might be called the sources of U.S. conduct and, in particular, its ideological aspects.

Ideologically, the U.S. way of being in the world has been at once massively traditional and strikingly arbitrary. On the one hand there is the inclination to invoke vast master narratives about the nation's place in world history; on the other there is the tendency to abrupt changes and arbitrary action in actual policy. The constancy here, then, has to do with the necessity of placing public action within an account of what the United States has always been about, or is imagined to have been about, in universal history. The United States been grasped throughout as a world-historical project, the fundamentals of which have not changed since 1776 (or 1789). The United States, one might say, is the original end of history: nothing, qualitatively, can improve on the original idea. This is why all political attempts to reshape the nation, inside or outside, perennially appeal to origins and tradition, to the truth of the beginning.[5] Tradition is then combined, intermittently, with extraordinary leeway and arbitrariness in concrete policy. Witness, in the respective period, Thomas Jefferson's Lousiana Purchase and James Polk's war against Mexico, two (largely) individual actions that resulted in staggering expansion.

Their material condition of possibility has to do, most immediately, with the constitutional division of power and the quasi-monarchical role of the executive, not least his (still his) power as commander-in-chief. Conceived as deliberately dysfunctional, the federal system in effect opened up, unexpectedly, for the imperial presidency, as the mini-state model on the North American continent came to be embroiled spasmodically but increasingly, and after 1941 irrevocably, with the geopolitical outside. The constitutional aspect both produces and reproduces the fractured domestic and continental structure of the ruling class. The system, in the end, makes it difficult to do decisive things at home while permitting, at times, decisive things abroad. The White House, historically, has been at considerable liberty not only to choose which particular external policy to pursue but also the particular American manner in which to situate it.[6]

We are familiar with this phenomenon in more recent times. George W. Bush chose to respond to the September 11 event with wars against Afghanistan and Iraq, suspension of the Geneva international convention in the name of an alleged threat to freedom everywhere, promulgation of the salvational role of the United States, and so forth. The frame here was a general "war on terror(ism)." Concrete policy was thus grounded in an appeal that was outstandingly American. Bush, however, might have chosen another, equally American frame, that of law and legitimate order, where the terrorist deeds would have been defined exclusively as crimes and the perpetrators not as warriors but criminals. Such a legalistic approach would also have featured a properly world-historical role for the United States, but the ensuing policy scenarios would have looked quite different. Executive license, it should be underlined, is not a product of modern (or postmodern) spin machines and mass media: consider, again, Polk's inventions in engineering the war against Mexico in 1846.

This license then operates within, and is overdetermined by, the fundamentals of America. Moments arise when these signifiers become controversial, or, more precisely, concrete application renders their actual meaning questionable. Is bombing Vietnam compatible with the universal value of freedom? Is colonial annexation of the Philippines compatible with the postcolonial identity of the United States? Is the opening of acquired territory to slavery compatible with the notion of a free society? Controversial policy not only connects directly to ultimate principle as mere appeal but also serves to problematize the principle itself. This is what happened in the 1970s with detente. It began as an American policy of negotiation, stability, and, above all, avoidance of nuclear confrontation, then turned into the closest the United States has ever come to geopolitical realism, only to disintegrate, denounced left and right as essentially amoral and so un-American: by the liberal left for its murderous effects in the third world, by the right for the appeasement of the Evil Empire. Detente, as practiced by Henry Kissinger, illustrates the difficulties of conducting foreign policy in an idiom that is unequivocally realist: realism, a discourse on timeless identity and sameness in international politics, is in that sense un-American. Never properly legitimate, realism works, half disguised and momentarily, only as long as it is an unequivocal success or at least not an unequivocal debacle.[7]

My remarks here will pursue the constitutive frame commonly referred to as Manifest Destiny, articulated explicitly in the nineteenth century but recast and reused on several occasions in the twentieth, expression as it is of that powerful mixture of Protestantism and liberalism from which there is no escape when one tries to think "America." At first sight, Manifest Destiny appears a very crude piece of ideology. Originally, it was deployed to sanction territorial expansion across the continent by appeal to the putatively self-evident edicts of higher authority, namely, God, Providence, and History. Lofty references corresponded to the astoundingly successful process itself, as the already sizeable federation grew into a transcontinental one. What could be more obvious: a self-serving ideology for massive, material gain. This is true enough, in a way. The simplicities, alas, turn out to be rather knottier than that and certainly more interesting. One must be quite precise, in fact, about the manner in which the United States imagined itself doing God's (and thereby History's) work, first on the North American continent and then many thousands of miles across the Pacific Ocean. For one thing, all Western powers in the nineteenth century would have insisted, if asked, that they were doing God's work in expanding their possessions, colonial or not. It would have been impossible to say otherwise, Western civilization essentially being understood as Christian. Initially, the distinctive feature of Manifest Destiny, as it turns out, is not the providential appeal itself but the absolute differentiation of that godly work from the rest of the West and the concomitant, utopian dimension, especially as it pertains to democracy and space. That differentiation, to complicate matters, is then partly elided in the second moment around the turn of the century, the moment of classical imperialism overseas when the ideology becomes civilizational. Even in that moment, however, the United States remains essentially a utopian project of world-historical significance.

Arguments along these lines would seem to land me in the diffuse debate about American exceptionalism. Alas, I do not want to go through all the preliminaries and caveats necessary to say anything substantial in that context. Manifest Destiny is certainly an ideology that centers around propositions about the United States as a unique and anointed agent in the world, but its specifics, which are very specific indeed, tend to disappear if the analysis is immersed in the wide array of concerns and issues that typically fall under the rubric of American exceptionalism.[8] My intention, instead, is to offer some considerations on the two central episodes when Manifest Destiny gains currency as a political term, moments which are both about territorial expansion and so about a certain inscription of space as it relates to distinctions between inside and outside. I will also say something necessarily sketchy and episodic about what happens to the concept in the twentieth century and into the present.

Manifest Destiny became a political catchword in the 1840s courtesy of John O'Sullivan, a foreign-born New Yorker of Irish-English background, a young Jacksonian who had turned into a prominent organic intellectual of the movement by publishing the influential *Democratic Review*.[9] By the standards of the time, then, O'Sullivan was a "progressive." He certainly perceived himself as a pioneer of the new, open and democratic future, if not as a radical. This is why he liked expansion. To get the rhetorical flavor, by no means extreme for the period, an extended quotation from an early programmatic statement (1839) may be in order:

> We are the nation of human progress, and who will, what can, set limits to our onward march? Providence is with us. . . . The far-reaching, the boundless future will be the era of American greatness. In its magnificent domain of space and time, the nation of many nations is destined to manifest to mankind the excellence of divine principles; to establish on earth the noblest temple ever dedicated to the worship of the Most High—the Sacred and the True. Its floor shall be a hemisphere—its roof the firmament of the star-studded heavens, and its congregation of an Union of many Republics, comprising hundreds of happy millions, calling, owning no man master, but governed by God's natural and moral law of equality, the law of brotherhood . . . For this blessed mission to the nations of the world, which are shut out from the life-giving light of truth, has America been chosen; and her high example shall smite unto death the tyranny of kings, hierarchs, and oligarchs, and carry the glad tidings of peace and good will where myriads now endure an existence scarcely more enviable than that of beasts of the field.[10]

O'Sullivan's argument, then, is simple. Democracy, the end of history, had come to its culmination and final expression in "the nation of nations," the space which Providence had evidently set aside in the western hemisphere "to manifest" to the world the meaning of divine truth. Democracy and Christianity, two aspects of the same thing, had thus come to its resting place in "the great nation of futurity," the glorious example to the world known as the United States. Expansion, it followed, was intrinsically a good thing. Believing divine democracy inherently peaceful, however, O'Sullivan never thought war in the traditional sense was the way to do it. Militarism was monarchical, European, and old-order. Yet it was actually in the heady conjuncture of impending war against Mexico, conflict with Britain over the Oregon Territory, and the inclusion of the gigantic republic of Texas into the Union that he actually introduced the expression "manifest destiny," the idea that the United States was predestined "to overspread the continent allotted by Providence for the free development of our yearly multiplying millions."[11]

As homogeneity of democratic institutions was basic to providentially decreed experiment, O'Sullivan came to have qualms about the Mexican venture and just how much of the continent one could include for the unblemished order of the same to stay the same. On similar grounds and for the sake of his party, he was explicitly against all discussion of that great problem of difference within the Union, namely, slavery. Perhaps he had a dialectical inkling somewhere that providentially predestined expansion might well spell the end of the glorious example as he knew it, as new territories would exacerbate difference over slavery to the point of breaking up the delicate internal balance.[12]

Though that conflagration was already being envisaged by some pessimists, it was still some distance away. For now, despite biting critiques (chiefly in New England), the whole complex of ideas articulated in the concept of "manifest destiny" held the day. Its very prevalence, in a way, was the novelty. For on many an occasion before, arguments had been voiced to the effect that God had some preordained layout clearly in mind for the United States that involved vast expansion. So, for instance, policy-makers would muse intermittently that Cuba, given its position on the map, surely belonged "naturally" to the Union. The massive expansionist moves of the 1840s, however, entailed a much more centered politics of "destiny." Destinarianism (to coin a phrase) became the very idiom of the whole project of expansion.[13]

What is its deep structure? Is there one? If Manifest Destiny is reduced to the few elementary propositions O'Sullivan typically voiced, it appears to be nothing more and nothing less than what it states. To reiterate: God, and so History and Nature, has evidently singled out the United States as the exemplary sanctuary for the final stage of history and thus opened up the continent for the expansive playing out of that mission of freedom. "Expansion," *ipso facto*, is inherently good, opposition to it, *ipso facto*, inherently wrong. End of argument. All that remains then for us retrospectively is empirically to account for how this was carried out and explore how the thematic came to return in a different register during the expansionism of the late 1890s. Yet O'Sullivan's position, which condensed in particularly clear form the whole destinarian thrust, deserves further elucidation. Again, it is an error to be simple about the seemingly simple. At the outset, accordingly, I need to say something fairly abstract about its conceptual history.

———

Ultimately, of course, Manifest Destiny is a concept of religious derivation. More precisely, it is Christian, Protestant and Calvinist, though this can easily be over-emphasized.[14] From its colonial beginnings, the United States had certainly shown a broad streak of destinarianism, a strong notion, in short, of being involved in something decisive in the historical trajectory of true Christianity. This is what gives the posture its typical radical aspect, its tendency to either/or, the desire for the absolute and the conviction that, essentially, one really embodies it. The underlying perspective can readily be summarized. History has a rational direction towards a given purpose, planned and guided as it is by Providence. In this unfolding, comprehensible drama, all agents are called upon to perform certain set roles and missions, callings they can choose to live up to or not. Choice is thus central to the proceedings, the act of constantly choosing, not between a potentially open series of options but between doing what one has been appointed to do and turning away from it. This way of being towards the world is at once individual and collective: the mission, responsibility, and choice are necessarily features of one's community insofar as it is conceived as such. Strict, one might say Puritan, versions generate strong boundaries and an aversion to contaminating contact with the outside. The pure is conceived as exemplary and difference is absolute. Hence, too, the policy orientation becomes explicitly "isolationist."[15]

Yet the very same axioms can result in quite the opposite stance: when the Calvinist trope is fused, as it easily was, with a vibrantly secular and republican ideology, conceived around a spatio-temporal opposition between the New and the Old World, there opens up the possibility of a kind of interventionism drastically to redo the outside, to purify and clear it so to speak. In the nineteenth century, this 'solution' to what the United States ought to be about in the world remains largely an obscurity; but it would begin to come to the fore in the imperialist moment at the turn of the century and, later, differently, in Woodrow Wilson. Originally products of the same conceptual frame, the two opposing postures have since remained central reference points for all domestic controversies about the general U.S. role abroad. Notions of a world-historical, Christian mission should not be conflated, as frequently happens, with messianism. On the face of it, the transformative function of redeeming the world clearly implies some affinity with the idea of the messianic. Surprisingly, however, Manifest Destiny in its nineteenth-century version is only thinly connected to it. Christianity, unlike Judaism, is obviously founded on the messianic notion, the coming of the Messiah and savior being the central event of history after creation itself, the next event being his return. The space of the Messiah in Christianity (again, unlike Judaism) is thus pre-empted, which is why imitators and substitutes beware. That said, there is room for intra-historical simulacra. The original Puritan-Calvinist undertaking had been modeled on the idea of the sacred remnant, a proto-Judaic project where God's purposes have come to reside in the particular doings and choices of a rigidly bounded community of the Elect, whose role is thus decisive to the movement of history. Still, this is not to be confused with the messianic as such. The formative sense of election and mission is then expanded and tremendously reinforced, albeit in modified form, with the advent of the secular, liberal United States and the Empire of Liberty: here is not only a sanctuary for freedom but a model vehicle for its inevitable victory in historical time and space.[16]

Once history is thus conceived as providentially designed progress to be played out in exemplary form in the United States, the notion of ultimate crisis also vanishes or is at least put in brackets. Intramundane redemption is then reduced to quantitative expansion of the universal principle of the United States, more of the same in short. This is perhaps messianic in some attenuated form: redemption is taking place all the time under the agent auspices of the ever-progressing, outwardly mobile United States, anointed to demonstrate for humankind where history is heading and so redeeming it or at least providing the preconditions for that happy event. Playing out the purposes of providential democracy on the North American continent, then, is a necessary step for the liberation of humankind; without it, liberation could not take place. Concretely, however, this is about the extension of already existing freedom in the United States, not about some erupting intervention into the historical world to remake and save it so as to establish eternal peace. The destinarian will become clearly messianic, to be sure, at certain critical points in the future: Woodrow Wilson's attempt to recast international relations in 1917–1919 and the early Cold War posture are two clearcut examples. The expansive mission in the 1840s in the name of Manifest Destiny is not essentially messianic.[17]

Hence, relatedly, Manifest Destiny is not apocalyptic either. It is obviously not apocalyptic in the conventional (and erroneous) sense of some massive cataclysmic crisis. Manifest Destiny represents no such upheaval. On the contrary, it represents democracy and property, as rationally consecrated in the principle and predictability of law, inherently peaceful, indeed the very meaning of peace. People in freedom are restlessly moving ahead in rational pursuit of whatever happens to strike their fancy; and they do so in transparent conditions of peace and legal order. If, by contrast, the apocalyptic is taken more accurately as revelation, Manifest Destiny seems directly related. Yet, peculiarly, it both posits revelation and declares the end of it.[18] Truth, Christian and secular, has been revealed in history, more precisely in the United States. Rigid providentialism now proclaims that the ancient mystery with no visible or at least certifiable solution has been replaced by self-evident clarity of purpose and agency.

Apocalyptic strands, interestingly, survive instead powerfully among some of the most ferociously anti-expansionist forces: the Abolitionists, for whom the Republic bears within it the unmistakable and sickening signs of destruction in the monumental sin of slavery, the very antithesis of freedom. These are the people for whom aggressive expansion seems a conspiracy of "the slavocracy" and its allies, indicating death and destruction and what not, the kind of catastrophic denouement that did in fact ensue. Manifest Destiny, in polar contrast, entails no room for such interpretative and contestational moves: its predictive certainty is absolute. The moving limit in space westwards is the line where history comes to a stop, not apocalyptically but rationally and peacefully.[19]

***

In a more concrete vein, I now want to connect this to the geopolitics of O'Sullivan's actual world. His operative frame here, evolved since the early Republic, is constituted by a polarity between the United States and Europe. Whereas Europe is marked by the "exterminating havoc" of the balance of power, by war and retrograde monarchy, the United States signifies peace, rationality, and freedom. This polarity, one should note, is resolutely undialectical: the United States or the sphere of freedom, being the natural state of humankind, has no need of Europe, either conceptually or functionally.[20] The federation stands alone, founded on a logic purely its own. No interaction with the outside is presupposed. Yet, normatively and actually, the United States favors interaction of another kind, not with Europe specifically but, all things being equal, with everyone everywhere. A proper international system, exemplified by the United States itself and to a lesser extent by the western hemisphere of which the federated republic is both the emblem and the guardian, is one of trade and peace. The axiom, laid out by Washington and Jefferson, is quite clear:

as much trade as possible, as little politics as possible, which is another way of saying that international relations should be about economics, maximum openness for individual exchange, as regulated in the last instance by law. The United States provides a perfect republican model how to do this, a federated model of freedom for the world: local self-determination but overall economic permeability and individual initiative across borders.[21] The implementation of that model in the conquered virgin lands of North America, which seems to O'Sullivan so manifestly preordained, was really a product of a great deal of chance and unrepeatable historical circumstances. Ironically, the material foundation was indeed industrialization in Western Europe, which provided people and the ultimate basis for the valorization of conquered land. The U.S. economy, oddly enough, was more globalized in the agrarian nineteenth century than in much of the industrialized twentieth. Yet, the destiny of the United States is experienced as radically different and removed from Europe, chiefly because of the overwhelming reality of continental expansion in relative geopolitical autonomy. That autonomy, to compound the irony, turns out also to depend ultimately on European factors: the British found it in their interest after 1815 to acquiesce and to use their naval supremacy accordingly.[22]

The Monroe Doctrine of 1823, or what gradually becomes known under that name, is symptomatic. The United States declares itself the self-evident guardian of the entire western hemisphere, which is defined as a space of progressive republican principle in contrast to backward monarchy in old Europe. History on the western side of the Atlantic has moved irreversibly to a new and, by implication, final stage, and the relation between the new and the old is one of political separation, a separation curiously enunciated in the name of an antipolitics of sorts. What is wrong with Europe is in fact that it is (geo)political. At no point is it recognized that the whole idea is actually unenforceable and is only allowed to flourish imaginatively because the British chose not to demonstrate its unreality.

———

The unreality of the Monroe Doctrine is, however, part of a destinarian ideology whose effects in the continental theatre itself are very real indeed. The rationality and efficacy of the process of implementation are devastating. Its organizational device, politically, is a fundamental reason destiny could be imagined in the way it was. I call this unique model "cellular replication." Originally set forth in the Northwest Ordinance of 1787, it became in every way constitutional, though it predated the actual Constitution two years hence. A machinery was established here whereby new member republics could create themselves in extant U.S. territories, citizens-to-be thus contracting with one another as constitutive powers and after a probationary period entering the Union on a footing completely equal to that of existing member states. It was in part this novel system that Thomas Jefferson, a central figure in its genesis, had in mind when he was referring to the "Empire of Liberty" and the "Empire for Liberty."[23]

Once the distinction from "Europe" has been made, the space of the United States as "America" becomes curiously indeterminate. It was not evident where the mobile "United States of America" actually were and/or at any rate where they would finally be (only the Civil War made the union singular). No defined territory or land attached to the union as a national mission. No one imagined that the United States would eventually be coterminous with the world; very few believed the entire western hemisphere would be a single union; and, before the railroads, many had logistical doubts about the possibility of a genuinely transcontinental republic. Still, if other unions came into being further afield, they would not constitute any essential difference: they too would be more of the same, an American union of true America. Meanwhile (and it was a very important meanwhile), the United States as actually existing freedom, would go about its business of expanding as best they could.

By imperial standards a very odd bird, it was really an enormously effective, decentralized way of recreating identity in space: the original, consensual union of republics reproducing and growing by means of more of exactly the same, reiteration where historical time is frozen. In the democratic 1830s and 40s, cellular replication across the West, vigorous and open-ended, was still for most an unmitigated good. The expansion of the Empire of and for Liberty, the timeless, universal principles of Man, was by definition a good thing. How could it be otherwise? One might quarrel over the proper way of dealing with the Amerindians or the British, and about how far the existing union could feasibly be extended. One could quarrel, in short, over means. But about the notion that expansion of the United States, as embodied in the unique principle of federative replication, was world-historically legitimate and fervently to be desired, about that idea there could as yet be no disagreement.[24]

It is useful to compare this replicating union of sameness with the concurrent notions of European nationhood (and quite similar ideas in Latin America). The United States is not a "homeland": it has no myth of a single people inhabiting since times immemorial a single land and speaking a single language, supposedly reproducing vertically generation after generation, with all the attached genealogies, traditions, and histories that go with that process. Moreover, there is none of the liberal vision of European nationalism one finds, say, in Giuseppe Mazzini, the idea of the world as a mosaic of equally worthy nation-states in peace, all reveling in their differences as peoples and cultures, indeed not only tolerating but celebrating each other's differences and peculiarities (one recognizes the argument in more recent odes to multiculturalism). In polar opposition, a "clean" and homogeneous space of absolute freedom, grasped as the indispensable vehicle for the world-historical future of that principle, can have no equals. For, absent any identical, adjacent federations, "the United States" as a concept does not permit any notion of equality with the outside. What is beyond can only be understood as a "not-yet," mired in various degrees of retrograde unfreedom. That domain can and certainly will be liberated at some point, if not by actual inclusion into the United States, then perhaps by following its radiant example at some distant time, or, as mentioned, because the Empire of Liberty itself finds a way to undo the shackles. Nevertheless, at all given times, there remains between the United States and the outside a constitutive gap of absolute difference, a difference of inequality in the name of equality, a difference ultimately between the free and the unfree. The United States is the world or the truth of the world, but the world is not the United States.[25]

The United States, then, comes to stand (incipiently in 1776 and certainly after 1800) metonymically for the whole of the New, the Republican, the Free, and the Western in the world, a place to be imitated and in fact the essence of the future. This is what O'Sullivan is referring to when he is imagining his nation as the essence of the world, though by his time, the condensing concept has become "democracy." The future, then, has already arrived in the nation of futurity, the nation of nations. The United States, equipped as it is "with the truths of God," the "arena" is exclusively about "the expansive future," an "untrodden space" to be entered "with a clear conscience unsullied by the past." Thus the European past has no meaning for O'Sullivan except as "lessons of avoidance," as a realm of error.[26]

When historical time has ceased qualitatively to develop on the inside and only pertains, as a series of stages, to the outside, it follows, critically, that outside opposition is irrational, if not downright criminal, while political quarrels on the inside can only take the form of an appeal to the principles and promise of the timeless, universal truth of the Origin. Authorized violence on the frontier, to name but one effect, is thus always conceived not as war but as "pacification," the repression of violators of the peace and the clearing of the way for the final transformation to order, independence, and freedom for those who are eligible to participate. Others can legitimately be punished with large-scale violence. And so, to devastating effect, indeed they were.

The border, the line moving constantly outwards, is accordingly invested with decisive importance. In the most immediate, concrete sense, it becomes, famously, "the frontier," a zone of transformation where freedom is created from scratch, as it were, out in the open. Land beyond, always by definition untouched, properly virginal, is turned into land proper when it has been cleared and subsequently surveyed. Wildness is eliminated. The settlement of what will become the United States is colonial in the true sense of the word. Land, then, is either not yet occupied or insufficiently occupied by people whose capacity to contract with one another and thus to be free and independent is next to nil. It is one of the signal features of the Empire of Liberty, accordingly, that it is keen on land but not on people, especially if the people in question happen to be different and already on that land. Amerindians, not being the same and irrationally in possession of the land, were thus an obstacle to be overcome by, in effect, whatever means necessary. Contrary to a great deal of obvious evidence, the conventional justification assumed that Amerindians, being naturally savage, were incapable of being American in the sense of fulfilling the criteria for what passed for a rational person.[27]

Crass self-gain aside, the foundational argument here was forthright and ingenious: property, not vague possession, was the essential characteristic of true self-hood; property meant independence and the capacity to make the land productive; Amerindians had no property and were apparently incapable of production; hence they were not real selves; hence they had no intrinsic right to the land. To relieve them of their land, one should nevertheless (contradictorily, but as a sign of superior civilization) enter into the kind of purchasing contracts they were presumably unqualified to conclude. Amerindians, until well into the nineteenth century, were thus defined as sovereign nations capable of concluding (unequal) treaties at the same time as they were constitutionally unfit for sovereignty. Whatever the means, in short, law and exchange are the master signifiers of the process, the politically correct way of dispossessing peoples.[28]

Such theorizing is of course not limited to colonial North America and the United States, but it reached its purest and most lethal expression here, and it becomes an integral part of the larger destinarian schemes of the 1840s. By then, however, the Amerindians had ceased to be a major obstacle and, by their very dispossession and expulsion, turned into evidence of the very freedom, independence, property, and democracy that had presumably replaced them—all, again, plainly according to the irrefutable historical edict of Providence. Their destiny, so to speak, has already been established: graphically removed, legally subordinated, militarily reduced to a disturbance on the frontier.

If various earlier forms of destinarianism, not least as doctrines of natural right, had thus informed the uneven development of pacification, one must emphasize that when O'Sullivan and the Jacksonians begin to talk about "manifest destiny," Amerindians are not the polemical concern. Geopolitically, O'Sullivan is concerned to contrast American space not with any indigenous world but with the distant European one of hierarchy and oppression. This opposition, again, is not a dialectical struggle in contradictory unity but nothing more and nothing less than a contrast with an absolutely separate universe where the true purposes of humankind are manifestly to be shown. Europe, in short, is what needs to be discarded, the polemical enemy, though by the end of the war against Mexico, when O'Sullivan himself had gone on to other things, the enemy had become Europe as refracted through the Spanish, supposedly backward Catholic legacy in that country. Conceptually, moreover, the governing Jacksonian notion of democracy (and, synonymously, freedom) evades the indigenous issue on the whole.[29] When Alexis de Tocqueville writes *Democracy in America* in this period, he notes with exemplary lucidity that democracy is heavily racialized in its actual content. The Jacksonian order is indeed massively white and in many ways far from democratic. It contains, in particular, a racialized component (of sorts) in the increasingly prominent, imaginary Anglo-Saxon heritage, a component that is enormously reinforced through the war against Mexico. Manifest Destiny in that sense comes to foreground over time in the 1840s ethnic essentialism over democratic principle.[30] Yet O'Sullivan's operative concept of democracy, the very essence of the providential dispensation, says nothing as such about race, much less slavery. Democracy in his conception is not a doctrine of conquest or displacement. Conquest enters into the proceedings only as a contingency and then preferably in the form of empty space to be settled, not as displacement or subordination of other people. Democracy, in effect, is a discourse of political community based on the principle of equality of its constituent members; it appears, as it were, in a vacuum. The crucial issue, consequently, is eligibility of membership. Who counts? Who is equal? On what grounds are certain categories excluded (Mexicans,

Catholics, women, people of color, immigrants, individuals younger than 18)? The answer is subject to political struggle in the present. Exclusion, then, is intrinsic to constitutive inclusion. Displacement, however, is not. It is historically specific.

Displacement is, however, latently problematic precisely in raising the issue of eligibility to the level of principle. Thus O'Sullivan liked to imagine Amerindian displacement as a vanishing act that had nothing inherently to do with the establishment of providential democracy. Insofar as Amerindians come into play, it is really as historical validation or prop of the basic truth of America, not in being displaced by conquering white settlers but as part of the objective process of receding wilderness and wildness, the opacity that is rapidly being turned into the translucent space of democracy. Indeed, it had become possible by O'Sullivan's time to feel a certain remorse and nostalgia about what was imagined as the Amerindian disappearance, if not extinction.[31] Even Andrew Jackson, ruthless remover-in-chief, manages to persuade himself that he has actually been saving Amerindians by expelling them from the Southeast and sending them off, at the cost of enormous native suffering, to a western wildness commensurate with their allegedly natural way of life. Henceforth, the Amerindian position becomes, by means of legal permutation and happenstance, a bizarre anomaly: domestic dependent nationals.[32] Their space, then, lies within but is excluded from America proper. America has no place for Amerindians. It is for one thing and one thing alone: democracy for eligibles. It is utopian, it is total, and it is homogenous.

In the Canadian provinces, perhaps the closest comparison, Amerindians were less vulnerable in theory and practice, ironically because of the supposedly retrograde and tyrannical imperial system: they were just one kind of imperial subjects among many other differentiated ones, ultimately covered throughout by the Royal Proclamation of 1763. Imperial authority performed a mediating role, then, that was missing in the pure and unadulterated space of freedom where everything was clearly taking place on direct authority of Providence, which is to say white democracy. The conceptual cleanliness of liberal, subsequently democratic, contractualism proved much worse for the indigenous peoples than the diversity of royal subjection.

The anomaly of an alien Amerindian space within the Republic fit the Manifest Destiny of Jacksonian democracy well because it allowed bracketing the whole native problem without wreaking conceptual havoc on foundational principles. Moreover, as Amerindians do not constitute a systemic problem, they require only limited attention, rather like the present-day anomaly of Puerto Rico and numerous other U.S. dependencies. The racial problems which emanated from slavery and free blacks assumed an altogether different magnitude, the functional silence commensurately more conspicuous. To put it a little too simply: democracy in the south liked slavery and increasingly came to see it as a foundation for (white) freedom, while democracy in the north disliked blacks, thought them inimical to (white) freedom and so wanted to exclude them, preferably sending them off to some appropriately exotic location. As O'Sullivan knew (along with his sometime mentor Martin van Buren), Jacksonian democracy could only harbor both of those two positions by means of another bracketing operation, hoping in a way that somehow the problem would go away.

—•—

As it happened, the Manifest Destiny of continentalist democracy, the bracketing move itself, vastly exacerbated the problem by adding more territory and more inflammatory questions as to what exactly constituted a free, democratic, and truly American space. In 1845, the Jacksonian task seemed simple: the purely quantitative one of creating, *ex nihilo*, pullulating democratic republics across the continental universe. The object of Manifest Destiny, then, has to do with space, not time. It has to do, specifically, with a certain theater or setting where the democratic purposes were hitherto hidden but are now revealed with complete clarity for the benefit of universal history. It is an irrefutable justification for the acquisition of that setting: Manifest Destiny is about a certain destination, the outer edges of the North American continent (though I doubt that O'Sullivan was clear on where those edges really lay). This is not only a unique project; it is the world-historical project to end all other political and civilizational projects. The dividing line between inside and outside is thus absolute. A single thrust, the war against Mexico engineered by James Polk, achieves the continental goal with apparent ease. Outstanding territorial issues with Britain in the Northwest, meanwhile, are resolved.

Stunning as this ratification of Manifest Destiny seemed to be, dialectical history would shortly stage an equally stunning reversal. Temporality returned in the form of staggering internal carnage. Continental success, Manifest Destiny, turned out to be a disaster just as the apocalyptic Abolitionists had predicted. Contradictions over the authority of the center to decide whether sameness would include or exclude slavery broke the union of freedom violently apart in one of the bloodiest conflicts in the nineteenth century. Not surprisingly, the Civil War gave simple expansionism abroad rather a bad name.[33]

This was not the end of expansionism, however, as there was ample room in the already existing acquisitions for the astonishing capitalist accumulation and industrialization that had begun even before the Civil War. Demonstrating American purposes, *sans* slavery now, was still the order of the day, as was the continuous replication of new states within. Race, at length, was transformed into a pseudo-scientific category designed to legitimate the widespread institution of white supremacy after the end of Reconstruction. Such seemingly rational concepts of racial hierarchies allowed white society to congeal nationally once again, at the same time as they served to curb much of the enthusiasm for expansion in places with lots of racially dubious people. "Destiny" did not disappear, but it largely faded from visibility in the boom and bustle.

A would-be humanitarian exercise in 1898 to help the Cuban insurrection against imperial Spanish rule (or at least to quell its disastrous effects) brought back, unexpectedly, Manifest Destiny to public debate with a vengeance. Its context and use were, however, radically different. The democratic element, for one thing, had disappeared, space was historicized, and race was everywhere. Most decisively, the United States connected up with Europe and the world in lines of continuity, thus replacing absolute distinction. What had happened?

Above all, empire; racialized, scientific empire. The last third of the nineteenth century had seen a formidable drive by the imperial powers of Europe to subordinate territories in Africa and Asia and to formalize their imperial systems. This process was conceived in two divergent registers. Taken as a collective unit, European imperialism was grasped as a civilizational and thereby Christian project for the good of all—even when Japan enters the game seriously in 1895, it does so explicitly in the collective name of civilizational superiority (less the Christian element). Within, however, imperialism was conducted as competition, as a struggle in the name of national greatness, size, and exclusivity. Navies, increasingly, provided the indexical measure here, the force that had made the British the hegemon of the century and now expressed more than anything else how well a country could combine industrial and military prowess. Important figures in the United States worried about this competition and what appeared to them as a national failure, not necessarily the failure of the world's first postcolonial power to become properly colonial but certainly to maintain a geopolitical posture commensurate with its enormously expanded economic base. According to this view, while the United States was well on its way to becoming the world's largest industrial and agricultural producer, it was failing signally to translate that prowess into political advantage on the international arena.[34]

The vast majority of the public cared not one whit about this; nor the majority of the politicians. The smoldering Cuban issue, however, served to bring geopolitics inadvertently to the surface. By going to war against Spain for the sake of Cuba, the United States ended up making the island into a protectorate and Puerto Rico, the Philippines, as well as Guam into colonies, in addition annexing Hawaii. At the end of 1898, the United States suddenly looked just like one Great Power among a very select number of others, an impression deepened by the addition of the Panama Canal Zone five years later. The historical particulars of this astonishing shift are of the greatest interest, but not for my purposes here. What is of interest instead is how "the United States" could be recast in destinarian terms now that it was apparently doing exactly what every old-style imperialist power was doing. Whither, in short, essential difference?

The advent of imperialism, it will be remembered, coincided with the advent of what is usually referred to as the Progressive Era in the United States, a period of reform grounded in a certain (let us say) rationalist, middle- and upper-class sense that the country had lost its bearings and was in urgent need of better order and better management along scientific lines. The colonial break divided this movement. Some of the most articulate and unfaltering anti-imperialists were Progressives. Nevertheless, the predominant Progressive view was not only to acquiesce but to see in the U.S. version of empire an opening precisely for quintessentially intelligent, enlightened reform, a project related to other imperialist endeavors, yet profoundly different. "Civilization" was the conceptual terrain on which this problem was fought out and eventually settled.[35]

It became possible, in effect, to grasp the endeavor entirely in civilizational and humanitarian terms, as the bringing of peace, prosperity, health, education, and so forth, to needy natives, or at least eligible and capable ones. Humanitarian guardianship was always coupled with a liberal, scientific racism, a scheme of classification according to which certain allegedly inferior types would naturally be consigned to the dustbin of history, as had, however regrettably, the Amerindians at home. Evolution would, so to speak, take care of them. Not coincidentally, the Progressive Era is one of those intermittent moments when America decides that the collective, ethnic, alien space of Amerindians is an irrational affront that must be abolished, the natives to be individualized and expeditiously Americanized. All of this is indeed put on brilliant display in the St. Louis World Exposition of 1904: the extraordinary Philippine Reservation with its taxonomic exhibit of the new colonial possession and all the uplifting, intelligent reform imposed upon it; and the Indian model school, replete with women's basketball teams and other invigorating features for the mind and body.[36]

According to the Progressive view, then, to eschew guardianship over those indigenous elements that survived evolutionary rigors was to shirk from responsibility, duty, and obligation; in short, from the nation's Manifest Destiny. Essentially, in other words, Progressives identified with the civilizational aspect of Western imperialism (only a few arch-imperialists in the United States would choose to accentuate the strictly geopolitical dimension). The United States, on this view, was the most advanced and sapient part of the most advanced and sapient part of Western civilization, namely, the Anglophone world. The modifier "most" here is crucial. It indicated that the United States, though "different," was actually part of something larger, the vanguard, to be sure, as evidenced for instance by the selflessly enlightened reforming and recreation of the Philippines, but nevertheless a project integrated in a line of continuity with other civilizational uplifters. The absolute divide, in other words, of the original Monroe Doctrine had been eliminated. Symptomatically, Teddy Roosevelt's famous Corollary to it in 1904 situated the United States as the regional Great Power in the western hemisphere with the right to discipline and punish, all of which indicated that other Great Powers would not only be within their right but be obliged to carry out a similar role in other regions.[37]

The elision of absolute difference was in fact typical of the Progressive Era, one of the few in U.S. history when it became possible to say in polite society that the Constitution really was rather an old and dated document in need of severe revision for modern times.[38] Continuity or not, talk of Manifest Destiny in this context was (again) largely a progressive or reformist concern: it was manifestly the destiny of the United States qua United States to help the little Brown Brothers that, unforeseeably, had come under its benevolent jurisdiction. The project as such, the election campaign of 1900 notwithstanding, had far less impact on the political structure than the destinarian expansion of the 1840s. After the Panama incident, the brutal repression of the Philippine insurgency, and the celebratory excitement of the St. Louis Exposition of 1904, colonial concerns faded from public purview.

Another fundamental problem of difference remained, however, a problem not in relation to Europe but to the new imperial possessions themselves. For it was clear that no person from, say, Guam, however radical the uplifting, would ever become a proper "American," and that as long as the island remained within, it would also remain outside the United States proper. Cellular replication had come to an end (though it would take half a century of probation before Hawaii would mark the actual end). The Empire of and for Liberty could now have territorial possessions in a state of enduring inferiority. This was a fact. There was, alas, no immediately obvious solution to what these facts really were in a legal sense, the simultaneous status of being both inside and outside. Not for the first time, it was the courts that eventually resolved the issue for the political system: with an invented category, the new territories were said to be "unincorporated," as distinct from "incorporated" acquisitions such as Alaska and Hawaii. To be "unincorporated" meant that the territory was in principle an instrument of the U.S. Congress, a thing to be disposed as Congress saw fit. That the instrumental status is still very much with us is scarcely well known in the United States, though it certainly is in Guam.[39]

History, cast in evolutionary concepts, thus made possible a new inscription of space(s) and the peoples that inhabited them, at the same time as it brought the nation of nations back into its fold. No longer was the United States a sacred space for the implementation and demonstration of providential purposes of democracy. The United States was still exemplary, but chiefly in the role as pioneering, superior agent in the transformation of the imperial world. Progressive empire is not about democracy but about mastery of self and others; and governing the self is primarily a problem of being able to master the art of governing others and their unwieldy, irrational ways. One of those ways is actually excessive democracy. Progressivism is about supposedly intelligent management of the real. Destiny is about evolutionary development and the capacity to understand and direct it. It is about conquering spaces peopled by inferiors. In short, it is about difference, hierarchy, and heterogeneity, not about identity, democracy, and homogeneity. The corresponding advent of segregated, racial spaces within is a graphic expression of the same shift.

The colonial moment was thus a large-scale, destinarian "intervention" in the outside world but not in response to any massive crisis of a world-historical kind. Apocalyptic sentiments, as in the 1840s, were more a mark of opponents, who predicted, wrongly this time around, that expansion would ruin the Union. The effects on the body politic were in fact limited, except insofar that it actually made that body into a body that could have extremities, though paradoxically unincorporated ones. The civilizational aspect entailed no messianic element. Rhetorically overblown as its antecedent, Manifest Destiny was now carried out in the name of providential, historical inevitability and the world-historical role of the United States in that process.

—◆—

World-transformative uniqueness combined with the apocalyptic was, however, about to appear with unexpected power and speed in the shape of Woodrow Wilson, a prototypical Progressive at the outset, who eventually came to revolutionize the ordering process to entail the entire globe, imputing to the United States (and himself) the messianic role of accomplishing this mighty change in history. In epically destinarian but now also apocalyptic language, he articulated the absolutely decisive calling for the United States to seize the moment and change the world finally into something identical to the United States itself, that is to say, to bring about the democratic and peaceful end of history. The United States, then, is both agent and model.

He failed. Yet he would also leave a curse on all his successors since. There is no way of escaping Wilson, because he enunciated the ultimate American destinarianism, ultimate in scope of application and world-historical magnitude. Wilson became an unavoidable reference point, a navigational landmark even when his legacy was in fact eschewed. Thus Franklin D. Roosevelt, the ostensible Wilsonian, often invoked destiny but in fact espoused none of the messianic convictions, always remaining (after the Japanese attack in 1941 had put the United States irrevocably in the world of geopolitics) a Progressive committed to law and order, stability and predictability, all sanctioned by genuine commitment to wartime collaboration with allies of a quite different ilk. With the idea of absolute difference with the outside world, he had very little patience. When the wartime collaboration breaks down and is followed by the most intense antagonism conceivable under formal conditions of peace, there is also a return to the "American" matrix: a messianic response to an apocalyptic crisis, a perceived and perhaps artificial crisis. What is known as the Cold War is indeed originally how the United States, more particularly the Truman administration, resolves the problem of legitimating peacetime globalism: perpetual U.S. engagement everywhere in the name of war for the sake of saving the world from destruction. In creating the division between the free world and the unspeakable netherworld that tries to invade it, the United States actually remains absolutely apart within its own sphere. The free world is not uniform. To lead that world is not merely to be indispensable, it is to have absolute authority in the last instance to do whatever it takes to carry on the war.[40]

Arguably, this version of Manifest Destiny expires around 1963, after the threat of nuclear conflagration had come graphically close to effecting a truly apocalyptic ending of everyone involved. It is hard to be messianic or for that matter destinarian about mutually assured nuclear destruction. To be one "superpower" out of two is to engage in geopolitical management, not to be on a quest for transcendence. Nuclear parity implies similarity, if not identity. Neither Richard M. Nixon nor Henry Kissinger is any exemplary exponent of Manifest Destiny, however "fateful" the political fate of the former. Reaganism briefly resurrects the Cold War format, almost as postmodern pastiche, but the very brevity of the exercise demonstrated how weak were its historical underpinnings. For one thing, behind the binary rhetoric of the Evil Empire and the Free World about to battle it out at Armageddon, Reagan's policy entailed intimate strategic relations with the other Communist giant, the People's Republic of China. Yet, to repeat, the United States does not have to be right to be successful, and in a mind-boggling twist of history, for reasons much more contingent than now recognized, the Evil Empire self-destructed, to the monumental surprise certainly of its erstwhile enemies.

The ensuing period, the clichéd "after the end of the Cold War," was not a propitious one for destinarian thinking. Destiny, so to speak, was over. Manifestly, destiny had happened. The role of the United States in the globalizing world of more and better markets, indeed more of the same everywhere, was certainly conceived as indispensable; but the space for world-historical transcendence and massive intervention had obviously disappeared. What remained? Mopping up operations and brushfire wars? Improving the World Trade Organization? Not much heroic material to be found for the organic intellectuals of "the only superpower" (the other ubiquitous cliché of the era).

An eruption of unimaginable magnitude then opened up once more for the return of the destinarian formula. The War on Terror(ism), modeled on the Cold War, thus once again featured a United States manifestly destined by higher authority to combat the forces of evil in the world and assuming the right to do so in whatever fashion and place it might see fit: the messianic is inherently beyond the law because the present is by definition degraded, in need of transcendence. This marked the return, then, of the United States as a world empire proper. However, the open-endedness and de-territorialized nature of the project ensured its failure: there is no possible end to a war, at once metaphorical and real, against a historical phenomenon which has no territory and is not actually an existing enemy (terror) in the first place. It is one thing to carry on an endless war on drugs where relative failure is recognized from the beginning; it is quite another to fashion one's position in the world on an endless war on terror which one expects to "win" and to mobilize one's incomparable military machine accordingly. Whether being wrong about the why and the wherefore in going to war in Iraq will exact a punishing toll is yet to be seen.

There was, however, another side of the destinarian thrust of the George W. Bush administration which O'Sullivan, Wilson, and Truman would all have recognized. I am referring to democracy, self-determination, freedom, and the auxiliary free enterprise. This is the conviction that people (i.e. those who count as such) are everywhere the same and, if allowed truly to determine their own selves, will naturally be free. Rational people everywhere, when given a chance, will constitute themselves politically in parallel ways to the Land of the Free itself, the actions of which are therefore always greeted by true people everywhere as liberation, even if this actually means coming under U.S. occupation and guardianship. Opposition, in this seamlessly circular argument, is thus at best mistaken or, at worst, subversive.

The century, then, that has passed since the imperialist surge, has seen, in fits and starts, the emergence of the United States as a world power. Manifest Destiny, which began as a spatio-temporal notion pertaining to the North American continent, was transformed into a global aspiration and became in the process messianic. As a political trope, it has had the advantage of being malleable and open to new content. Manifest Destiny, from that angle, is a function: it has no given concrete goal. Its axiom is world-historical, providential chosenness. The actual task of that function can vary. In a continental setting, it was not about intervention but contiguous expansion. In an imperial-colonial setting, it was about peerlessly enlightened uplifting of appropriate natives. At Versailles, it was about recasting international relations and letting people truly be people. In the Cold War, it was about saving the Free World and vanquishing totalitarianism. In the current era (about to pass, as I write), it is about saving the world from terrorism and making it safe for democracy. From another angle, I have argued that Manifest Destiny, variations aside, did not become messianic until the object was the whole world and a catastrophic crisis was at hand; and that the messianic variant, once continentalism has been fulfilled and superseded, is the strongest conceivable one when it comes to separation between the United States and the outside.

Yet I have also argued that Manifest Destiny is not an ideological given or absolute feature of U.S. history. Its use is not random, but it is certainly contingent. Manifest Destiny, to reiterate, is conspicuous by its absence in the massive, global emergency of the Second World War: a combination of FDR's Progressive disdain for U.S. separation ("isolationism") and the realities of the wartime alliance precluded destinarianism. In the end it must also be said that Kennan was right about the peculiarities of the social and political structure of the United States: mixing a strongly decentralized and domestically oriented ruling class, politically expressed in the locally anchored Congress, with an equally strong, nationally elected executive, who is also, monarchically, commander-in-chief, makes for a certain license in the choice of ideological framing that few other regimes can afford or even contemplate. What these frames are and how they are made is of monumental concern for the world outside the United States, regrettably often more so than for the United States itself.

Notes

1. George F. Kennan, *American Diplomacy* (Chicago: University of Chicago Press, 1984), 59.

2. Eric Hobsbawm refers pithily to this feature of the U.S. posture as "the power of knocking things down," recently more in evidence than the otherwise much vaunted soft power (Hobsbawm in conversation with the author, 6 June 2008, London).

3. See my *Manifest Destiny: American Expansionism and the Empire of Right* (New York: Hill & Wang, 1995). The present essay, while drawing extensively on this short little book, is otherwise an attempt to rethink it, above all on two matters: space and messianism. The classical work (and still the best) is otherwise Albert K. Weinberg, *Manifest Destiny: A Study of Nationalist Expansionism in American History* (Gloucester, MA, 1958 [1935]).

4. A peculiar lesson of the debacle in Vietnam, however, was that the critical evaluation of counterinsurgency ceased within the U.S. military, overtaken by

a will to forget. I have benefited much here from conversations with Lt. Colonel Conrad Crane (ret). Meanwhile, it would be easy, all too easy, to retort that while the United States lost, it really won in the end, what with Vietnam turning into an efficient low-cost factory run by the Communist Party for the benefit of the capitalist metropolis.

5. A good example, now hard to remember, was Newt Gingrich's so-called Contract with America (1994), according to which America had lost its way after years of Democratic waywardness and now had to return to its original truth. Much of Ronald Reagan's rhetoric of return was similarly phrased.

6. Executive power everywhere tends to have a certain license, a certain "geopolitical privacy," but the de-centered structure of the U.S. government lends itself especially to it. See Michael Mann, *States, War, Capitalism* (Oxford: Blackwell, 1988), chs. 5–6. My nineteenth-century examples of Jefferson and Polk notwithstanding, clearly there is a qualitative change here after 7 December 1941: the Second World War marks the beginning of the permanent national security state and a massive expansion of executive power in foreign affairs. The distance between Woodrow Wilson's travails in 1919 and the ease with which Harry S. Truman pushed through his Doctrine in 1947 is testimony enough. In the present, a cursory glance over the global map of the U.S. military power is enough to see the point. One of the few to pay proper attention to the political implications here is Andrew Bacevich. See e.g. his *American Empire: The Realities and Consequences of U.S. Diplomacy* (Cambridge: Harvard University Press, 2002).

7. On realism in the United States, see the edited volume, Nicholas Guilhot, ed., *Realism in the United States* (forthcoming).

8. The topic of exceptionalism has invited a vast literature, much of it misplaced in my view. I am sympathetic to Ian Tyrrell's well-known intervention here: "American Exceptionalism in an Age of International History," *American Historical Review* 96 (Oct. 1991), 1031–55.

9. O'Sullivan was from a lineage of Irish-English mercenaries and adventurers. His mother ended up in the United States, where O'Sullivan eventually graduated from Columbia College. His subsequent life (he died in 1895 on the eve of the resurgence of Manifest Destiny) was as every bit as checkered as that of his forebears: after selling the *Review* in 1846, for instance, he became heavily involved in sundry conspiracies to acquire Cuba. See Julius W. Pratt, "John L. O'Sullivan and Manifest Destiny," *New York History*, July 1933, 14:3, 213–34; Sheldon Harris, "The Public Career of John Louis O'Sullivan," Ph.D. dissertation, Columbia University, 1958; and most recently, Robert D. Sampson, *John L. O'Sullivan and His Times* (Kent, OH: Kent State University Press, 2003).

10. The quotation is from his seminal editorial in the *Democratic Review* (official if unused name, *The United States Magazine and Democratic Review*), July-August 1839, 427, 430.

11. The last quotation is from O'Sullivan's editorial "Annexation" in the *Demo-*

cratic Review, July/Aug 1845, 5, which referred not to Mexico but the annexation of Texas and the dispute with Britain over the Oregon territory. He used
a similar formulation in the *New York Morning News*, 27 December 1845.

12. The aforementioned (n. 11) editorial expressed, p. 8, very plainly the rationale for its structural silence on slavery: "National in its character and aims,
this Review abstains from the discussion of a topic pregnant with embarrass-
ment and danger . . ."

13. One prominent predecessor will suffice as illustration. In a letter to his father
in 1811, John Quincy Adams wrote: "the whole continent of North America
appears to be destined by Divine Providence to be peopled by one *nation*,
speaking one language, professing one general system of religious and political principles, and accustomed to one general tenor of social usages and customs." Adams also thought Cuba and Puerto Rico natural parts of the future
continentalist power. His abolitionist reorientation in the 1830s changed this
attitude completely. *The Writings of John Quincy Adams*, vol. IV: 1811–1813
(New York: McMillan, 1914), 209.

14. O'Sullivan, for instance, was an Episcopalian but his family background was
in good part Catholic. Nonetheless, the basic structure was always Protestant,
radically Protestant.

15. See my *Manifest Destiny* for more on this highly condensed account. Among
the numerous primary and secondary sources I have used, the one I would
single out is Sacvan Bercovitch, *The Rites of Assent: Transformations in the
Symbolic Construction of America* (New York: Routledge, 1993).

16. See Gershom Scholem, *The Messianic Idea in Judaism and Other Essays on Jew-
ish Spirituality* (New York: Schocken Books, 1971); Peter Duncan, *Russian
Messianism : Third Rome, Holy Revolution, Communism and After* (New York:
Routledge, 2000); and Thomas L. Thompson, *The Messiah Myth: The Near
Eastern Roots of Jesus and David* (New York: Basic Books, 2005); and Anders
Stephanson, "Law and Messianic Counterwar from FDR to George W. Bush,"
in Luca Baldissari and Paolo Pezzino, eds., *Guidicare e punire: i processi per cri-
mini di guerra tra diritto e politica* (Naples: L'Ancora del Mediterraneo, 2005).

17. Nor is to be conflated with the related Puritan mission of the sacred remnant,
the quasi-Mosaic trek across space to preserve truth in a new and promised
land. The land is certainly promised and the providential mission is about
eternal truth, but the democratic project is not about a chosen people in the
Mosaic sense. What defines the chosen agent in this case is in a way that it is
not a "people."

18. On this thematic, see Malcolm Bull, *Seeing Things Hidden: Apocalypse, Vision
and Totality* (London: Verso, 1999).

19. Richard J. Cawardine, *Evangelicals and Politics in Antebellum America* (New
Haven: Yale, 1993), 146–57; Reginald Horsman, *Race and Manifest Destiny: The
Origins of Racial Anglo-Saxonism* (Cambridge, MA: Harvard University Press,

1981), 257–71 (which deals with the more incisive moderate critique as well).

20. A similar aspect appears in the Cold War: "the Free World" is thus the natural one which can stand on its own, the totalitarian one essentially parasitic and dependent. The difference is that O'Sullivan's Democracy/Freedom exists as an isolated space, whereas the Cold War vision assumes the lethal threat of the evil parasite.

21. David C. Hendrickson, *Peace Pact: The Lost World of the American Founding* (Lawrence: University of Kansas Press, 2006), explores the origins of the United States as a model for international relations.

22. Generally, see D.W. Meinig's marvelous *The Shaping of America: A Geographical Perspective on 500 Years of History. Volume 2: Continental America, 1800–1867* (New Haven, 1993).

23. On Jefferson and the state system generally, see Robert W. Tucker and David C. Hendrickson, *Empire of Liberty: the Statecraft of Thomas Jefferson*, (New York: Oxford University Press, 1990); Peter S. Onuf, *Statehood and Union: A History of the Northwest Ordinance* (Bloomington: Indiana University Press, 1987); John Lauritz Larson, "Jefferson's Union and the Problem of Internal Improvements," in Peter Onuf, *Jeffersonian Legacies* (Charlottesville: University Press of Virginia, 1993).

24. See my "A Most Interesting Empire," in Lloyd Gardner and Marilyn Young, eds., *The New Empire* (New York: The New Press, 2004), for a more extensive treatment of the idea of cellular reproduction.

25. ibid.

26. The quotations are from O'Sullivan's "The Nation of Futurity," *Democratic Review*, 426–7. For a stimulating account of the Protestant precedents, see James Simpson, *Burning to Read: English Fundamentalism and Its Reformation Opponents* (Cambridge: Harvard University Press, 2007), ch. 6. The notion of creation *ex nihilo* in a pristine space was modified and indeed contradicted, depending on the day-to-day relation with Britain, by the element of Anglo-Saxonism, viz. the United States as the preservation and fulfillment of ancient Anglo-Saxon (i.e. Teutonic, pre-Norman) liberty.

27. On the spatial issues of expansion, see Meinig, *The Shaping*. See also Thomas R. Hietala, *Manifest Design: Anxious Aggrandizement in Late Jacksonian America*, (Ithaca: Cornell University Press, 1985).

28. The legal and political issues are analyzed with great rigor in Lisa M. Ford, "Settler Sovereignty: Jurisdiction and Indigenous People in Georgia and New South Wales, 1788–1836," Ph.D. dissertation, Columbia University, 2007.

29. Sean Wilentz, *The Rise of American Democracy: Jefferson to Lincoln* (New York: Norton, 2006), elaborates well the democratic credentials of Jacksonianism, though perhaps a trifle too far.

30. On the racial issue, see Michael Hunt, *Ideology and American Foreign Policy*

(New Haven: Yale University Press, 1987); Patricia Nelson Limerick, *The Legacy of Conquest: The Unbroken Past of the American West* (New York: Norton, 1987); and especially Horsman, *Race and Manifest Destiny*.

31. Compare his passage in the *Democratic Review*, December 1842, 621, on Amerindians: "It is melancholy to reflect that, judging from the past, no future event seems more certain than the speedy disappearance of the American aboriginal race, when these now broken, scattered, and degraded remnants of a primitive and once cultivated branch of the human family, will scarcely be remembered, save in poetry and tradition." On other occasions, the *Review* articulated the more conventional view that it was all really their own fault: "Doubtless the Indians have suffered in contact with us; but they have suffered, because of their own inherent vices of character and condition, such as their obstinate idleness and apathy, and their want of, and revulsion from all political institutions.... rather than by reason of any fault of ours. It is our misfortune, quite as well as theirs, that they cling so tenaciously to their native degradation." *Democratic Review*, September 1838, 129. By the time O'Sullivan had left, the *Review* became more overtly racist and vulgar: "The Mexican race now see, in the fate of the aborigines of the north, their own inevitable destiny. They must amalgamate or be lost, in the superior vigor of the Anglo-Saxon race, or they must utterly perish. They may postpone the hour for a time, but it will come, when their nationality shall cease." *Democratic Review*, February 1847, 100.

32. On peculiar legal history here, see Lindsay Robertson, *Conquest by Law: How the Discovery of America Dispossessed Indigenous Peoples of Their Lands* (New York: Oxford University Press, 2005).

33. The so-called Gadsden Purchase of 1853, which added some Mexican territory, turned out to be the last gasp, though no one expected this to be case at the time. The Northern Whig and later prominent Republican William Seward, ardent expansionist and Abolitionist at the same time, added enormously to the federation after the Civil War of course by buying Alaska, but his "Folly" was widely conceived as nothing but an Arctic waste; and so it raised none of the now paramount problem of alien peoples and their threat to republican purity. Ernest N. Paolino, *The Foundations of the American Empire: William Henry Seward and U.S. Foreign Policy* (Ithaca: Cornell University Press, 1973), remains the best treatment of Seward.

34. Generally, see Stephanson, *Manifest Destiny*, ch. 3; for an argument about executive power, see Fareed Zakaria, *From Wealth to Power: The Unusual Origins of America's World Role* (Princeton: Princeton University Press, 1998).

35. For more on this, see Stephanson, "A Most Peculiar Empire."

36. See Paul Kramer, "Making Concessions: Race and Empire Revisited at the Philippine Exposition, St. Louis, 1901–1905," *Radical History Review* 73:1999, 74–114; on the taxonomic aspect, Vincente L. Rafael, *White Love and Other Events in Filipino History* (Durham: Duke University Press, 2000); and

Theresa Ventura's forthcoming dissertation (Columbia University), "Empire for Reform: American Agrarianism and the Control of Nature in Colonial Philippines."

37. Stephanson, *Manifest Destiny*, ch. 3.

38. Compare Teddy Roosevelt here with his distant relative and equally Progressive follower Franklin: neither had much devotion to the Constitution as an expression of timeless truth, both thinking presidential power should be stretched as far as it possibly could, which, in Franklin's case, was very far indeed. On the line of continuity with Europe in the Progressive Era, see Daniel T. Rodgers, *Atlantic Crossings: Social Politics in a Progressive Age* (Cambridge: Harvard University Press, 2000); and on the geopolitical aspect here, Warren Zimmerman, *First Great Triumph: How Five Americans Made Their Country a World Power* (New York: Farrar, Straus & Giroux, 2002).

39. Generally, see Arnold Leibowitz, *Defining Status: A Comprehensive Analysis of United States Territorial Relations* (Dordrecht: Martinus Nijhoff, 1989); on Puerto Rico, see C.D. Burnett and B. Marshall, eds., *Foreign in a Domestic Sense: Puerto Rico, American Expansion, and the Constitution* (Durham: Duke University Press, 2001); and the path-breaking work of Efrén Rivera Ramos, *The Legal Construction of Identity: The Judicial and Social Legacy of American Colonialism in Puerto Rico* (Washington: American Psychological Association, 2001).

40. I have written about the Cold War as a conceptual problem from this angle on several occasions. See "The United States as Cold War," in Silvio Pons and Federico Romero, eds., *Reinterpreting the End of the Cold War: Essays, Interpretations, Periodizations* (London: Frank Cass, 2004); "Liberty or Death: The Cold War as US Ideology," in O. A. Westad, ed., *Reviewing the Cold War: Approaches, Interpretations, Theory* (London: Frank Cass, 2000); and "Fourteen Notes on the Very Idea of a Cold War," in G. O'Tuathail and S.Dalby, eds., *Rethinking Geopolitics* (New York: Routledge, 1999). Much of the ensuing attempt here to provide a periodization of the postwar epoch may also be found in these articles.

3

The "Conquest of the Desert" as a Trope and Enactment of Argentina's Manifest Destiny

Claudia N. Briones and Walter Delrio

In Argentina's official history the so-called Conquest of the Desert refers to the military annexation of the Indian territories of Pampa and Patagonia. The expression had been construed as a necessary condition to achieve "order and progress" (a Comtean injunction that appears on the Brazilian flag) and a solution to the constitutive dilemma of the national project, "civilization or barbarism." In contemporary indigenous memories, however, the Conquest is known as the "white raid"—a reversal of the hegemonic characterization of "raids" as instances of indigenous savagery.[1]

From both points of view, the Conquest is an epitomizing event (Landsman and Ciborski 1992). On the one hand, it simplifies the very complex array of relations, practices, and significations that such a state venture set in motion. On the other hand, it was (and still is) powerful enough to cement a national image based upon the negation of any indigenous contribution to the configuration of Argentineness and Argentina itself. For both reasons, the Conquest is the subject of renewed historiographic debate, and the academic literature about it is abundant. It also triggers debates among citizens that often result in demonstrations for and against it in public spaces.

Scholars debate three main topics: (a) whether the military campaigns were a necessary and legitimate national undertaking or a genocide; (b) the extent to which the Indians to be conquered were foreign invaders with no rights or native inhabitants who should have been protected by the state; and (c) the admirable or despicable profile of Julio Argentino Roca, general in charge of the military campaign of 1878 and twice president of the Republic (1880–1886 and 1898–1904), who is seen either as a "patriarch of Argentineness" or as an oligarchic, self-absorbed ruler. Ordinary citizens argue about the removal of monuments honoring General Roca, and about the acceptability of current Mapuche claims because they may come from inauthentic Indians. Inauthenticity is attributed to the Mapuche either because they are seen as once and forever Chilean nationals, or because they have changed so much that they cannot be considered Indians anymore. In this regard, one of our arguments is that the notion of aboriginality made up of cultural traits put together into a sort of essential and immutable "cultural capital" misses the historicity, materiality, and dynamics that characterize indigenous and other social forms of identification, and ignores the complex effects of consistent yet varied politics of "othering."

We cannot exhaust here the meanings and effects that the Conquest brings together. Rather, our contribution intends to identify some of the material and symbolic implications of the military annexation of Pampa and Patagonia for the configuration of Argentina's national identity in two broad areas. First, we focus on hegemonic materials to ponder the role that they have played in the shaping of the nation-state. Second, we explore the images created by these materials as well as specific and deliberate omissions within these official memories. In order to do so, we pay attention not only to official sources but also to the controversies that the Conquest provoked, which swing from depicting it as a quasi-genocidal event to seeing it as the only way of putting barbarism in its place. To achieve our purpose we bring indigenous testimonies to the fore, not only to provide the point of view of subaltern memories, but also to enliven Argentinians' contemporary sense of being a heterogeneous people.

Scholarly opinions on Argentina's Indian Policy have diverged. Some writers have argued that the state policy was the absence of sustained policies (Carrasco 1991; Slavsky 1992; Martínez Sarasola 1992). Some of us have pointed out that the spasmodic creation of reservations (Briones 1998) and "circumscribed responses to concrete cases" are evidence of a state activity that was the outcome of complex negotiation, and hence far less erratic than it seems to have been (Briones y Delrio 2002; Delrio 2005). Focusing not only on the land policies but also on the confinement policies that continued over more than a decade after the official end of the Conquest, we now offer a slightly different argument. The subordination of the Indian Policy to broader policies on land and colonization since the beginning of the twentieth century operated on the basis of an older design, which was to transform Pampa and Patagonia into a sociological "desert" through de-tribalization and practical extermination that extended well beyond the period of the military campaigns. As a result, later strategies of "incorporation" could be presented as grounded in the necessity of placing mere "tribal remnants."

Conventional and New Thoughts about the Conquest

In 1979, on the occasion of the centenary of the Conquest of the Desert, the most brutal military dictatorship in Argentina declared June 11 a holiday to commemorate the day when the troops commanded by the General Julio Argentino Roca had arrived at Rio Negro. In November of that same year, a history congress was held in the Patagonian city of General Roca. The military Minister of Internal Affairs at the time, General Albano Harguindeguy, addressed the academic audience on the "epic event." Harguindeguy seized the opportunity to support the "tradition" of the National Army as guardian and promoter of order in opposition to "the barbarism" of the past—the aborigines—and that of the present—the "stateless subversive." His opening speech also condensed the official reading of the event:

> The Conquest of the Desert was the response of the nation to a geopolitical, economic and social challenge. The 1879 campaign managed to expel the foreign Indian who was invading our Pampa, [as well as] to dominate the territory politically and economically, to multiply the companies and the yields of work, to assure the south border and to populate the inner lands. (Academia Nacional de Historia, 1980, vol. l: 42–3)

From the same historical viewpoint, the minister elaborated on the "achievements" that followed. In the short term, the Conquest represented the solution to a problem that had lasted several centuries (Indian control over Pampa and Patagonia), thus setting the foundation for the emergence of the modern state as envisioned by the so-called Generación del '80, the moral elite who sought to engineer a civilized, unified, and unique nation-state. In the mid-term, the effect of the Conquest was to turn the Argentine Republic into "one of the leading countries of the world, for God's grace and the vision and action of its men" (ibid., 43).

The perspective introduced by Harguindeguy is neither novel nor limited to the military (Briones 1999). It has come up at various periods and circumstances, because the Conquest of the Desert has been a functional and structuring narrative of the territory-nation-state matrix (Delrio 2005). Extended and legitimized by the Argentine academies of history and anthropology, this master statement has been reproduced in public speeches as well as in the names of cities, monuments, and streets. It was also found in school texts used during the twentieth century. By the turn of that century, when the indigenous struggle gained momentum and managed to obtain recognition of special rights under the constitutional amendment of 1994, school texts had to be modified. Nevertheless, beyond its reformulation or deletion from the school curricula, the master statement on the Conquest still continues to manifest itself in different ways.

To begin with, the Conquest has been symbolically transformed into a circumscribed, supposedly bloodless event, mainly tied to the determination and vision of General Roca. It consisted, however, of a series of military campaigns between 1878 and 1885. The first campaign involved the advance of several columns that converged from different points of the line of military forts to occupy the shores of the Rio Negro. Hence June 11, 1879—the military and political celebration by which Roca consolidated his self-image of a desert conqueror—only meant the achievement of a very basic goal: the gathering of troops on the island of Choele Choel, on the lower Rio Negro. Other major goals would be reached later, when subsequent campaigns gained partial military control of the territory. One of these goals was to secure positions along the mountain chain of the Andes—the central element in the border disputes with the Chilean state. Another objective was to establish the presence of what came to be called the "police of the desert" on the interior of the Patagonian plateau, so as to have direct control over the social groups that were living in a supposedly uninhabited territory or, in any case, a territory only populated by "foreign Indians."

Second, the Conquest eliminated the problem of "internal borders" posed by "foreign Indians," a problem that interprets a border not simply as a limit of state territory, but as a separation of distinctive and homogeneous groupings that can spread back and forth in time. As a result, membership in indigenous groups is also nationalized on a permanent basis, as if Indians had already been Chilean or Argentine before the creation of either nation-state. Moreover, once the arrival of the railroads and the telegraph became the by-product of "the removal of internal borders," the saga of civilization and progress obscures the fact that the development of society (embodied in state apparatuses such as peace courts, schools, civil registry offices, etc.) worked at an uneven pace and did not reach everybody or every place alike. Understandably, therefore, many indigenous and Creole inhabitants of the mountain regions had to integrate their economic activities with the Chileans (Bandieri 1993) and to register the birth of their children in offices across the Andes, the only ones available in the area (Cerruti et al. 1996). Against such a backdrop, one could say that the Argentinization—or "foreignization" as its counterpart—of the indigenous people was an ideological device that operated symbolically at first, and proceeded materially only with time.

Third, the dominant belief has been that the Conquest succeeded as an immediate solution of the indigenous problem. This assumption contributed to obscuring genocidal practices that persisted. It also helped to turn state policies into a non-topic, avoiding discussion of a process riddled with contradictions,[2] which was criticized and debated by the moral elites while it was taking place.[3] That is, taking the success of the Conquest for granted made it easy to assume that the indigenous groups either "went to Chile, where they came from originally" or "died of diseases and poverty," or even "turned out to be decimated during the conquest." Denial of the existence of indigenous people legitimized the idea that the Argentine state—unlike other Latin American countries—did not need to produce a continued and coherent policy to incorporate the native population of Patagonia into the nation-state after the end of the military campaigns. In this context, the settlements and distributions of land to indigenous people would appear as circumscribed responses to concrete (and few) cases. These actions also appeared to be independent of state policy, both continuous and comprehensive, that worked to further the alienation of native lands and promote colonization. In this way, minimizing the weight of the indigenous issue allowed the state not only to activate it as a *problem* when needed, but also to simplify the variety of agencies and interests at play when it was time for solutions (Briones and Delrio 2002). In time, both movements aligned with a national self-image that closed in on any legitimate hint of cultural heterogeneity. Thus the narrowing of the field of vision and debate on the Indian policies gradually buttressed the idea that what was done was as necessary as it was inevitable.

Finally, ethnic categories not only were nationalized but essentialized in ways that failed to account for the deep transformations produced on the internal borders. On presupposing a kind of sociological continuity among the defeated groups and those settled in reservations or colonies, the historical-anthropological hegemonic explanation also ended up minimizing the differences and contradictions between both policies (military neutralization and relocation). In turn, considering the existing communities to be "tribal remnants" in process of "civilization"—or modernization, according to the times—the academy constructed the indigenous topic as a question of paleo-ethnography. The attribution in the present of characteristics that applied in the past has resulted in ignoring not only the redefinition of ethnic boundaries that followed the transformation of "sovereign Indians" to "Argentine (indigenous) citizens" in the decades immediately after the Conquest (Bechis 1984, Delrio 2002), but also the subsequent complex processes of communalization (Brow 1990) that were activated by successive evictions from assigned lands. Instead of understanding the social memory of survivors as the product of subaltern subjects who had undergone selective policies of cultural marking and unmarking, it was interpreted as the reconstruction of the real indigenous way of life before the campaigns. In this fashion, the silences and ellipses that populate indigenous memories were interpreted as indicators of a permanent state of "whitening" and cultural loss.

Indigenous memories work in a less linear way, however. The campaigns are seen as the end of a mythical stage of abundance and autonomy and the start of persecutions, the struggle for survival, and the beginning of successive expropriations under a constant threat to life and integrity of the family groups. To these survivors, the decades following the Conquest seem to lay the foundation for exploitation. Stories about detention in concentration camps, massive deportations, tortures and division of families may be followed by narratives of the escapes and the meandering itineraries of the grandparents in search of the lands that would foster a sense of place for the new communities they would form. These memories, then, proliferate in statements about new families and new alliances, though always in spaces progressively marginalized and under permanent threat of new evictions. But they also point to practices of extermination and social dismemberment that were prolonged beyond the period of direct military actions (1885) and were applied to subjects not involved in these actions (elders, women, and children). This leads us to postulate a twofold argument. First, the plan of de-Indianization did not operate only or mainly on the level of socio-symbolic identifications. Second, the indigenous policy was far from being spasmodic or inactive at this stage. On the contrary, it aimed at emptying "the desert" of populations self-identified as Indians mainly after its military conquest.

Let us now anchor this twofold argument on the procedures for state territorialization in its extension towards Pampa and Patagonia.

Keys to the Symbolic Geography of the Argentine Nation-state

In her analysis of the historiographic debate on the Conquest, Martha Bechis (1983) has argued that in early 1980s the key analytical issues involved either the figure of the hero, Roca, the consecrated icons of progress—mainly the triad of telegraph, railroads, and Remington—or the increase in cattle productivity that sought to correlate the numbers of heads of cattle with dead Indians. The author introduced a perspective that, from then on, would become unavoidable. It consisted in extending the frames of analysis to the set of relations between the native peoples and the processes of state formation and consolidation of Chile and Argentina. This went against the former tendency of separating the subject into two temporally discrete and separate areas of study: one concerning history-border relations from the state's point of view; the other an essentialist and a-historical ethnology.

In the last two decades, fields of investigation that had been unexplored were expanded. Academic literature began to include indigenous politics and to find active and significant indigenous participation in small and large-scale commercial movements. The links between the transformation of sovereign tribes into subaltern groups and nation-building processes within the parameters of the territory-nation-state matrix also became part of the picture. Nevertheless, most lines of work continued supporting the temporal division—before and after the state conquest—as separate developments, and hardly abandoned the state's point of view.[4]

Now then, to appraise critically the idea that, in all aspects, the Conquest had been a definite temporal cut, as well as an abrupt break in practices and relations, it may help to delineate the symbolic geography of the nation as it has been condensed into different hegemonic narratives that developed from regarding the Conquest as a key event. To place the relations between native peoples and the nation-state in a wider context, we will need to summarize previous state processes and practices of territorialization.

In official versions and conventional perceptions, the roots of Argentineness are always anchored in a territory that is viewed as Argentinian since a very remote past. This territory is the one contained by the colonial boundaries of the Viceroyalty of the Río de la Plata. Created in 1776, this district was drawn by King Carlos III as one of the new Spanish circumscriptions in America that would facilitate better administrative control. Once the Viceroyalty was established, Buenos Aires became the capital of an extended region independent of Lima. Extending from Lake Titicaca to the Strait of Magellan, the imagined area included the present territories of Argentina, Paraguay, Bolivia, Uruguay, and part of Chile as Spanish domains. Even the Chaco and Patagonia, at the time independent Indian territories, were part of this new area.

Once independence movements started at the beginning of the nineteenth century, the Creoles accepted the Borbonic geography and assumed the colonial boundaries as part of their own territories. Thus, when the rebels overthrew the viceroy in 1810, the self-proclaimed First Government Board of the United Provinces of the Rio de la Plata claimed the political representation of the Viceroyalty of the Rio de la Plata, though not as a sovereign entity but in the name of King Ferdinand VII while his imprisonment in Napoleon's hands lasted. As a result, Indian lands that had never been under Spanish control were also seen by the rebels as part of their colonial legacy.

Beyond the complex events that led to a relatively definitive shape for the independent states of the Southern Cone, the elites' interests surely lay in preserving and eventually extending the colonial territories as an inherent and inherited part of the new Argentine Republic—a perspective that, in time, would be contested by the Chilean state. Hence the lamentations (and wars) upon the loss of some provinces of the Viceroyalty, such as the Alto Peru (today Bolivia), the Banda Oriental (today Uruguay), Asunción-governed area (today Paraguay), and the recurrent and extended border conflicts with Chile. In this context it is striking that the successive hegemonic parties that struggled for power before the definitive constitution of the Argentine Republic[5] regarded the extensive territories, at the time considered Indian lands, as if these were subject to recovery rather than expansion.

It had been clear, if difficult to admit, that vast extensions of the already imagined Argentine geography were out of immediate Creole control. This knowledge led the Generation of 1937—intellectuals with romantic undertones such as Juan Bautista Alberdi, Esteban Echeverría, and Domingo Faustino Sarmiento himself, who were key figures in the early imagining of a unified central state and a European-laden Argentine nation—to forge the idea that those extensions were nothing but a desert: a part of a territory already owned by the Creoles but characterized by a cruel and indomitable nature that still needed to be controlled. In this trope, there was much more than a description of environmental characteristics. Not only was the military advance on Pampa and Patagonia later named the Conquest of the Desert, but the corresponding advance on the Chaco region was in turn catalogued as the Conquest of the Green Desert (Wright 2003).

As Indian lands were renamed a desert, their inhabitants were symbolically turned into foreigners. The political discourse of the 1870s was especially influential in formulating the stereotype of the aborigines of Pampa and Patagonia as a by-product of a Chilean migration-invasion that transformed and extinguished the real native population.[6] Hence the Conquest could be rationalized as the mission that would expel the savages to Chile, their real motherland. Ironically, what was going on had much in common with the parallel Pacification of the Araucanía underway in Chile. Hence, the only thing left to the Republic was to mourn the extinction of the

Tehuelche, the "real Argentine aborigines," at the hands of the indigenous invaders. At the same time, this would lead the state to adopt limited measures to settle the few "tribal remnants."

The relevant point here is that the urgency of populating empty lands with desirable citizens was seen early on as a vital constituent of the national project and destiny. Though men of the Generación de '80 appear as originators of the axiom "governing is populating" and of the annexation of the desert, they just put an existing plan into motion. Selective migration policies had been in place much earlier, and the military campaign of 1879 against the Indian lands was neither the first nor the only one. It was launched, however, in a specific context and invested with meanings that have conferred it an aura of uniqueness.

To begin with, the proposal that the Conquest was an enterprise of legitimate recovery instead of one of expansion was central to deem it as a more public than private enterprise.[7] However, the effective recovery of the Indian lands would have to wait until other crucial steps secured the process of state-building. The Conquest thus followed other key events such as the end of the civil war between the state of Buenos Aires and the Confederación Argentina (confederation of provinces) that lasted from 1853 to 1862; the war with Paraguay (1865–1869); and the defeat of the last *montoneras,* social and political movements led by charismatic individuals who commanded uprisings of the *gauchos* against the federal government during the 1860s and 1870s. Only after these convoluted events were settled could Argentina's state borders and internal frontiers become a central issue for the elites' politics. Only then was the expansion of the southern frontier over the Pampas, Patagonia, and Araucanía depicted as a source of conflict that required immediate action, although the governments of Argentina and Chile had already agreed to establish state borders by using the Andes as point of reference in the mid-nineteenth century, that is, almost three decades before of the real subjection of those territories.

More specifically, the mental construction of Indian lands as a remote part of the state's territory, whether "desert," depopulated, or populated by "savages," made it possible to conceive the venture as a task of military rather than civil competence (Trinchero 2000). Thus when General Roca, by then already president, reported the success of the military expeditions to the Indian lands in his 1885 State of the Union address to the National Congress, he announced that the problem had been solved:

> Today the absurd barriers that still remained are raised, those that
> the barbarism opposed from the North and from the South of our

own territory, and when one speaks about borders from now on, we will understand that we refer to the lines that divide us from the neighboring nations, and not to those that have been synonymous with blood, grief, insecurity and discredit for the Republic. (Dirección de Información Parlamentaria 1991: 205)

Let us examine how these ideas—of recovery and of an uninhabited land—echoed not only in the spatialization and temporalization (Alonso 1994) of the nation, but in the economic, sociological, and political directives that would convey the forms of consolidation of the territory-nation-state matrix.

In spatial terms the internal borders, or borders with the Indians, were represented as lines of forts. They were, however, spaces of interaction and exchange in an economic region trading in the continental markets and inhabited by a heterogeneous population. Yet insofar as the internal borders were seen as an abrupt limit with the wild, irredeemable, asocial "otherness," the Conquest could be presented as an operation "against the Indians and other marauding upstarts who dominate our long and unknown borders of the south" (Manuel Olascoaga, in Ramayón 1978: 207). In maps drawn to outline the incorporated territory and within a symbolic geography of a country that spread from the mountains to the Atlantic Ocean, the lands assigned to the native population—before really being known and occupied—were already called "national territory." Unlike other provinces, the national territory would not be limited by geographical accidents but by the arbitrary tracing of lines. The cartographic design of the territories is thus reminiscent of the supposed linearity attributed to the borders with the Indians.

As regards the temporalization of the nation, to mark Roca's 1879—or even 1885—as unequivocal threshold of the indigenous neutralization is to forget that the military campaigns to Chaco lasted until 1913 at least. The dating also ignores that the Parliament continued debating whether and how to proceed with the advance and the aborigines' submission for several years (Lenton 2005). As mentioned, the effective arrival of the state institutions to the different regions of Patagonia was slow and uneven, and the transformations that the Conquest presupposes did not happen immediately.

As for substantive evidence, it seems to be as suitable as it is paradoxical to trace the roots of Argentineness to the Tehuelches whenever a complete denial of aborigines' existence is impossible. It is suitable because the Tehuelches were the fewest, the most southern or remote at the moment of the Conquest, as well as the most dispersed. Yet it is paradoxical because the Tehuelches, mobile hunter-gatherers who used to live in tents made of guanaco leather, were considered to be the most alien to civilization. To this day, the juxtaposition of "Argentine" Tehuelches versus "Chilean" Mapuche (who are held responsible of the annihilation of the former) is used to put into question the indigenous rights and claims of the latter. This formulation disregards both the long-lasting practices of mixed marriages among indigenous groups and the fact that the families which call themselves Mapuche had lived on Argentine soil for many generations.

From an economic perspective, spatialization took form in the homestead and land policies. Indeed, the fact that Indian territory was seen as an "inheritance" made it possible in the short term to pay for the costs of the campaign with the sale of shares from the lands to be "recovered." In contradiction with the project to install farmers, this practice ended up encouraging the formation of large estates. Soon, land policies characterized by accumulation benefited the power elite, and were denounced even by Domingo F. Sarmiento, one of the main supporters of the ideology of annihilation of barbarism (Viñas 2003).

These settlement policies reflected the existing tension between the overall liberal spirit of the national Constitution—which, for example, established religious freedom for the inhabitants—and Article 67 clause 15, which called for the national Congress "to assure the peace in the borders, to promote the pacific dealings with the Indians and their conversion to Catholicism." In time, this may explain why de-tribalization policies fostered effects opposite from those intended. In any case, the early legislation established only that the indigenous population should submit to religious "missions." These laws did not refer primarily to indigenous affairs but to immigration and settlement (Avellaneda's Law, 1876) or to the powers of the Governors of National Territories. That is to say, it was assumed that the Indians had to be first Christianized in order to be incorporated into the nation's civil body. Responding to national priorities, though, religious missions were established only in the national territories of the north of the country, where the growing industries were in need of seasonal labor force, and where the local natives, mainly hunter-gatherers, were thought to be the most primitive.[8] In Pampa and Patagonia these missions were never active, except in the island of Tierra del Fuego, to deal with the Selk'-nam population that was considered extremely archaic and regressive. In consequence, indigenous groups that stayed or came back to Pampa and Patagonia and whose claims for settlement were answered ended up under the juridical status of intruders, or settlers with precarious permission of possession of public lands, or settlers with precarious occupation of lands reserved for future settlements. Very few would obtain lands with definitive title of property, only those who could invoke the Ley de Premios Militares (Law of Military Prizes), which was created to benefit those—natives included—who collaborated with the conquering army in the Conquest campaign (Briones and Delrio 2002).

"Settler" or colonist status was meant for the European immigrant population in the Law of Settlement and Immigration of 1876. Later, the 1501 Law of 1884, also called Argentine Home Law (because it was related to the Homestead Acts of the United States), contemplated giving colonists' status to "poor gauchos," the deprived population already deemed Argentine. Towards the end of the 1890s decade, a dozen colonies were created in agreement with this law; many of them were intended to solve the settlement of "tribal remnants" or "scattered aborigines."[9] Implementation of this regulation ended around 1907, and only a handful of indigenous people received colonists' status for agricultural-pastoral colonies.

In sum, Argentina never acted to solve the problems of indigenous people, as Chile did with the distribution towards the end of the nineteenth century of almost three thousand land titles in compensation, which would be the basis of the "reductions" (Bengoa 1985). Nor were solutions of this sort discussed, as they were in the United States, with the project to settle all the indigenous peoples in a state of their own, in Oklahoma (Kelley 1979). Rather, in Argentina we encounter general juridical outlines that may include some reflection on the righteous treatment of the aborigines—though seldom materialized—and decrees and laws drawn to solve specific cases. As a result, today most indigenous communities still do not possess titles of property for their traditionally occupied lands, even though these titles were envisaged in the settlement permissions, and communal possession and property became a constitutional order since the 1994 reform.

From a sociological perspective, the trope of the "desert" blurred the fluency and social complexity of the "internal borders" where aborigines and non-aborigines coexisted and interacted in hostilities and commercial exchanges.[10] It also left not only the aborigines but all the pre-Conquest Creole inhabitants out of the national project. In a country that constructed itself as a by-product of immigration, the national self-image increased the importance of the European newcomers after the Conquest, for these appeared as exclusive beneficiaries of the state "civilizing" action but not, in contrast to the United States, as actors themselves. The exception to this generalization is probably the Welsh colony that started to develop in 1865 and would eventually join the national territory of Chubut. Even this private project in Indian lands, thousands of kilometers away from the line of forts, was permanently monitored by the national authorities that viewed it as a possible source of conflict more than a solution for the occupation of the desert. Thus, even two decades after Chubut's incorporation to the state control, the Welsh community was suspected of favoring the annexation of some Chubut lands to the United Kingdom (Delrio 2005).

In political terms, the incorporation of the conquered areas was seen as recovery but with a peculiar twist, since they were not established as provinces in agreement with the Constitution, but as national territories. In practical terms, this made them completely dependent on federal decision-making. The governors appointed to the first administrations by Buenos Aires were all military men. Moreover, the inhabitants lacked political rights. Thus even though the Conquest was declared a single event that restored republican territory, it created strongly militarized, anomalous gaps in the area of citizens' rights at least up to the middle of the twentieth century (Favaro 1999).

Without minimizing the ambiguities in status of all the inhabitants of the territories, these became more obvious when related to their native inhabitants. For example, immediately after the occupation of the mountainous borders that would presumably divide the Argentinean and Chilean territories, the indigenous settlers ceased to be called "savages" in army documents, only to be categorized as either "Argentine aborigines" or "Chilean aborigines" (Delrio 2002). Originally, this classificatory system represented an attempt to apply *jus solis* to the indigenous population. In order to determine competences and state jurisdictions, people who had not yet formally submitted were to be considered "rebels to their nation," while those who had escaped from one army or another and were crossing the Andes were labeled as "emigrants" or "refugees."[11]

The transformation of indigenes into foreigners continued to be a discretionary device used to reduce the number of those who had to be looked after or settled. Projecting the symbolic geography of the nation backward in time and replacing, in certain cases, *jus solis* for *jus sanguinis*, the lowering of the degree of "barbarism" demanded for diverse settlement policies or labor force regulations gave way to the idea that certain Indians and their descendants were Argentine, while others, like the Mapuche, were and always would be Chilean (Briones and Lenton 1997). Therefore not only was much of the Conquest justified as an effort to stop Chilean expansionism, but also the concept of Araucanization (though this was

not the name given to it at the time) was—and still is—a way to symbolically empty the desert (there are no Indians as the majority are foreigners).
In addition, "foreignization" also exonerated a civilized state from providing merciful Indian policies, since foreign invaders had no right to be
redeemed by civilizing practices.[12]

From another perspective, residents of Mapuche communities in the
current territories of Chile and Argentina generally refer to their grandparents as the "real" Chileans or Argentinians, in opposition to military
expeditions composed by "foreigners." Likewise, they regarded the large
estate owners' businessmen and the small and big traders as foreigners
insofar as they took active part in state policies inclined to genocide and to
indigenous expropriation.

Founding Images and Ethics of the Nation-state

The significance of the Conquest in the history of the country continues
to be debated periodically among academics and prominent intellectuals.

For example, Juan José Cresto, during his tenure as President of the
Argentine Academy of History and Chair of the Museum of National History for more than one term, has stated clearly the tenets of the most conservative, official perspective:

> In recent times, a historiography based upon no trustable documen-
> tation whatsoever maintains that Roca's expedition against the Indi-
> ans in 1879 was a genocide. This claim either shows extreme
> ignorance or hides the interests of territorial claims. The indigenous
> issue is complex, because it involves very different regions . . . races
> that were not and are not comparable, like the Diaguitas, the Abipons
> or the Mapuches. In the South, the Araucanian peoples came from
> Chile and penetrated into the national territory at the beginning of
> the eighteenth century, as many historians of this country tell us,
> some of them in a laudatory tone.
>
> The wild Pampas were totally empty, with some clusters of isolated
> inhabitants . . . the Indian was frightful when he learnt to ride horses
> brought in by the Europeans to steal cows that also came with the
> Spaniards, to sell them in Chile. He was also frightful when he learnt
> how to use iron knives which were obtained as well from the white
> man's industry. The Indian camps were full of female captives, white
> women whose feet were cut to prevent them from running away . . .
> The Argentine history is full of small and big Indian raids during the
> eighteenth and nineteenth centuries, until the final occupation of the

desert by Roca . . . Was Roca occupying Indian lands? The answer is absolutely no. These empty lands started being occupied by the Spanish expeditions in the sixteenth century, which brought horses and cows with them. The Indians started occupying these lands one hundred and eighty years after that . . . Roca organized the expedition, and not only the military but also journalists, scientists and public servants joined in . . . is it believable that all these persons and the others that followed the venture step by step were silent accomplices of a genocide? Is a secret involving five thousand persons conceivable? . . . The only truth is that the Pampas were freed of Indian raids and that the Indians were put into big reservations, although it is also true that dishonest individuals took over many of their lands later . . . On the other hand, speaking of Indians nowadays is an insult. Why Indian? He simply is one more Argentine among the thirty seven million inhabitants of the country, with the same rights and obligations as all of the rest . . . Fortunately, any professional researcher, any scholar interested in learning from the past through documentation will ask astonished: what genocide? (Cresto 2004)

Cresto's perspective on the glorious profile of General Roca, on the unsuitability of thinking about the Conquest as a genocidal enterprise, and of the cruel and foreign temperament of the Mapuche in particular and the Indians in general conflicts with the points of view of academic historians such as Daniel Campione:

What is the relationship between the repudiation of Julio Argentino Roca and the struggle to abolish the so called Día de la Raza (Columbus Day)? To understand this, one has to notice some continuity among the different "conquests," all of them involving land alienation, economic exploitation, and the subjugation of the "vanquished," whose only choice was to submit silently or to "disappear" . . . The Spaniards destroyed and conquered on behalf of the superiority of their religion . . . The Argentines did it on behalf of their racial supremacy and of Western civilization, overcoming the "barbarism" with the scientific weapons provided by Darwin and Gobineau, the leading theorist of nineteenth-century racism. This was the ideological cover-up of landlords who wanted more lands, of businessmen who benefited from loans, of tradesmen who supplied the Army, of military men who earned new medals and also lands. And the Argentine state sought to consolidate itself by means of extending its territorial control over lands only one-third of which it controlled effectively . . . Both conquests match in the construction of an "other" who is put outside, undesirable, with no acknowledged human dignity whatsoever, who deserves to be annihilated physically or spiritually . . . It would be thus confusing to criticize the Dia de la Raza and the glorification of the Spanish conquest with the resulting extermination of the indigenous peoples, while worshiping Roca and the so called conquest of the desert . . . To accept the exaltation of past slaughters keeps the door opened for future crimes. It is not by chance that the last military dictatorship indulged itself through the celebration of both "conquests" . . . At the same time, it devoted itself to "exterminate" the new "stranger," the one who was considered "subversive" not because of his/her race or origin, but because of his/her ideas . . . (Campione 2004)

Disagreements show up in intense exchanges of readers' letters in both national and provincial media whenever a particular situation leads civil society to understand the present in the light of the past. In this sense, exchanges of letters to the editor exploded, for example, when the Mapuche people requested the removal of the Roca statue placed in the town hall square of Bariloche, in the province of Rio Negro (Briones 1999), or when the neighborhood assemblies of Buenos Aires favored a similar removal after the 2001 crisis, as symbol of the need to rethink the historical agreements of the country. Controversy flared again at the beginning of 2006, when the Constitutional Assembly of the province of Neuquén discussed whether and how indigenous rights—the Mapuches' obviously included—should be incorporated in the constitutional amendment under examination. In this last regard, a neighbor from Bariloche sent the following letter to the most prominent newspaper of the region:

If the National Constitution says that every Argentine and every foreigner who chooses to live under our flag has the same civic rights, and Neuquén's Constitution abides by the National Constitution, then Neuquén's administration's stance is inappropriate vis-à-vis the Mapuche ethnic group, which is native of the Mapocho River, in Santiago de Chile. They are not indigenous to this land, for they are living in the land of the *puelches* [people of the East, where the sun comes out, Argentine people]. These two peoples [Mapuches and puelches] are divided by the Andes and the language . . . The Mapuche descendants have no special indigenous rights whatsoever, for all of them are *ngulluches* [people from the West, where the sun comes down, Chilean nowadays] . . . It seems that our old soldiers of the Conquest of the Desert (1879/1885), dead people whose tombs bloomed with crosses throughout the vast Pampas and the Cordillera to honor the mandate of the National Executive Power on behalf of the Argentine people, have no value whatsoever nowadays. (*Río Negro On line*, 01/29/2006, available at http://www.rionegro.com.ar /arch200601/29/cartas.php)

What is interesting is how debates about the Conquest bring out conflicting self-images. Briefly, these images continue to clash because they refer to unsolved historical problems, such as the recognition of the indigenous peoples' past and present contributions to the mainstream. But they can also be conflictive because of the way reviewing past flaws brings out contemporary tensions in individuals, as, for example, in seeking to ascertain whether the Argentine state has shown a genocidal predisposition from its very emergence.

In this last regard, those who seek to emphasize these readings frequently find intimate relations between the elimination of the aborigines at the end of the nineteenth century and the state terrorism carried out one century afterwards (from David Viñas 2003 to Osvaldo Bayer 2005; see Campione above). Conversely, those who restrict and transform the concept of genocide as foreign business—up to the point of considering it to be improper to speak in such terms about Argentine history—emphasize as well the foreign aspect of the Indians of Pampa and Patagonia and the alleged "stateless" quality of the 1970s "subversives." They also consider, for both cases, that the numbers of casualties are exaggerated (as if the quantitative aspect were to define the qualitative one).

Both parties of this ideological divide concentrate their arguments solely on the period of the military actions (1878–1885), thus reinforcing the characterization of the Conquest as an epitomizing event that must be understood in opposing ways. As such, the Conquest gains cross-temporal significance that continues to activate and re-articulate representations of aboriginality with residual efficacy (Jameson 1991). Yet it provides little material to explain what lay behind the Argentine state's Indian policies and indigenous peoples' trajectories. Because of that, in the previous section we illustrated how the state's territorialization imposed different approaches and tempos in the economic and political incorporation of the indigenous population and the so-called national territories as well. In this section we will explore how the hegemonically determined realities within which the indigenous peoples have had to make sense of themselves reverberate in and affect their memories.

In the representation of the Conquest of the Desert as a mere account of the clashes between the military and the aborigines, neither the hegemonic memories nor the subaltern ones reveal the crudeness of the clash or the defeat of the former and the victory of the latter (as in the battles of Little Big Horn or Wounded Knee).

In various and now popular descriptions, the images of the Conquest are stereotyped images of Indian raiders taking their loot and captives, or else of the army led by Roca arriving at the Rio Negro empty of inhabitants.[13] This simplification of actions—indigenous raids and military parades—corresponds with that of the indigenous groups themselves. None of the subjects that led the resistance remain in the official history or in the popular media culture as individuals with distinctive personal profiles. Prominent figures who contributed to the complexity of Indian diplomacy and the development of the frontier's economic, political, and social life, such as Sayhueque (Vezub 2002) or Calfucura (Bechis 1983), blur into the desert stereotype woven by the official history. They are seen as characters within a plot logic that overcomes them, rather than subjects capable of taking political decisions. Together with the absence of indigenous protagonists in the national heroes' pantheon (unlike in Chile and Peru, for instance), the idea of Friendly Indians (*Indios Amigos*)[14] tends to operate as a collective noun, or as a personal labeling that equally blurs any individual identity. Probably saintly Ceferino Namuncurá is the best known individual figure, as a young man who, once the Conquest was concluded, embraced civilization and initiated the way of "redemption" by joining the Salesian seminary to become a Catholic priest.

In terms of images that have shaped the popular culture, it is still paradoxical that *Martin Fierro*, the literary piece that buttresses the canon of Argentine literature, recreates notions that link the Indian camps on the other side of the frontier with savagism and absolutely irredeemable customs. And this is paradoxical because the *Martin Fierro* is one of the first items of that canon that has a fair view of the gauchos (Shumway 1991), although it ignores miscegenation and leaves Indians out of a shared way of life. Many years later (1945), the movie *Pampa Bárbara* follows the same line in its vision of the border as menaced by an indigenous savagery that pollutes the bonhomie and ethics of the suffering gaucho, confined to the forts.[15] It is not irrelevant either that the media culture lacks prominent figures such as Daniel Boone or the Lone Ranger, who at least appear in a friendly relation with a tarnished but existing indigenous mate.

In sum, these hegemonic imaginaries leave out any indigenous character that is valued or presented as a companion with whom a non-indigenous character can form a lasting friendship based—though with asymmetries—in reciprocal confidence and loyalty.[16] Instead, the national formation of alterity has sought to "whiten" or render invisible those aborigines who were capable of being civilized (who showed, for example, an ability to make political alliances), and to keep at a distance those who somehow were seen as a threat to the values of civilization (the reluctant and objectors). Both movements can be exemplified with the double stereotype of the personalities of Valentín Sayhueque and Miguel Ñancuche Nahuelquir. These two indigenous leaders had formed a political alliance and shared destinies, after the campaigns, in the same concentration camps. Nevertheless, the state and missionary agencies would permanently present them through contrasting images. While Sayhueque represents rebelliousness and the impossibility of full incorporation to civilized life, Miguel Ñancuche stands for a straight path of change (Delrio 2001). The paradox here is that Sayhueque had been considered by the state as the most plausible chief for an alliance before the Conquest and had even been named as indigenous Argentine Governor by Roca (Bechis 1999). However, within the concentration camps, he was the one who refused to give up polygamy and tribal rituals and was thus punished with the deportation of the families under his leadership to the province of Mendoza (Delrio 2001).

Adding to the distance constructed against anything indigenous was the singular blend of biological positivism that characterized Argentina's moral elites (Soler 1979), according to which the elimination or extinction of inferior races was inevitable and legitimate. In practical terms, this ideology militated against any policy based, for example, on the type of seductive appeal of Rondón's Brazilian positivism (Ramos 1995). It also meant that honoring the agreements that had been signed with the aborigines up to one year before the military campaigns of 1879 was unnecessary (Levaggi 2000, Briones and Carrasco 2000), another clear contrast with the United States and Canada.

In turn, the ambiguities concerning the Indian—a race doomed to become extinct because of its own inadequacy or that had to be actively neutralized—correspond to the contradictory visions that hegemonic discourses fostered. For these emphasize the campaigns as a heroic military endeavor, yet at the same time minimize the violence of the actions and highlight the knowledge gained by means of an enterprise depicted, at times, more as scientific than military.[17] The statements that diminish the crudeness of the army are precisely those that are invoked today by people who deny the epithet of "genocide" to explain the ways in which the annexation of the territories of Pampa and Patagonia came to be. From their point of view, the purpose of the military endeavor was to bring about "civilization" and "progress" to the region. As summarized by a commentator who was until recently the director of the Museum of National History:

> Roca organized the expedition and it included not only military bodies, but also journalists, scientists and civil servants . . . there were also nurses and helpers. The Indian prisoners and the children, women and elders were examined for ailments, vaccinated and many of them were sent to diverse hospitals of the very precarious Buenos Aires of those days. (Cresto 2004).

This bloodless[18] quality serves not only to minimize the numbers of indigenous "casualties of war," but to defend, on the basis of its civilizing effect, the different "destinies" of the prisoners and those who submitted and surrendered (Mases 2002). In this regard, it is interesting to note what subject becomes a topic of public debate, as well as what stays out of it.

One idea proposed as a solution was to send the defeated to Tucumán as the labor force for the sugar cane harvests, or to distribute them in private houses as domestic personnel, or to assign them to the army (Briones 2004; Lenton 2005). Other contemporaries doubted the effectiveness of these proposals to achieve the civilizing objective and even questioned its humane correctness.[19] The remarkable point is that almost nothing became public in relation to the forced peregrinations, the massive deportations, and the confinement in concentration camps of certain groups, until the nation-state decided what to do with them (Delrio 2005). Though the existing documentation in historical files does not register these practices, these are described—as we will see next—in other sources.

Silenced Counterarguments of the Bloodless Venture

From the indigenous perspective, descriptions of the campaign period are flooded with pain and suffering, to the extreme that sometimes the *wigka* (white, non-Indian) invader is not even directly mentioned (Golluscio 1990, Briones 1988). Bringing together (Briggs 1986) communicative, interpretive, and genre-specific contexts to relate in a condensed manner the mistreatments of various periods, "the triplex sign 'the arrival of the Spanish'" refers to the necessity of escaping and hiding. It also introduces stories that tell the fear in which the ancestors lived, their inability to light a fire to cook or to warm up during the escapes to the other side of the Andes in order not to be discovered; and the strategy of burying belongings and valuables that could not be transported in the flight.

The trauma of the elders—as well as present interethnic relations— reinforce the silences. That is why, before beginning to share one of these stories, an elder said to one of us once: "you should forgive me my child because I know that your dad is Spanish, but when the Spanish came . . . " When the distance between the speaker and the listener narrows, more explicit statements may emerge. These stories embody the otherwise epitomized event as family history, with names and known faces:

> They took my grandmother captive and they took her to Buenos Aires . . . they had them locked up, in a regiment, say, that they were guarded there by the military men. They [the military men] locked them in the barrack and they walk them, herding them like animals. (Mauricio Fermín, Vuelta del Rio, Chubut, January 2005)
>
> In the time of this captivity, the lady when tired, when she couldn't [walk] any more, they cut off her tits. She was a captive, my grandmother was a captive, an Argentine captive, and when they took her captive she had to go then . . . there. There was where she had to go, [but] ran away, went out, she came here, and made a family here. My grandmother used to cry [when she remembered]. (Laureana Nahueltripay, Cushamen, Chubut 1997)

Statements of this type take us back to the scarcely known "meanwhile" of the solution to the indigenous problem. Beyond the various strategies with which the native peoples faced the Conquest campaigns in the southern border,[20] the common destiny of many of the submitted and voluntarily assembled groups was departure to concentration camps under military control, until the state officers decided what would be done with them, whether placement in the labor force or "tribal remnants" settlement. These camps, set up mainly along the Rio Negro and in Valcheta, were centers from which large numbers of people were moved towards other parts of the country (mainly to Buenos Aires, Tucumán, and Cuyo). This "meanwhile," in some cases, took more than ten years.[21]

The indigenous people are not the only ones that keep a memory record of these practices. As a Welsh colonist of the territory of Chubut wrote:

The path that we were crossing went across the tents of the Indians that the government had imprisoned in a reformatory. In these reserves, I believe that there was the majority of the Patagonia's Indians. The most important nucleus was nearby Valcheta. They were surrounded by weaved wire fences of great height, in that court the Indians walked. (John Daniel Evans, in Clery Evans, 1994: 92–93)

Though Evans's memories have nourished the official history of the province of Chubut, this fragment has been neglected. Perhaps selective oblivions relate to three main areas of practices that became self-fulfilling prophecies of the irrelevance of "the indigenous problem," or of the lack of specific or substantial material of native senses of being and belonging.

First, these practices resulted in a relative depopulation of the conquered regions after the indigenous surrender, which tautologically fed the metaphor of the desert that must be populated by European pioneers or colonists from other parts of the country. However, here the subaltern memories turn out to be very explicit when individuals describe the events that preceded the settlement in present-day communities.

My granny used to cry, she cried, she remembered. And when all those elders who escaped from the war got together . . . they said how they [the white men] tied them, when they were tied, they say they [the white men] herded the persons. Those that were pregnant, as they delivered, they [the white men] cut the kids nape and the woman who delivered stayed there lying down. They [the white men] killed them. They [the elders] came barefooted or with guanaco leather boots. This is what my grandmother said. They [the white men] led them to the place where they killed them all. From different places, those who escaped came here. (Catalina Antilef, February 2005, Futahuao, Chubut)

The so-called tribal remnants were a product of silent policies on the disposition of contingents that were systematically concentrated and deported to different parts of the country according to the needs of the regional elites. Because of their small size, tribal remnants would not have made it necessary for the state to formulate a uniform settlement policy. Other practices of de-tribalization, like renaming people and separating family groups, meant to deny to the expelled population self-recognition as indigenous settlers. There were other mechanisms of denial of their culture, such as forbidding polygamy and certain rituals, as well as the banning of religious figures. Thus, when the remainder of the confined population was removed from the military centers in the 1890s, it was hoped that many of them would seek work as rural laborers in the new *estancias* or large ranches in the region. Nonetheless, there were still some who persevered in requesting collective settlements.

Those natives who remained or came back to Patagonia and asked for collective settlement permissions encountered bureaucrats who questioned either the autochthony of people self-identified as Mapuche, or alleged that the indigenous families could not demonstrate the minimal conditions or potential for civility and civilization ("they continue living in tents") to be recognized as settlers. The indigenous people kept being accused of being Chileans or uncivilized, not only to deny them possession of the land throughout the twentieth century, but also to legitimize evictions from lands that had been previously granted. Even the double self-recognition as "Argentinian" and "civilized" would not be a guarantee of permanent status, as is dramatically attested by the eviction of the Nahuelpans (Briones and Lenton 1997; Chele Diaz 2004, Delrio 2005; Lenton 2005).

If, following the indigenous peoples' surrender or capture, their paths were far from linear, so too were their itineraries after the deportations and the concentration camps. They had to move anew, either from denied spaces (for not being the "original ones"), or from granted ones (promptly given to or appropriated by tenants and new owners of large estates). Displacements were also the result of voluntarily abandoning granted spaces that gradually became inadequate because of the growth of families and their flocks (Olivera and Briones 1987).

The cultural integrity of the peoples of Pampa and Patagonia thus suffered various transformations. In some ways, instead of leading to de-tribalization, the settlements were producing the opposite effect, as happened in other contexts (see, for instance, Bengoa 1985 for the Chilean case). Permission to settle that was granted to a certain chief and his "people" or his "tribe" gave way to processes of communalization for many communities that today are recognized or claim to be recognized as such. The "manifest destiny" that the state envisaged and created resulted in uncertain and heterogeneous destinies for the native peoples. However, the more extreme state plan of material and symbolic de-Indianization was only partly fulfilled.

It is worth pointing out that the processes of community formation were far from being mere relocations of "tribal remnants"—as the official discourse would label those populations. On the contrary, communities have undergone successive development by means of adoptions, ritual kinship, and the establishment of new alliances among groups permanently marginalized and compelled to prove—and to unfold under multiple pressures—strategies to obtain lands and the state's recognition.

Many ethno-historical and ethnological interpretations fail because they disregard the vicissitudes and painful experiences of indigenous people. Historians tend to focus on specific periods and hence they link the current Mapuche self-recognition with an "Araucanization" (adoption of a borrowed Mapuche identity and culture) that looms as definite in time as the Conquest does. Besides, they remain trapped in the arguments on how much Mapuche or how much Tehuelche—and so how much Chilean or how much Argentinian—these settlers are. Without even listening to what these subjects have to say, their interpreters lose the possibility of understanding the power and need to extend in time the diverse practices of communalization for the collective survival of heterogeneous groups. More regrettable still is their failure to admit that even today and in spite of constitutional mandates, the recognition of an indigenous sense of belonging remains vulnerable to arguments, pressures, and disqualifications. We refer to hegemonic practices that involve the constant questioning of the aboriginality of certain citizens for having migrated, or the denial of legal standing as "indigenous community" to families in rural or urban places that today request it, justified by the argument that they cannot exhibit any type of "traditional" organization, or that they are distanced from the "original places" they were forced to abandon.

From the point of view of the processes of construction of cultural hegemony, the effects of what has been done, said, and concealed are several. Explicit imputations of foreignness and incivility, as well as the silences imposed on practices and policies of extermination and de-Indianization, contributed to produce the conventional certainty, almost undisputed up to the end of the twentieth century, that Argentina is an Indian-free country, or a country in which aborigines do not exist in a significant proportion. Moreover, it is generally believed that the few remaining Indians would have or would lack nowadays whatever they used to have or lack before, and are thus held responsible for not having known how to adapt to civilization. In this, the residual efficacy of the nationalization of indigenous memberships is still important, given that in the ongoing twenty-first century Mapuche land claims continue to be described as a vehicle of "Chileans' dark interests in Argentine territory" (as stated, for instance, in Casamiquela 2004 and 2007).

From the point of view of subaltern memories, some of the hegemonic imaginaries have been embodied as self-images of irreparable loss or cultural deterioration, or even as the belief that indigenousness expresses itself only, or better, in rural contexts. These images coexist with statements about indigenous belonging that are anchored in the memory of diverse sufferings and displacements. The interesting point is that such recollections have not only circulated inside the communities, but also traveled across time and space, through oral transmission and along their forced migration paths. These migrations took them and continue taking them to other communities, to rural places, to Patagonian ranches and towns, to the most important cities of the country, or abroad. Thus indigenous senses of belonging are not based only upon community-based experiences or face-to-face interactions, but also woven in and through heterogeneous and apparently detached circuits—circuits in fact connected by clandestine stories and suppressed memories.

To make silenced statements audible seems to be the only way to grasp the strength of indigenous identifications that still hold today in Argentina despite having been historically vilified; identifications which still are derogated nowadays, when they are labeled as "emergent" or opportunistic. In the social sciences, it might be helpful to consider the limitations of scholars who continue anchoring group-formation processes in structures of resources and opportunities, without considering that indigenous senses of belonging are often cemented together by memories of sufferings that only euphemistically can be defined as "cultural capital."

In any event, by taking into account subaltern memories we have not simply tried to understand Mapuche perspectives, trajectories, and claims. We have mainly aimed at unraveling past and present state practices that official memories and hegemonic discourses tend to hide from us all.

Notes

1. The word "raid" (in Spanish *malón*) had been used to describe indigenous military actions (both small incursions and large mobilizations of warriors). Especially in the second half of the nineteenth century, raids were typically ascribed to "savages," given their "natural" tendency to robbery. Therein the significance of naming the Creoles' actions of retaliation and invasion with the same word, "raid."

2. For example, Law 215 of 1867 stipulated that settlement policies should be made by agreement with "voluntarily presented" or surrendered Indians chiefs, and decided unilaterally for those who continued to rebel. In practical terms, however, it seemed easier for the state to grant a more immediate and

negotiated "solution" to leaders identified as "rebels," such as Namuncura, than to leaders who had performed as "soldiers" of the National Army.

3. Often, commentators who refute the contemporary critiques of the Conquest accuse such critics of historical anachronism—the projection to the past of values related to the present—in making the charges of disrespect for an idea of human rights that would appear much later in time. However, Diana Lenton's study (1992) on the parliamentary debates concerning the implementation of submission and settlement policies shows that opposing voices were raised among the moral elites themselves at the time. While invoking humanism, clemency and commiseration to the defeated, these voices could not, however, affect the prevalent views of the successive administrations.

4. As an example, the so called Frontier Studies in Chile were intended to renew previous debates. Recognizing the publication of *Relaciones fronterizas en la Araucanía* (1982) as a precedent of such an enterprise, the set of works that follow this line of inquiry take the explanation of complexity as their key aim. In Sergio Villalobos's words, the Frontier Studies would become the Chilean version of the "history from below" paradigm, by claiming the impossibility of understanding the Chilean history without considering "the indigenous perspective." In time, however, most analyses cannot overcome a one-sided standpoint that eschews consideration of the indigenous agency. Thus Villalobos himself describes how, after agonizing for three centuries, the Pehuenches have gone into extinction and physical and cultural miscegenation (Villalobos 1989). In sum, he advances an explanation that takes their present away from the current Pehuenches.

5. The Argentine constitution was written in 1853, adopted by the province of Buenos Aires only in 1860, and put into effect in 1880, with the federalization of the capital city.

6. This "foreignizing" discourse on the indigenous population uses episodes of the political indigenous history as an index of a "Chilean invasion." This way, the presence in the Pampa of groups from the Andes, registered from the first moment of the Spanish conquest, is showed as an invasion that still threatens the republic (see for instance the rationale of Estanislao Zeballos's argument, in Zeballos 1986).

7. Because of the nature of the state and the role it took in indigenous affairs, management of these fell to the executive power rather than the legislative or the judicial powers. Thus, in Argentina, Supreme Court rulings on indigenous cases are very scarce. Besides being highly unfavorable to the native peoples, these rulings recreate widespread stereotypes (Carrasco 2000). This makes an interesting contrast with the United States, where the judiciary was able to produce concepts like that of "domestic dependent nation," creating jurisprudence and at the same time directives for the procedures of the other two state branches (Cornell 1988a and 1988b; Deloria 1979; Strong and Van Winkle

1993). For another element of comparison, in Argentina the indigenous affairs agency was never defined in contrast to the SPI/FUNAI (see Pacheco, this volume) in Brazil or the BIA in the United States (Champagne 1992), for it never lasted in time and had little importance. On the contrary, what occurred was a scattering of indigenous agencies—twenty-one between 1912 and 1980 (Martínez Sarasola 1992: 387–9)—some with frequent changes of ministerial jurisdiction, and sometimes there was no agency.

8. Much of the population submitted in the south was moved to the north as labor force, for the wood workshops and the sugar cane harvests. They were also moved to Cuyo to serve the equally subsidized wine industry.

9. The government of Julio Roca, in his second presidential period 1898 to 1904, used "Home Law" to keep an extensive territory of approximately 300,000 hectares, intended for the settlement in colonies of the still dispersed indigenous groups. These lands were afterwards subdivided and destined for other purposes. Situated between two different national territories, this wide swath resembles the Great Navajo Reservation of the United States, defined in territories of four states (Baca 1988). Yet it was neither devoted to the settlement of a single people, nor experienced enlargements in time. On the contrary, it was a seemingly generic space for diverse "tribal remnants" and was reduced in time.

10. Many commentators have discarded the idea of "desert" and "wild world," along with nomad life of "equestrian vandals." The most important authors in this field are Raúl Mandrini (1984), Martha Bechis (1984), Lidia Nacuzzi (1996), Miguel Palermo (1986), Leonardo León Solis (1991), José Bengoa (1985), Claudia Gotta (1993), Pedro Navarro Floria (1996) and Marcela Tamagnini (1997), among others.

11. This comes up in the correspondence exchanged by the commanders of the Chilean and Argentinian armies, especially between Gregorio Urrutia and Enrique Godoy, who repeatedly used the terms "emigrated Indians" to talk about those who had traversed the Andean passes. They also pointed to the "asylum" and to the "Ley de Gentes" or Law of Peoples to refer to those who were considered either Argentine or Chilean Indians (*National File of Chile, Department of War*, Vol. 1045, F. 105–110).

12. Ethnologists of the first half of the twentieth century consolidated these theories in the concepts of "Araucanization" and "Tehuelche complex" (Mandrini and Ortelli 1995; Lazzari and Lenton 2000). They reaffirm the nationalistic discourses that extrapolate the nation-state borders to a remote past in phrases like the "the first settlers," the "Argentine aborigines," "provincial aborigines," etc. that are part of textbooks, ethnic maps, academic articles, and encyclopedias.

13. The picture by the Uruguayan painter José María Blanes, in the National Historical Museum of Buenos Aires, has been used several times as the icon to

illustrate this historic episode. On the $100 bill still in current use, however, the reproduction has cut off a scene on the left that shows a few aborigines listening to a priest.

14. The "Friendly Indians" refers to certain political or familiar indigenous units that served or collaborated with the state forces. On the subject, see for instance Bechis (1999), Delrio (2002).

15. There is an American version of this film, the remake *Savage Pampas,* released in 1966.

16. An exception may be found in the comic strips by Dante Quinterno that show a relationship between "Patoruzú" (Patagonian Indian) and "Isidoro Cañones" (pampered and naughty son of urban parents). The complexity of the strategies of indigenous "othering" that this series promotes prevents us from a deeper analysis here. All the same, it is enough to mention that the origin of the Indian character's Tehuelche lineage goes back to ancient Egypt.

17. "The army that has achieved this work, does not need, in order to be worthy of the country's eternal gratitude, to be remembered by the martial actions that it executed. It will be enough to exhibit only the itineraries of its march, the immense sum of knowledge that it has produced, and the important problems that it has solved" (Manuel Olascoaga, in *Ramayón* 1878: 207).

18. "Only when historians analyze the war of the desert and its development will numerous interesting descriptions be seen, and only then will be perceived, with the greatest certainty, an idea of the *bloodless sacrifices*" (*Ramayón* [1921] 1978: 123; our emphasis).

19. As Diana Lenton indicates (1992), these procedures were also denounced in the Congress. Aristóbulo del Valle, opposition legislator from the province of Buenos Aires, argued in 1879 that "what did we do in the campaign of the Patagonia? We reproduced the barbarian scenes from the time of the slave trade . . . we have enslaved the man, prostituted the woman, we have torn the child from its mother's bosom, the elder has been taken to serve as slave somewhere."

20. On this subject see Bechis (1999), Delrio (1996, 2002, and 2005).

21. For example Delrio (2005) reports that "Domingo Milanesio in 1894 visited a Tehuelche camp at the Lak-naik Lake (27 miles to the south of the Mayo River, Chubut), where a woman told him that she knew him from his previous missions in Valcheta, in 1884. In 1896, Vacchina mentioned that he found part of Prane's tribe in Gualjaina, where two women told him that they had been already baptized, one in Chichinales and the other one in Junín de los Andes."

References

Academia Nacional de la Historia. 1980. *Congreso Nacional de Historia sobre la Conquista del Desierto.* Buenos Aires: Academia Nacional de la Historia. 4 tomos.

(Autores varios). 1982. *Relaciones Fronterizas en la Araucanía.* Santiago de Chile: Editorial de la Universidad Católica de Chile.

Baca, L. 1988. "The Legal Status of American Indians." In *Handbook of North American Indians.* W. Sturtevant (general ed.). Washington: Smithsonian Institute. Vol. IV, W. Washburn (vol. ed). "History of Indian-White Relations." IV: 230–37.

Bandieri, S. 1993. "Actividades Económicas y Modalidades de Asentamiento." En *Historia de Neuquén.* S. Bandieri *et al.* (ed.) Buenos Aires: Plus Ultra. pp. 147–261.

Bayer, Osvaldo. 2005. "De Estatuas y Genocidas." Primera Jornada. *Políticas genocidas del estado argentino: Campaña del Desierto y Guerra de la Triple Alianza*. Legislatura de la Ciudad de Buenos Aires, Mayo 9.

Bechis, Martha Aurora. 1984. *Interethnic Relations during the Period of Nation-State Formation in Chile and Argentina: From Sovereign to Ethnic.* New York: New School Publication no. 8409728.

———. 1999. "La 'organización nacional' y las tribus pampeanas en Argentina durante el siglo XIX." Paper presented at XII Congreso Internacional de AHILA. Porto, Portugal.

Bengoa, José. 1985. *Historia social del pueblo Mapuche. Siglos XIX y XX.* Santiago de Chile: Ed. Sur.

Briggs, Ch. 1986. *Learning How to Ask: A Sociolinguistic Appraisal of the Role of the Interview in Social Science Research.* Cambridge: Cambridge University Press.

Briones, Claudia. 1988. "Caciques y estancieros mapuche: dos momentos y una historia." Paper presented at 46° Congreso Internacional de Americanistas, Ámsterdam, Holland.

———. 1998. *La alteridad en el cuarto mundo. Una construcción antropológica de la diferencia.* Buenos Aires, Ediciones del Sol.

———. 1999. "Weaving 'the Mapuche People': The Cultural politics of Organizations with Indigenous Philosophy and Leadership." Ph.D. Dissertation, University of Austin, Texas.

———. 2004. "Construcciones de Aboriginalidad en Argentina." *Bulletin de la Société Suisse des Américanistes,* 68: 73–90.

Briones, Claudia y Morita Carrasco. 2000. *Pacta Sunt Servanda. Capitulaciones, convenios y tratados con indígenas en Pampa y Patagonia (Argentina, 1742–1880).* Bs. As., International Working Group on Indigenous Affairs, Serie Documentos en Español no. 29. VinciGuerra Testimonios.

Briones, Claudia y Delrio, Walter. 2002. "Patria sí, colonias también. Estrategias diferenciadas de radicación de indígenas en Pampa y Patagonia." En: Teruel, Ana, Lacarrieu, Mónica y Jerez, Omar (comps.) *Fronteras, ciudades y estados.* Colección Mnemosina. Córdoba: Alción Editora.

Briones, Claudia y Diana Lenton. 1997. "Debates parlamentarios y nación. La construcción discursiva de la inclusión/exclusión del indígena." En: *Actas de las Terceras Jornadas de Lingüística Aborigena,* Instituto de Lingüística, FFyL-UBA: 303–18.

Brow, James. 1990. "Notes on Community, Hegemony, and the Uses of the Past." *Anthropological Quarterly,* 63(1): 1–6.

Campione, Daniel. 2004. "De la Conquista española a la conquista del 'desierto.'" *Argenpress,* 17 de octubre (available at http://argenpress.ar4.toservers.com /nota.asp?num=015200).

Carrasco, Morita. 1991. "Hegemonía y Políticas Indigenistas Argentinas en el Chaco Centro-Occidental." *América Indígena* 51(1): 63–122.

———. 2000. *Los derechos de los pueblos indígenas en Argentina.* Asociación de Comunidades Indígenas Lhaka Honhat e International Working Group on Indigenous Affairs. Serie Documentos en Español # 30. Buenos Aires: VinciGuerra Testimonios.

Casamiquela, Rodolfo. 2004. "Los Mapuches verdaderos son muy pocos." *Diario Río Negro on line,* 6 de septiembre. (Available at www.rionegro.com.ar /arch200409/06/o06j04.php).

———. 2007. "Hay mucha hipocresía y demagogia con los pueblos mapuches." *Diario El Bolsón on line,* Río Negro (Available at www.bolsonweb.com.ar /diariobolson/detalle.php?id_noticia=8553).

Cerutti, A. et al. 1996. *Las usinas del prejuicio antichileno en el territorio del Neuquén en el período comprendido entre 1895 y 1930.* Informe final. Facultad de Derecho y Ciencias Sociales. Departamento de Ciencias Políticas y Sociales, UNCOMA.

Champagne, D. 1992. "Organizational Change and Conflict: A Case Study of the Bureau of Indian Affairs." In *Native Americans and Public Policy.* F. Lyden and L. Legters (eds). Pittsburgh: University of Pittsburgh Press, pp. 33–61.

Cornell, S. 1988a. *The Return of the Native. American Indian Political Resurgence.* New York: Oxford University Press.

———. 1988b. "The Transformations of Tribe: Organization and Self-concept in Native American Ethnicities." *Ethnic and Racial Studies,* 11(1): 27–47.

Cresto, Juan José. 2004. "Roca y el mito del genocidio." *La Nación Digital,* 23 de noviembre. (Available at http://www.lanacion.com.ar/opinion/nota.asp ?nota_id=656498&origen=premium)

Deloria, V. Jr. 1979. "Self-determination and the Concept of Sovereignty." In *Economic Development in American Indian Reservations.* R. Dunbar Ortiz (ed.).

Santa Fe, NM: Native American Studies, University of New Mexico, Development Series no. 1, pp. 22–8.

Deloria, V. Jr. and C. Lytle. 1983. *American Indians, American Justice*. Austin: University of Texas Press.

Delrio, Walter. 1996. *Estrategias de relación interétnica en Patagonia noroccidental hacia fines del siglo XIX. El caso del linaje de Miguel Ñancuche Nahuelquir y el proceso de comunalización en Colonia Cushamen*. Buenos Aires: Universidad de Buenos Aires.

———. 2001. "Confinamiento, deportación y bautismos en la costa del río Negro." *Cuadernos de Antropología Social,* Inst. De Ciencias Antropológicas-UBA, no. 13.

———. 2002. "Indios amigos, salvajes o argentinos. Procesos de construcción de categorías sociales en la incorporación de los pueblos originarios al estado-nación (1870–1885)." En: Nacuzzi, Lidia e I. De Jong. *Funcionarios, militares y exploradores. Miradas sobre el otro en la frontera pampeano-patagónica*. Sociedad Argentina de Antropología (en prensa).

———. 2005. *Memorias de expropiación. Sometimiento e incorporación indígena en la Patagonia (1872–1943)*. Bernal: Universidad Nacional de Quilmes.

Díaz, Chele. 2003. *1937: El desalojo de la tribu Nahuelpán*. El Bolsón: Editorial Musiquel.

Dirección De Información Parlamentaria Del Congreso De La Nación 1991. *Tratamiento de la Cuestión Indígena*. Buenos Aires: Estudios e Investigaciones no. II.

Evans, Clery. 1994. *John Daniel Evans, El Molinero* (C. A. Evans, pub., 92–93), citado por J. Fiori y G. De Vera, *Trevelin, un pueblo en los tiempos del molino* (2002: 24–25).

Favaro, O. 1999. *Neuquén. La construcción de un orden estatal*. Neuquén: Universidad Nacional del Comahue.

Golluscio, Lucía. 1990. "La Imagen del Dominador en la Literatura Oral Mapuche y su relación con lo 'no dicho', una Estrategia de Resistencia Cultural." *Annales Littéraires de l'Université de Franche-Comté,* París, 416: 695–707.

Gotta, C. 1993. "Una aproximación histórica al problema del ganado como moneda en norpatagonia, siglos XVIII-XIX." En: *Anuario IEHS*, no. VIII, Tandil.

Jameson, Frederic. 1991. *The Political Unconscious. Narrative as a Socially Symbolic Act*. Ithaca: Cornell University Press.

Kelley, K. 1979. "Federal Indian Land Policy and Economic Development in the United States." In *Economic Development in American Indian Reservations*. R. Dunbar Ortiz (ed.). Santa Fe, NM: Native American Studies, University of New Mexico, Development Series no. 1, pp. 30–42.

Landsman, G. and S. Ciborski. 1992. "Representation and Politics: Contesting Histories of the Iroquois." *Cultural Anthropology,* 7(4): 425–47.

Lazzari, Axel y Diana Lenton. 2000. "Etnología y Nación: facetas del concepto de Araucanización." En *Avá. Revista de Antropología*, 1: 125–40.

Lenton, Diana. 1992. "Relaciones Interétnicas: Derechos Humanos y Autocrítica en la Generación del '80." En *La problemática Indígena. Estudios antropológicos sobre pueblos indígenas de la Argentina.* J. Radovich y A. Balazote (comps.). Buenos Aires: CEDAL, pp. 27–65.

———. 2005. "De Centauros a Protegidos. La construcción del sujeto de la política indigenista argentina desde los debates parlamentarios." Tesis Doctoral. Facultad de Filosofía y Letras, Universidad de Buenos Aires.

León Solís, Leonardo. 1991. *Maloqueros y conchavadores en Araucanía y las Pampas, 1700–1800.* Temuco: Ediciones Universidad de la Frontera, Serie Quinto Centenario.

Levaggi, Abelardo. 2000. *Paz en la frontera. Historia de las relaciones diplomáticas con las comunidades indígenas en la Argentina (Siglos XVI–XIX).* Buenos Aires: Universidad del Museo Social.

Mandrini, Raúl. 1984. "La base económica de los cacicatos araucanos del actual territorio argentino (siglo XIX)." Ponencia presentada en: *VI Jornadas de Historia Económica.* Vaquerías, Córdoba.

Mandrini, Raúl y Sara Ortelli. 1995. "Repensando viejos problemas: observaciones sobre la araucanización de las pampas." En: *Runa*, vol. XXII, Buenos Aires.

Martínez Sarásola, C. 1992. *Nuestros paisanos los indios.* Buenos Aires.

Mases, Enrique. 2002. *Estado y cuestión indígena. El destino final de los indios sometidos en el sur del territorio (1878–1910).* Buenos Aires, Prometeo libros/ Entrepasados.

Nacuzzi, Lidia. 1996. *"Los tehuelches del norte de la Patagonia."* Tesis de Doctorado. Universidad de Buenos Aires.

Navarro Floria, Pedro. 1996. "Ciencia y política en la región Norpatagónica: el abordaje ilustrado a la ocupación militar (1779–1879)." En: Jorge Pinto (ed.), *Araucanía y Pampas. Un mundo fronterizo en América del Sur.* Temuco: Ediciones Universidad de la Frontera, pp. 93–101.

Olivera, Miguel y Claudia Briones. 1987. "Proceso y estructura: Transformaciones asociadas al régimen de 'reserva de tierras' en una Agrupación mapuche." *Cuadernos de Historia Regional*, Buenos Aires, 4(10): 29–73.

Palermo, M. A. 1986. "Reflexiones sobre el llamado 'complejo ecuestre' en la Argentina." En: *Runa*, vol. XVI, Buenos Aires.

Ramayón, Eduardo. [1921] 1978. *Ejército guerrero, poblador y civilizador.* Buenos Aires: EUDEBA.

Ramos, Alcida. 1995. "Seduced and Abandoned: The Taming of Brazilian Indians." In *Questioning Otherness: An Interdisciplinary Exchange.* V. Domínguez and C. Lewis (eds.). Iowa City: The University of Iowa Press, pp.1–23.

Shumway, Nicolás. 1991. *La Invención de la Argentina. Historia de una idea.* Buenos Aires: Emecé.

Slavsky, L. 1992. "Los indígenas y la Sociedad Nacional. Apuntes sobre política indigenista en la Argentina." En: *La Problemática Indígena. Estudios antropológicos sobre pueblos indígenas de la Argentina.* J. Radovich y A. Balazote (comps.). Buenos Aires: CEAL, pp. 67–79.

Soler, Ricaurte. 1979. *El positivismo argentino. Pensamiento filosófico y sociológico.* México: Universidad Nacional Autónoma de México.

Strong, P. and B. Van Winkle. 1993. "Tribe and Nation: American Indians and American Nationalism." *Social Analysis,* 33: 9–26.

Tamagnini, Marcela. 1997. "Fricción interétnica en las fronteras del cono sur 1850–1880." Tesis de Maestría. Universidad Nacional de Río Cuarto.

Trinchero, Héctor. 2000. *Los Dominios del Demonio. Civilización y Barbarie en las Fronteras de la Nación. El Chaco Central.* Buenos Aires: EUDEBA.

US Commission on Human Rights. 1992. "A Historical Context for Evaluation." In *Native Americans and Public Policy.* F. Lyden y L. Legters (eds). Pittsburgh: University of Pittsburgh Press, pp. 13–32.

Vezub, Julio. 2002. "La 'Secretaría de Valentín Sayhueque.' Correspondencia indígena, poder e identidad en el País de las Manzanas (1860–1883)." *Revista de Estudios Trasandinos,* no. 7.

Villalobos, Sergio. 1989. *Los pehuenches en la vida fronteriza.* Santiago: Editorial de la Universidad Católica de Chile.

Viñas, David. 2003. *Indios, Ejército y Frontera.* Buenos Aires: Santiago Arcos Editora.

Wright, Pablo. 2003. "Colonización del espacio, la palabra y el cuerpo en el Chaco argentino." *Horizontes Antropológicos,* 19: 137–152,

Zeballos, Estanislao. [1878] 1986. *La conquista de quince mil leguas.* Buenos Aires: Hyspamérica.

4

"Wild Indians," Tutelary Roles, and Moving Frontier in Amazonia: Images of Indians in the Birth of Brazil

João Pacheco de Oliveira

Introduction

Indigenous peoples have been and are an essential element of Brazilian national existence, defining institutions and customs which are associated with Brazilian identity and also the territory which frames these socio-cultural processes. The goal of the present article is to critically consider representations of these autochthonous populations. The interpretation which we put forth here is supported by observations of both the legal dimension[1] and of quotidian uses and practices, paying special attention to iconographic representations. Our effort at denaturalizing these representations takes the form of a historical (though non-chronological and non-linear) narrative that reveals the social conditions in which they were created and reflects upon the incongruities between what available sources and registers have to say and the explicative schemes commonly mobilized to interpret said images.

Our work here makes reference to a series of attempts developed within Brazilian anthropology by such authors as Roberto Cardoso de Oliveira,[2] Otávio Velho,[3] Darcy Ribeiro,[4] and José de Souza Martins[5] to look at Brazil through the analytical lens of the expanding frontier. In particular, this text has been inspired by two prior works, one by Velho (1976) and one by myself,[6] which refer to the late 19th and early 20th century debates involving economists, historians and ethnologists regarding colonization theory (Merivale,[7] Wakefield,[8] Marx,[9] F. J. Turner,[10] Nieboer,[11] Domar[12]).

We will begin by analyzing the most apparently evident of certainties. Common sense categorically affirms that the Indian problem in Brazil is an Amazonian question, as it is only in that region where small native collectivities survive, protected by the vast rainforest. Artistic and erudite representations do not much differ from those offered by the common citizen when it comes to this point: the omnipresent stereotype is that of the Amazonian Indian. This being's participation in the country's life and history, understood as non-existent in the past, is today merely virtual, limited to philosophical concepts and to his understanding of the unique environment in which he lives. The international scientific bibliography tends to reinforce this conviction, as anthropologists reaffirm that the old taxonomic category, the "lowland cultures of South America," is now purely and simply a synonym of "Amazonian." It's also quite common to hear descriptions of "the last frontier" when people talk about the Amazon, giving one the (erroneous) impression that a wide variety of professionals (planners, journalists and etc.) are using the frontier concept as a tool for analysis.

Majestic Nature and the Desert of History

Let's begin with a wider look at the scenario. What is the image of the Amazon that every Brazilian carries within himself? What set of representations move him to act upon and think about the *real* Amazon? How does he express his ideas and concepts about its original inhabitants, their history, and their current situation?

Such images do not belong to us as individuals, even though we carry them inside us. They are made up of conventions which we have not created, the presuppositions and implications of which we often do not understand. They are deposited in our mind as ripples or echoes of concepts created by earlier generations in a clear example of Pierre Bourdieu's[13] aphorism, "les morts saisient les vifs." Thus, if our question has as its focus Brazilian representations of the Amazon, we must be aware that such an investigation cannot be rigidly limited in spatial terms: such representations were and are often formulated at a great distance from the Amazon, in places that are much closer to home than one might think. Nevertheless, it is these representations which govern our thoughts regarding the region, at least to a certain extent.

In order to begin talking about the Amazon, we should start our story not in 1500 (with the discovery of Brazil), or 1492 (with the arrival of the Spanish in the Americas), or even in 1542 (with the first successful navigation of the Amazon River), but in the 19th century. It was during this rather more recent period that most of the ideas which we today understand to be timeless, eternal, natural and objective were formulated. We need to turn history on its head, move back and forth between the past and what will be the future, utilizing what Marc Bloch calls a "prudently regressive method"[14] in order to come to grips with how we currently think about the Amazon.

Nineteenth-century thinkers have deeded us scientific and artistic representations of the Amazon which lead us to think about the region in a stereotyped and preconceived way, as if it were unquestionably a natural totality. According to these descriptions—which still inform many of today's ideologies, "green imperialism"[15] being one of the most obvious cases in point—the Amazon is a world of water and forest, in which nature functions as an integrated and harmonious system, ruling with an almost absolute hand. It is that privileged spot on earth where the most perfect expression of nature's ultimate dominion over man is expressed, a sort of "paradise lost" which supposedly echoes the conditions on Earth before the appearance of mankind. In other words, within this view of things, the Amazon represents the empire of Mother Nature, the planet's final bulwark against the advance of civilization, the dominion of water and life and the desert of history.

Within this complex of images, the evaluation of nature's role oscillates. Sometimes, it is presented as a decadent or perverse force and at others as splendid and magnificent. The representations generated by Von Martius and Orton, as well as many other travelers, fall into this first category. They emphasize the adversity of the environment and the inadequate adaptation of living species (above all, man) to such a scenario. Fashionable writers such as Jules Verne[16] and Ferreira de Castro[17] presented the forest's capacity to devastate man and his works in vivid colors, giving this the feeling of inexorable destiny. Brazilian authors such as Euclides da Cunha and Alberto Rangel reinforced this essentially misanthropic view of the region, describing the Amazon as "a land without men" and "a green hell."

Then there are the thinkers who take what seems to be a radically opposite view. The greatest of these, of course, was Humboldt who, even without visiting the region's Portuguese colonies, expressed an optimistic view of the Amazon, describing it as the future "granary of the world." Other travelers, such as Bates and Agassiz, emphasized the region's possibilities. In an article written in 1865, before presenting many arguments in favor of Amazonian colonization, Agassiz belittled the region's detractors by saying: "The general opinion is, in effect, that the climate of the Amazon is most unhealthy. Not a single traveler describes it as anything but terrifying. It is the land of fever, so they all say."[18]

But if there are differences of opinion regarding the Amazon's natural potential, there are no doubts regarding its majestic character or the almost total insignificance of the human populations which reside within the region. French geographer Elisée Reclus,[19] in fact, once made a point of contrasting the Amazon's importance in the natural history of the earth with its absolute lack of influence upon the history of man.

It's important to understand that discourses such these are historically dated and, furthermore, were never exclusively applied to the Amazonian region and its inhabitants. The 19th century—and especially its second half—was a high point for colonial expansion and during this period European explorers and autochthonous populations faced each other in several different parts of the world. Eric Wolf and Eric Hobsbawm have mapped (each with his own emphasis) the impressive extent of the colonial enterprise which marked the structure and daily life of the 19th century in the West. According to Edward Said,[20] a fierce critic of the process of objectification which the West imposes upon other peoples, in 1800 the Western powers controlled 35% of the globe's surface but by 1914 this had increased to 85%. Never before in human history had such a large number of colonies existed, nor were differences in power between colonizers and colonized so marked.

The trope of a *virgin nature*, endowed with vast natural resources and immense swaths of free land uninhabited by humans was markedly present in the 19th century imagination, not only with regards to the Amazon, but also Africa, India and Oceania. Fictional works in English, such as those written by Conrad, Kipling, and Melville (among many others) eternalized certain types of characters and landscapes and propagated these images across the entire planet, incorporating the colonial worldview into humanity's intellectual and emotional patrimony. The emphasis of these stories was not upon events, which would have allowed the formation of a sort of proto-history—romanticized in the extreme, to be sure—of the colonial governing structures which were being integrated into the world system of nation states. What these works of fiction emphasized instead (and what still remains in readers' minds) was the scenery: the grandiose natural backdrop which determined both the horizon of the white protagonists and the destiny of their native opponents. Within these fictional narratives, the natives themselves are often represented as a quasi-natural counterpart to the civilized white man, serving mainly to disturb his inevitable advance in the same general manner as rivers or mountain ranges.

The new nations of the Americas also became involved in promoting internal colonization as a result of the political ruptures which these settler states engendered during their processes of independence. This is what occurred in the trans-Appalachian American West, and also south of the Bio-Bio River in Chile and on the Araucânian pampas of Argentina. In Brazil, this discursive genre resulted in a series of texts written in German by the colonists of Santa Catarina and Rio Grande do Sul. These reproduce memories of the saga of the white man in his expansion across the face of the Earth, recounting this movement as a narrative of heroism, sacrifice, and dedication.

The social system at the cutting edge of the colonial enterprise, the *frontier society*, can be installed on any continent or in any ecosystem without altering the rhetoric of "the last frontier." *Virgin nature*, which is to be subjugated and domesticated in order to produce wealth (merchandise, in other words) is a constant element in the representations of frontier agents and also in official discourse. It also serves as a euphemism for the treatment applied to autochthonous populations.

In 1882, the French intellectual Ernst Renan wrote a famous article in which he claimed that nations construct feelings of unity not only through memories which are celebrated and recognized, but also through strategic forgetfulness. Both memories and forgetfulness are transformed into conventions which soon become so consensually accepted that it no longer becomes necessary to speak of them. In this sense, autochthonous populations were not considered to be relevant during colonial expansion, nor during the formation of the new nation states of the Americas. Their needs and desires were minimized or even ignored by the national elites, and even the most positively disposed intellectuals saw them as a mere footnote to national history, at the very most.[21]

In the first attempts to systematically create a history of Brazil, undertaken in the decades following independence, indigenous peoples were confined to the very first chapters of our history. The most famous works[22] of the *Instituto Histórico e Geográfico Brasileiro* (IHGB; Brazilian Historical and Geographical Institute), the academy created by Emperor D. Pedro II in order to produce and disseminate knowledge about the land, people, arts, and sciences of Brazil, the indigenous populations situated within the country's borders are presented in a completely unfavorable light, considered only as a pure expression of primitive simplicity. Such views were supported by repeated comparisons between Brazil's native populations and those of the pre-Columbian states situated in the Andes and Central

America, fixing the Amazonian populations in the intellectual and public mind as among the simplest human forms on earth.

Colonization and Indian Labor

It thus causes a sense of unreality when one reflects upon the fact that the available colonial sources, read and utilized in an extremely tendentious manner by Brazil's 19th century historians, do not support in any way, shape or form these interpretations. The early colonial chroniclers such as Diego de Carvajal and the Jesuit Father Gaspar de Acuña, who traveled down the Amazon River in 1542 and 1639 respectively, reported extensive populations grouped together in large riverside settlements, practicing diverse forms of agriculture and husbandry. These were complex and stratified societies that were characterized by elaborate religious and political structures and controlled large numbers of warriors trained in efficient combat techniques.

Carvajal described in extensive detail one of these peoples, which he claimed acted as if they were the true lords of the river, being lead by a great chief named Apariá. David Sweet[23] and Betty Meggers[24] identified this people as the Omaguas (also known as the Cambevas). Archeologist Ana Roosevelt ratified this hypothesis after repeated field investigations (initially begun by Sweet) identified the existence of *cacicatos* (chieftainships) among the people of the region. More recent archeological reports[25] express reservations regarding this hypothesis, but also reaffirm the complexity of the pre-colonial native societies as revealed through studies of their material remnants[26] and spatial distribution.

First contact between European explorers and autochthonous populations did not occur in the interior of the Amazon Basin in the same way as it had occurred along the Atlantic seaboard. On the coast, the Europeans stayed in their caravels or sheltered themselves in fortified bays and atop of hills and this allowed them to successfully perform (more often than not) acts of violence and power. Carvajal and Acuñas' narratives dramatically relate a different story, recounting the first European voyages along the Amazon as a sequence of friendly meetings, battles, and hairbreadth escapes from the local populations, which were generally much superior to the explorers in terms of numbers, logistics, and overall military force.

The narrative of the Spanish Fathers shows them wracked with hunger, lost in unknown terrain, and suffering from the progressive deterioration of their troops' military capacities. It is a clear image of the fragile condition of the supposed discoverers of the Amazonian world, one which is consistently set off in contrast to the opulence of the surrounding region and the great size of the populations found within it.[27] It's interesting to observe that while such reports were considered to be of secondary importance or even complete fantasies by the first Brazilian historians, they were also ignored by the artists who began, in the second half of the 19th century, to paint portraits of the most important moments of the young country's history. Only the historical registers of the more impressive initial contacts made between Europeans and the indigenous populations of the seaboard ever impacted upon the imagination of such 19th century artists as Vitor Meireles, whose famous work *A Primeira Missa no Brasil* (1861; *The First Mass in Brazil*) became quickly accepted as one of the most popular symbols of Brazilian national identity.

The differences between the seaboard and Amazon, however, did not pass unnoticed by the Portuguese colonial administration, which divided the two regions into separate colonies, administered in different manner and with quite distinct historical configurations and rhythms of development.

In the coastal colony of Brazil, the sites initially occupied by the Europeans were protected by forts and batteries. They sheltered commercial enclaves and opened up to the backlands with the installation of plantations and sugar mills. Farther out, they were ringed by an extensive cattle raising zone. Olinda, Recife, Salvador and Rio de Janeiro—and half a century later São Luís and Belém—among others, were cities created in the 16th century following this general layout, which was quite similar to that seen in medieval Portugal.

At first, indigenous populations provided decisive aid in the construction of the churches, forts, and other public works which composed these settlements. Later, export-orientated cultivation began to demand the use of more extensive plantations, creating territorial expansion and greater labor mobilization and resulting in increasing conflict between the indigenous populations and the colonists.[28]

Europeans (Portuguese, French, or Dutch) reacted with shock, fear and admiration when faced with a humanity which was radically different from anything which they had heard of before, and this permitted the 16th century chroniclers (most of them religious in orientation and/or training) to make varied ethnographic observations. As time went on, however, representations of native peoples became more strongly negatively stereotyped, with descriptions of cannibalism and nudity taking a prime role in the construction of visions of the Indian as pagan. The images of the first books in which white traveler's tales of the Americas where published, most particularly Hans Staden's narrative, were created by German engravers who had never been to Brazil and who took their inspiration for rendering scenes of cannibalism from the techniques which medieval butchers used on animals such as pigs, sheep, and bulls. These images exacerbated readers' horrified reactions, both against cannibalism and the peoples who practiced it.[29]

It is important to remember that the Portuguese, like the Spanish, had a prior experience of conflict and conviviality with the Arab caliphates of the Iberian Peninsula and that this history was an important element in the process of Portuguese national formation. The discourse of the *potential criminalization of difference*—in this case, of those men and women who did not recognize or accept Christianity—which underlay the policies directed against the Iberian Moors was virtually omnipresent during the colonial period. This helped to legitimize the capture and enslavement of Indians and justify the wars of extermination.

Different from the black African, the native American could not be enslaved. He could, however, be "reduced" or "brought down," being moved from his original region to another in order to receive religious assistance. *Tropas de resgate,* or "rescue troops," composed of Portuguese soldiers and missionaries who catechized Indians and mixed-blood *mamelucos,* swept through the backlands of Brazil, supposedly searching for *captives* in native villages. These people were presumably prisoners from other ethnic groups who were destined to be eaten. Instead of simply freeing these captives, the troops took them to catechism and baptism stations, where they were supposedly converted to Catholicism and taught, but, in any case, most definitely had to perform unpaid labor for selected families of colonists.

The law also provided for the declaration of *just war* against a given native people, which simplified military operations of extermination, as well as the capture, baptism, and temporary enslavement of numerous native families. The reasons for the declaration of a just war were many and varied and ran from prejudicial acts directed against colonists (such as death, robbery or pilferage) to simple refusal to receive religious instruction.[30] In reality, these conflicts were a re-elaboration, in the American context, of the Iberian crusades and pogroms against the Moors and Jews, and like these earlier conflicts, just wars were motivated both by greed and religious intolerance.

The explanations given by the majority of historians for the substitution of native labor by African slave labor in Brazil are generally anchored in a prejudiced view of the continent's autochthonous populations. In the first compilations of Brazilian history, such as that organized by Varnhagen (whose evolutionist perspective has been noted above), the characterization of the Indian as a nomadic gatherer was part of a complex of traits supposedly associated with his *primitivism*, a state which was practically defined as being non-agricultural. But Varnhagen did not attribute the colonists' shift to African slave labor to the Indian's supposed inability to farm: he indicated a series of other factors as also being responsible. The intellectuals of the early Brazilian republic, firm in their belief in economic determinism, would later explain this substitution almost exclusively through the argument that black slave labor offered greater profits than Indian labor and thus a greater comparative advantage.

Later investigations have made it clear that this substitution was the result of a series of factors—above all, the profits merchants and the Portuguese Crown made on the slave trade and the strategic interests that were involved in the Southern Atlantic triangular commerce (Brazil–Africa–Portugal). Because of this, the labor force utilized by the colonists became increasingly made up of African slaves, while native labor was progressively shoved off into a relatively restricted parallel market which attended to such non-exportation oriented activities as public works, subsistence agriculture, and domestic work.

The exploration and colonization of the Amazon would follow a different pattern from that of the Atlantic seaboard. It was conducted along rivers, emphasized extractive activities and was characterized by temporary occupations by expeditions in search of the so-called *drogas do sertão* (a category of extractive activity which took in everything from plant gathering to manatee and turtle hunting). This production was almost entirely geared towards exportation and it was not dependent upon the establishment of forts or urban nuclei in the backlands. These extractive expeditions became more common beginning with the third decade of the 17th century, and by the dawn of the 18th they represented an important source of profits for both the colonists and the Portuguese Crown.[31]

As the main source of labor of these expeditions was indigenous, they also served to promote the capture and "reduction" of Indians, bringing these to work on plantations, in domestic service, or on public construction projects and also on future expeditions as guides, soldiers, and canoe men.[32] New diseases brought into the continent by Europeans as well as losses caused by direct conflicts or by conditions on forced labor projects pushed the coastal native population into a vertiginous fall in the first century after contact. This obliged expeditions seeking to capture natives into ever longer voyages into the so-called "*sertões*" or backlands.[33]

The occupation of the Brazilian interior was carried out through the installation of missionary villages, which were productive units almost exclusively dependent on indigenous labor and thus upon native tolerance of religious conversion and missionary activities. Colonization nuclei in the Amazon Basin were effectively indigenous villages administered by missionaries in an undertaking which united the Portuguese Crown's religious, economic, and geopolitical interests. In 1696, 11,000 natives resided in the missions. By 1730 this number had grown to 30,000, and it was to increase even further to 50,000 by the middle of the 18th century.

The economic factor upon which the occupation of the Amazon, the work of the extractive troops, and the establishment of missionary villages rested was the labor of the native American, called by Father Antonio Vieira "red gold."[34] All of the region's wealth was ultimately constructed upon Indian work. It is in the struggle to seek out and control this crucial productive factor (for which no other alternative was ever successfully created) that colonists, missionaries, and government officials entered into disputes and around which they composed their interests.

Though imported disease and military activities ended up exterminating many peoples and interfered with the socio-cultural reproduction of others, drastically reducing native populations in many instances, it is important to keep in mind that none of these facts altered the basic presuppositions underlying the occupation of the Amazon. All activity in the region remained—and continued to remain for more than a century—entirely dependent upon native labor.

The Making of a *Mestizo* People

New policies for the region were outlined by the Marques de Pombal in his *Diretório de Índios* (1755/*Indian Laws*). These transformed villages into settlements and county seats whose administration was turned over to lay authorities, the so-called Indian Directors, judges, and city councilmen. The Jesuits, the order which had been the most consistent promoter of missionary villages for natives, were expulsed from the Amazon in 1757 and, in the following years, from the Portuguese colonies of Africa and Asia. Their goods were confiscated and passed along to other religious orders. A general commerce company was created in order to foment development in the region, exporting goods and importing black slaves with the profits.

The Pombaline argument was quite simple: if the Amazon needed to be occupied and if its current inhabitants were mostly Indians, then the logical solution was to declare these Indians to be citizens and to set up the legal instruments in order to effect this transformation as quickly as possible. The first step was to dismantle the indigenous villages implanted by the Jesuits, while maintaining the native populations in distinct groups according to their linguistic[35] and cultural affinities while subjecting them to closer tutelary political control. The legislation passed in the name of this project was clearly assimilationist in character,[36] imposing Portuguese as the official language and prohibiting the use of native or pidgin tongues. Interethnic marriage was encouraged and prohibitions against non-Indians residing in the villages were lifted. Civil life was held to be the best school for natives and public officials understood to be the teachers most capable of turning Indians into citizens.

Contrary to Pombal's expectations, however, these measures resulted in the collapse of the regional economy without the subsequent rise of any alternative. The commerce company was short-lived and agriculture did not expand, nor were large numbers of African slaves imported into the region. Many villages suffered significant population decreases as residents returned to living in family units along the main rivers. Frequent accusations of abuse leveled against village directors resulted in the Indian Directorate system being suspended by decree in 1798. The position of Director survived, however, and these continued to engage in negative activities in some parts of the region until the mid-19th century.

Three factors were important during this period. The first was the continuation of *just wars*. War was declared against the Mura between 1784 under the pretext that they were interfering with navigation along the Madeira River and thus with communications between Mato Grosso and Pará. The conflict ended with the tribe's final surrender in 1786, understood to be a "voluntary reduction in the name of peace."[37]

Secondly, some indigenous peoples such as the Omaguas, who had converted to Catholicism and had earlier inhabited the missionary villages, were "disappeared" through the new Indian Directorate scheme. Though these Indians still partially maintained themselves in urban nuclei, travelers along the Upper Solimões during the first decades of the 19th century declared this people (which had earlier controlled the rivers, banks and islands of the region) to be extinct.

Finally, a third important factor during this period was the increasing numbers of Indians in the Amazon who were not associated with any village at all but who instead lived in dispersed family groups, extracting their needs from the surrounding land and maintaining sporadic relations with traders, religious workers, and colonial authorities. These Indians continued to baptized and call themselves Christians and frequently used a Portuguese which included many terms taken from the pidgin "general language." This contingent would become known as the *tapuios* in the 18th century and would form the base of the *caboclo* social category in the 19th and 20th.

According to studies done thus far, these *tapuios* (Christianized Indians) and *caboclos* formed the social base of the *Cabanagem* rebellion, a movement which occurred between 1834 and 1839 and which was the result of economic stagnation and the worsening life conditions of the poorest sections of the region's society. Rebels took Belem twice during the revolt and were expelled both times, retreating to Vila da Barra (the future Manaus). Later they went up the Negro River to Maués, where they were given the support of the Municipal Council. The movement also had significant support along the Negro, Madeira and Tapajós rivers. Following the repression of the revolt and several outbreaks of smallpox and malaria, the Mura, estimated in 1826 at some 60,000 souls, were reduced in number to 1,300.

Contrasting Images of Indians in the 18th and 19th centuries

The Brazilian coast was visited by many travelers and chroniclers. By contrast, Portuguese authorities kept the Amazon shrouded in mystery, restricting access and limiting the distribution of information regarding the region. The decision to keep the region "hidden" (Tavares Bastos [1866], 1937: 383) began to change after border treaties were signed with Spain and the Portuguese Royal Family moved to Brazil during the Napoleonic Wars. This process continued with the reception of foreign scientific and artistic missions.

From 1783 to 1792, naturalist Alexandre Rodrigues Ferreira undertook voyages to the captaincies of Pará, Rio Negro, and Mato Grosso, traveling some 9,372 km, writing ample notes regarding the ethnography, botany, and geology of the Amazonian region, and forming several valuable scientific collections. He was accompanied in his travels by two *rabiscadores* (illustrators), J. J. Freire and J. J. Codina, and his book *Viagem Philosofica* contained numerous illustrations.

What do we encounter in this trip's reports, the terrible results of extermination or the no less depressing effects of cultural destruction? The reports surprise in this respect. Even taking into consideration the fact that the voyage was an official expedition whose principal goal was to emphasize the positive aspects of Amazonian life, the artistic and technological exuberance of the native peoples reported by the voyagers is surprising. Among the images, we find clear social constructions of people, personages (chiefs) and institutions which are particular to each native culture. We can see images of the *estólica* (a weapon) and of cranial mutilation being undertaken on a Cambeva Indian. There's a Miranha Indian with blowpipe and *carcaz*, and drawings of Mura and Uaupés body paintings, as well as a picture of a Curutú *maloca*.[38]

Other travelers and naturalists also visited the Amazon during the first decades of the 19th century, producing a rich iconography of the region's inhabitants. These still impressed travelers with their great cultural diversity and many voyagers left interesting reports documenting it. An example can be found in the engravings, drawings, and paintings created by Debret, Spix and Martius and Hercules Florence, who were among the many travelers to visit the region in the three to four decades following Ferreira's voyage.

These images were quite different from those produced at the same time of the Indians of the Atlantic Coast. Debret, whose trips were mostly confined to the southern reaches of Brazil, offers up a panel in which he presents a dozen indigenous habitations. Most of these sketches show temporary shelters and rustic dwellings that emphasize the nomadic, primitive, and technologically precarious state of these populations. One is left under the impression that these are very primitive populations or perhaps peoples who have undergone an intensive period of cultural decadence. The two *malocas* drawn by Debret, for example, are much less complex and beautiful than the Curutú *maloca* drawn by the artist of the Alexandre Rodrigues Ferreira expedition.

Another interesting contrast can be seen between two of Debret's illustrations. On the one hand, we have the picture entitled *Botocudos, Puris, Patachós, Machacalis*, which shows us a gathering of natives. On the other, we have images showing Guaicuru warriors. In the first illustration, the Indians appear as a primitive horde, almost without any identifying signs or corporal decoration; they have brutish physiognomies which suggest an animalistic analogy to the observer (the Indians in fact look like gorillas or orangutans). In the second illustration, which deals with Amazonian Indians, the political strength, domination over nature, and cultural resiliency which Debret saw in this people are clearly visible.

Another picture by J. J. Rugendas, entitled *Uma Família de Botocudos* (*A Botocudo Family*), shows us an example of the negative images generated about this people by the physical anthropologists of Brazil's National Museum in the second half of the 19th century, who understood them to be living examples of the most primitive peoples in the world, together with the African pygmies and certain Australian tribes. In this context, it's important to recall that the Botocudo represented in the picture had been the targets of a declaration of *just war*—the last in the colony's history—a few years earlier by the Portuguese King D. João VI, then resident in Brazil. The tribe had been attacked by the Imperial Army and had been almost completely exterminated. All its lands were confiscated and redistributed among surviving officers and local merchants.

Dead Indians before the Rising Nation

Let us now return to the 19th century after our brief excursion through the history of the Amazon and our discussion of how that region was constructed. In independent Brazil, according to the so-called Patriarch of Independence, there was no longer room for just wars against specific indigenous peoples. José Bonifácio de Andrade e Silva, a central figure in the first constitutional convention, several times Imperial minister (in diverse portfolios), councilor to Pedro I and Pedro II's tutor, wrote a document[39] which defined the main lines of what has since been Brazil's official stance regarding its native populations. In this document, the autochthonous condition of these peoples was clearly underlined. They were presumed to be the first and true owners of the land, as opposed to the Portuguese, who had arrived later and against whom the nation was now seeking its own emancipation. José Bonifácio emphasized the Brazilian state's obligation to treat these "primitive brethren" with comprehension and humility.

This state ban on the use of officially declared war against native populations was a highly significant and radical move at the time. According to a census of parishes, conducted in 1817–18 by Councilor Veloso de Oliveira, Brazil's population amounted to some 3.6 million people (including already baptized Indians who lived in regular contact with Brazilian society). The same census estimated the number of "Indios bravos" (or *wild Indians)* in the country to be 800,000, or 20% of Brazil's total population.

It was to these *"wild Indians"* that the attention of the Brazilian state and its dominant elite would now turn, bringing colonial political relations full circle.

Colonial activities had had as their focus the production of *tame Indians*: natives who submitted to the ritual of baptism and who were declared to be Christian and *vassalos d` El Rey*. These are the Indians who the state decreed could not be tortured or enslaved, as they were under the same royal protection as the rest of His Imperial Majesty's subjects. Other natives, the so-called "Indios bravos" (or *"wild Indians"*), constituted a residual category that was also transitory and clearly ambiguous, implying heterogeneous and even antagonistic social destinies. These natives could become Christians and be transformed into *colonial Indians*,[40] or they could resist catechism and be treated as enemies, even declared the target of a *just war*.

The national project that was put into practice in independent Brazil was not republican, as was the case in the neighboring South American countries, but monarchist and imperial. It was, in fact, a continuation of the state formative structures implanted by D. João VI who, following the French invasion of Portugal, removed to Rio de Janeiro along with some 15,000 members of his court to establish the capital of the Portuguese Empire in that tropical city. In order to maintain control of the imperial machine, it was necessary to create an administrative structure (that was totally alien to the colony) completely from scratch. In this fashion the institutions regulating national economic, political, and cultural life, such as the Mint, the Bank of Brazil, the Royal Press, the Naval Arsenal, the Astronomical Observatory, the Royal Library, and the Botanical Gardens came into being. All of these institutions, which were to form the basis of the Brazilian state, were in fact entirely molded in the imperial pattern of government.

Instead of questioning this administrative structure, those in favor of independence defended it. More than anything else, the Brazilian patriots feared that the return of the Portuguese Court to the metropolis would result in the dismantling of Brazil's imperial administration and the devolution of that country to the status of a mere colony. The republican movements which rose up during this period were all regionalist in character: the only political project which sought national unity also fought to continue the imperial institutions, only without the inconvenience of having the Portuguese running them.

In the Brazilian Empire—and especially during the reign of D. Pedro II, which lasted a half-century—a movement to homogenize administrative structures and representative forms was begun within the nation under a centralized monarchical model. All the regions of the country were to be represented in Parliament and in the bureaucracy, but to insist upon regional specificities was virtually to support local revolts and was seen as a highly unpatriotic act. The diversity of the historical models through which Brazil had been occupied thus began to fall into obscurity and the different ethnic configurations which characterized each of the two old Portuguese colonies were covered over with the rubric of one people, one state. In terms of the representations of native peoples, the categories *tapuio*, *caboclo*, *colonial Indian* were totally forgotten and these peoples were seen as composing part of the country's poor citizenry who were dangerously attracted to regionalist revolts and republican movements.

The indigenist program delineated by José Bonifácio was totally directed towards "Indios bravos" (or "*wild Indians*") and was based upon two principles: the refusal to use force against natives and the recommendation that humane treatment would lead them to civilization and to participation in the Brazilian national community.[41] This program would be implemented through the creation of tutelary structures, which began to be formed during the Regency period in order to resolve judicial questions involving Indians under the care of the office of the Judge of Orphans. During D. Pedro II's reign, administrative responsibility passed into the hands of a General Directorate of Indians, attached to the Ministry of the Interior. Local activities, however, were generally undertaken by Catholic missionaries who received financial support from the government (through the institution of royal patronage). Later, during the Republic, a specialized governmental branch inspired in evolutionary conceptions of society (most particularly Comtean positivism) was founded. Its organizing principles were based upon military hierarchy and the bureaucracy itself obeyed the routines of the federal civil service.

It was only possible to establish a humanitarian attitude towards the indigenous groups and establish protective (tutelary) mechanisms in the central state, with the political and economic costs such mechanisms entailed, given the important symbolic weight the autochthonous populations had in the independence process and in the consolidation of the Empire of Brazil. It was because they were considered to be the true and ancient lords of the land that "Indios bravos" were not to be persecuted and exterminated: alive, they constituted indisputable proof of the existence of Brazil before the arrival of the Portuguese. The indigenous populations of the country were understood to be the oldest and most authentic symbols of Brazilian nationalism, and it was in light of this condition that policies towards them were constructed.

It is within this set of images and representations that *Indianism*, an artistic and literary movement, would gain meaning and popularity in the second half of the 19th century, enjoying the support and approval of the Emperor. The Indian of the past was rehabilitated, given dignity in his values and motives, and transformed into a symbol of the young nation. All the early accusations which were leveled at native peoples in daily life (that they were cruel, treacherous, lazy, and so forth) were completely overturned by nostalgic idealization. Poets and novelists such as Gonçalves Dias and

José de Alencar used native words and institutions as props in their works to celebrate the originality and destiny of the Brazilian nation that was being born.

A small section of Gonçalves Dias' poem *The Timbiras* beautifully demonstrates this use of indigenous institutions and linguistic forms in order to express an affirmation of Brazilian nationality. In this fashion, the narrative voice of a new Brazilian poetry asks to be heard and attempts to purge itself of European symbols and the Greco-Roman tradition:

> Listen to me. The humble and modest singer,
> My forehead not ringed with laurel and myrtle,
> But with the green branch I have girthed it,
> And with wildflowers have decorated my lyre;
> .....
> Singer of the jungles, in the wild woods,
> I choose the rough trunk of the palm tree.
> United with it, I release my cry,
> While the wind makes the palms buzz,
> And rustles the long fronds.
> The wild beasts and death will not simply listen to me:
> The tears of dew suddenly
> Flung from my lyre's distended chords,
> Must make them somewhat peaceful and malleable. (*The Timbiras*)

Given this semantic axis, supported by romanticism and the Rousseauian figure of the Noble Savage, it is no wonder that native adornments and decorations would be used to decorate the mantle of the Emperor of Brazil, or that the country would be represented in such temples of culture as the Scala Theater of Milan with maestro Carlos Gomes' opera *The Guarani*, inspired by a popular novel of the same name by José de Alencar.

But this celebrated image of the Indian, based as it was on the 16th century chronicles, had little to do with the native lives of the present, nor did it recover travelers' representations of Amazonian Indians. The characters and facts utilized by the romantic *indianists*, as Gonçalves Dias himself made quite clear, belonged exclusively to the past and to an "American people, now extinct" (idem). Real contemporary Indians, in spite of being the descendants of this race, only supposedly expressed its slow death agonies. The indigenous populations of the Amazon began to be thought of and represented in the same way as the remaining wild Indian populations along the Atlantic coast—in other words, as a residual humanity that was headed towards inevitable extinction.

It was the dramatic images of the contemporary death and disappearance of these autochthonous populations which, years later, in 1883, inspired Rodolfo Amoedo to paint *The Last Tamoio*. The Indian subject of this painting, aided by a missionary, no longer shows clothes and ornaments specific to any given culture and doesn't even present racially pure phenotypical traits.

While in representations of the past the Indian (still portrayed in his aboriginal splendor) became a supporting character in the most significant episodes of the nation's formation (such as in the painting of the *First Mass in Brazil*), real and contemporary Indians began to be identified as primitive beings, mired in the most rudimentary stages of civilization. They were increasingly understood as having little to no capacity to adapt themselves to modern life and were thus in need of a complacent eye and protective hand, being totally dependent on tutelary and protective mediation.

The Invasion of Indian Lands

While coffee plantations advanced up the Paraíba vale and over northeastern São Paulo, producing the wealth which, during the second half of the 19th century, would be seen as the life-blood of the Empire, rubber production began its extraordinary expansion in the Amazon Basin, penetrating into the most remote corners of the land with an intensity which had not been paralleled before or since.

Up to the end of the 19th century, rubber extraction did not break with the colonial model already established in the region since the 17th century expeditions to collect *drogas do sertão*. Indians were the basic labor force along the rubber circuits and they continued in the role, exercising all the basic extractive activities, especially in those areas where profit margins were slimmer.[42]

The radical difference the new model presented lay in its scale and in the commercial connections which were utilized (involving suppliers and foreign banks). This gave rubber extraction a very different impact from earlier extractive models in terms of the volume of products produced, the intensity of the labor involved, and the extent of the areas affected. In order to respond to growing demands and rising prices, thousands of immigrants from the Brazilian northeast were brought into the Amazon as rubber collectors in forced labor schemes (debt slavery orchestrated through suppliers' monopolist control of trade).[43]

This enormous and diffuse credit network, which commanded virtual armies of rubber tappers, invaded the lands of the *"wild Indians"* of the Amazon (which constituted the majority of the 800,000 estimated by Councilor Veloso), crisscrossing these with rubber collection circuits. Numberless ethnic groups became extinct by the early 20th century as a result of this process, according to a study conducted by Darcy Ribeiro (1957). Other peoples, such as the Ticuna, the Cashinauá, and the Miranha, were brought into the extractive frontier, working as essential laborers both in latex collection and in sundry support activities (as oarsmen, guides, agricultural laborers) along the rubber circuits. If they managed to escape from immediate extermination, they suffered from a form of slavery that was even more arbitrary and brutal than that imposed upon the white tappers, with profound repercussions on their culture, forms of sociability, and demographic extent.

While the great debates which occupied the attention of national institutions and the intelligentsia concerned the problems of coffee production and agricultural expansion in the Brazilian south and southeast (most particularly focusing upon the problem of replacing slave with immigrant labor), other questions were discussed in the Amazon, typically involving only regional actors. Economic and political debates centered on the polarity formed by *native rubber circuits* (such as in the Amazon) and *cultivated rubber plantations* (such as those of Malaysia, grown from Amazonian stock acclimatized in London's Kew Gardens and transplanted to the British colonies of Asia); improvement of latex collection, preparation, and transportation techniques; the advantages of agriculture versus the region's extractive vocation; and the desired profile of foreign immigrants.[44]

Indian and rubber tapper perspectives were always absent from these debates. The "drama of the rubber circuits" was only dealt with by a few of the period's fictional works, where authors such as Ferreira de Castro, Araújo Lima and Guedes, among others, described in lurid prose the mechanisms which rubber bosses used to subjugate their labor force and the frequent armed incursions into native *malocas*. These are the only local registers to be found in public life of what was then a widespread historical process.

If the belief that the coastal native populations were in the last throes of extinction was arbitrary and incorrect, such invisibility was at least justified by the relatively low indigenous demographic presence in those provinces, which rarely reached above 10% of the total population. In the Amazon, however, even Tavares Bastos (who considered Indians to be a decadent race and preached biological miscegenation, free commerce, and salaried labor as mechanisms through which to "perfect" the autochthonous population) was forced to cite data which contradicted his belief in the Indian's little importance in that context. According to Tavares Bastos, in 1860 there were some 17,000 Indians "living in tribes" (in other words, autonomously) in the Upper Amazonian lowlands (p. 357). This was a significant portion of the region's population and it didn't even take into consideration the *caboclos*.

The first national census, undertaken during the reign of D. Pedro II in 1872, clearly indicated that 64% of the Amazonian population was classified as *caboclos* (in other words, Indians and their descendants). This contradicts the opinion of certain authors who believe that Amazon Indians passed from majority to minority status in the region at the beginning of the 19th century. We can now see that Indians and their descendants were a demographic majority in the Amazon well into the rubber cycle (1870 to 1910).

Though the term *caboclo* today carries less of an ethnic charge, no longer being immediately associated with natives, this was not the case at the end of the 19th century. Thus the French translation of the census of 1872 clearly distinguished the *caboclo* (translated as "*indien,*" or "Indian") from the *mestiço* (referred to in the census as "*pardo*" and translated as "*métis*"). One of Debret's most famous paintings, entitled *Caboclo,* shows an Indian supporting himself in a position for a long distance shot with a bow and arrow. Another Debret picture, entitled *Caboclos' Village in Cantagalo,* shows a scene taken from the daily lives of Indians in Rio de Janeiro. Both the references to cultural performances which are quite similar to those of the "*wild Indians*" and a portrayal which emphasizes these peoples' nudity and rudimentary technology demonstrate the difficulties which 19th century observers had in making radical separations between *Indians* and *caboclos*.

When Malaysia's rubber plantations entered into production for the world market in 1911, latex prices dropped brutally the world over and a deep and chronic economic crisis installed itself in the Brazilian Amazon. Except for brief favorable fluctuations resulting from the World Wars, rubber production in the region entered into terminal decline. Linkages to the international market became ever more fragile, but production relations (with suppliers controlling a commercial monopoly and indebting laborers) maintained themselves by operating with products of lesser value (such as fish, furs and wood) which were sold in local or regional markets. With the exception of the short episode of the so-called *rubber soldiers* (1942/1945; a government initiative to reactivate latex production for strategic reasons), flows of new workers into the rubber circuits and older production areas dried up.

The extractive frontier was neither extinguished nor abruptly dismantled: it simply became stationary and began a slow retreat. The march of rubber through the Amazon Basin was interrupted and pressure upon autochthonous populations was diminished. The number of violent attacks directed by invaders against relatively isolated native population also decreased. This was a factor which was as or more important than the foundation of the SPI (the Brazilian government's official Indian protective service, established in 1910 at the beginning of the rubber crisis), in terms of reducing the number of invasions of native lands.

The Tutelage of "Wild Indians"

During the reign of D. Pedro II, what attention was paid to Indians was generally symbolic, focusing on these peoples' ancient lineage and on facts, customs, and characters from before the Portuguese colonization. From the point of view of public policy, however, it was very rare for natives to have any visibility at all. One of these few moments was during the war with Paraguay (1865–1870), when the Kadiwéu and Terena Indians organized special platoons to fight alongside Brazilian troops against the Paraguayan soldiers which had entered their lands. Some talk was heard regarding boarding schools for Indians, but news regarding the Native population rarely reached Brazilian papers and when it did, it generally dealt with purely localized situations, denouncing how this or that group had been abandoned or praising the dedication of missionaries or government workers.

This situation was to change radically at the beginning of the 20th century, when newspapers began to repeatedly report conflicts between Indians and whites in several areas of the country. These reports talked of clashes which left dead and wounded and which ended up in the theft or destruction of goods and/or the kidnapping of children and generally ended with local authorities emphasizing that the Indians were threatening the security of farms, highways, and villages and generally hurting regional progress. The destruction (or fears thereof) tended to center on public works (such as railroads, highways, and telegraph lines) or productive activities which were strongly supported by the central government (such as the southern colonization frontiers) and which were penetrating into officially uninhabited lands which were nevertheless occupied by little known autochthonous populations.

The government was strongly pressured to act firmly and rapidly in these situations in order to protect investments which it had financed or in which it had a large stake. Not to act meant to let the conflict escalate, a situation which could generate grave consequences and result in criticisms from both sides. But how should the government act? Letting local work teams and colonists resolve the trouble on their own tended to lead to the extermination of the Indians involved and created a precedent which ran completely against the humane and pacific treatment of native populations outlined by José Bonifácio. This, in turn, risked offending the sensibilities of the nation's artists and intellectuals who had, thanks to *Indianism*, chosen the Indian as a sort of national relic. On the other hand, supporting catechism activities seemed useless or even counterproductive: useless, because in a situation of mutual distrust and confrontation, missionaries had little chance to make their message heard; counterproductive because each new failure of missionary activities only increased the probable necessity of military action.

The official government response to this dilemma grew out of a successful concrete experience. A governmental work crew directed by a military engineer and made up of army officials implanted telegraphic posts and stations throughout Guaporé territory in Minas Gerais from 1908 to 1910, blazing a wide trail several hundred kilometers long through the chaparral and forests. During its work, this team maintained friendly contact with dozens of indigenous tribes, pacifying even those considered to be the most treacherous and aggressive and even mobilizing some Indians to work at protecting the line and its associated equipment. This work was documented and photographed and was widely divulged by the media and the expedition entered into popular mythology as the *Rondon Commission.* Upon his return to the federal capital in 1910, the expedition's leader, Major Cándido Rondon, was lauded for his work and dined and paraded about town as the "explorer of the *sertões*"—a true "*sertanista,*" now recognized as a national hero.

What was the program of action which Rondon proposed? In his view, Indians should receive special attention from a state agency (originally the SPI, substituted later on by FUNAI), which would act to protect and assist them. In order to avoid continuing warfare between Indians and punitive expeditions supported by local political and economic leaders, it was absolutely necessary to place Indians under the tutelage of the Union, through an effective state bureaucracy.

Rondon was a soldier and an engineer, as well as an adept of the positivism of philosopher Auguste Comte. He considered indigenous populations to be human social forms which were mired at the most rudimentary stages of development. In religious and general terms, they were stuck at the fetishist state of social evolution and it was thus not easy to force them to abruptly pass over to monotheistic religious forms. So that they might become a part of Brazil, as José Bonifácio preached, it was necessary to treat them with "gentle and assuasive methods," establishing a "fraternal and secular form of protection" which would permit the Indians to slowly evolve. In this manner, Rondon delineated the precepts of a new *sertanismo*, one which was no longer oriented by the experiences of the punitive *bandeirante* slaving expeditions of the 17th and 18th centuries, but which sought to continue the nation's territorial expansion by treating the Indian in a humane and altruistic fashion.

Separating his views from that of the missionaries and counterpoising himself against people calling for extermination of Brazil's indigenous groups, Rondon became the center of a network of collaborators and followers who would build Brazil's new indigenous service in accordance with his principles and who inspired the admiration of the public and many sectors of the Brazilian state.

In his work for the Telegraph Line Commission, Rondon coined the phrase "die, if necessary, but never kill." He labored to attract and pacify isolated peoples who had often been attacked or threatened by rubber tappers along the extractive frontier and, because of this, were wary of the white man. By pacifying warring tribes and bringing them under federal tutelage, Rondon and his followers greatly contributed to lessening the violence practiced against Indians in the backlands of Brazil.

The successful foundation and maintenance of an indigenist agency was a much more challenging task, however. The one which Rondon and his circle set up was under the aegis of the powerful Ministry of Agriculture, Industry and Commerce (MAIC) and was originally called the Service for the Protection of Indians and the Localization of National Workers (*Serviço de Proteção aos Índios e Localização de Trabalhadores Nacionais;* SPILTN), having among its attributions the responsibility of organizing agricultural colonies for rural laborers. The following year, Rondon's team managed to free themselves from this subsidiary responsibility and their agency became known simply as the SPI. The administrative consolidation of the Service was extremely slow, however, and four years passed by before its internal regulations were approved (in 1915). Basic systematization of its procedures was only completed in 1928.

The Rondonian program was applied only in certain political and economic conjunctures, and the agency suffered from a chronic lack of funds and qualified personnel.[45] During its existence, the SPI passed through the hands of several ministries (moving from the MAIC, to the Ministry of Agriculture, to the Ministry of Labor, to the Ministry of War), having to adapt itself to the priorities and orientations of each of these different institutional contexts. As Darcy Ribeiro has commented, the SPI's strength (or lack thereof) depended upon Rondon's personal fortunes, and in the 1940s he removed himself from the Service's directorate, taking up the presidency of the recently created National Council for the Protection of Indians (*Conselho Nacional de Proteção aos Índios;* CNPI), an inter-institutional commission which had purely consultative functions, where he remained until his death in 1958. Less than a decade later, numerous accusations against employees of the SPI led to the formation of a Parliamentary Commission Inquiry (CPI) in Congress which, after two years of investigations, concluded by revealing an extensive list of corruption and injuries against natives carried out by members of the Service. The CPI recommended that the Service be shut down and this finally occurred in 1969.

The impact of Rondonian indigenism on the indigenous peoples of the Amazon Basin was quite varied, in some cases decisive and in others merely topical or eventual. The latter was the case in the states of Amazonas, Acre, Roraima and Amapá, which made up most of the region; in others, such as Mato Grosso and Rondônia in the first decades of the 20th century, Rondon and his followers had greater success. This was what occurred for example in the upper Xingu region, where the Central Brazil Foundation (whose cadres were partially incorporated into the SPI and FUNAI) had been working since the 1940s. In spite of their work and national and international visibility, the SPI's own analysts estimated that some 87 ethnic groups disappeared during the first half of the 20th century, 37 of these classified as "isolated" (Ribeiro, 1970: 217).

In terms of representations of the Indian, the SPI was not innovative. It simply continued the reversal of policies which began following independence, and which had been consolidated by romanticism. To Rondonian indigenists, the Indian was a primitive being who did not know or understand the white man and his civilized goods. Because of this, Native collectivities were understood to be fragile and hard to incorporate into the modern world. They were always understood to be on the verge of extinction. This is essentially the same Indian as that celebrated by 19th century romanticism: an illustrious ancestor of the modern Brazilian. He lacked the grandeur and splendor which the *indianists* attributed to him, however and was now transformed in to a pure and innocent being, eternally threatened by the present.

The Rondonian narrative, anchored in a humanitarian and romantic view of the world, focuses on the Indian as a character in a drama, underlining his unhappy condition on the one hand while on the other ennobling the brave *sertanistas* who dedicate their lives to his risky and almost doomed cause. For this reason, the indigenists' attention was almost exclusively focused upon "Indios bravos," or "*wild Indians*" (in the colonial sense of the term, meaning those who were not baptized and did not regularly participate in trade or labor relations with local whites), seeking to exercise a tutelary protection over these and incorporate them into the Brazilian nation. In the words and works of the Rondonian indigenists, José Bonifácio's intentions can be easily perceived, updated with the positivist jargon of a secular missionaryism.

In a study conducted in the SPI's archives during the 1950s, Brazil's indigenous population was estimated at between 68,000 and 99,000 Indians (Ribeiro 1957), who represented something on the order of 0.2% of the Brazilian population. One hundred and fifty ethnic groups were listed and regarding almost a quarter of these, the Service had absolutely no information at all. The population's profile indicates that it was mainly composed of micro-groups with fewer than 100 members. At the opposite pole, ethnic groups with more than 2000 members were few in number. The image one gets from this study is that more than half of Brazil's native population was made up of very small social units which were extremely threatened and which only managed to survive due to government tutelage and the efforts of a handful of selfless indigenists.

The Last Few Decades

With the rubber boom over, the daily existence of the Amazonian Indians was never again affected by a similar impact at such a general deep and integrated level. During the 1970s, the era of the so-called "Brazilian miracle,"[46] an ambitious plan was constructed to link up various frontier cities with the new Brazilian federal capital through highways. These transportation routes would be reinforced by INCRA-established colonies, settled by landless peasants brought in from other regions of the country (above all else from the northeast). If it had been transformed into a reality, this plan would have certainly deeply affected the life conditions of the country's Indians. It never got off the ground due to international economic conditions, but in the interim, the new national Indian service, FUNAI, used it as an excuse to mobilize resources in order to set up a minimal infrastructure and become more well established in the Amazon.

Later expansive frontiers had only intermittent and sectoral impacts, but these were grave enough to the peoples who found their lands in the way and thus under threat. This was the case with miners in the territories of the Cinta-Largas, the Yanomami and the Makuxi, in Roraima, in Pari-Cachoeira, and along the Negro River; with timber extraction on the lands of the Kayapó in Pará and the Marubo in the Javari Valley; and currently with soybean production in Mato Grosso, Rondônia and Roraima.

At the same time, other economic activities have sprung up in the Amazon, many of these centered no longer in the rural zone but in the region's capitals (most particularly in Manaus with the institution of the free economic zone). These activities are typically industrial, service, or tourist in nature. Recently made into states, the territories of Roraima, Acre, Amapá and Tocantins have created their own administrative structures, including state universities. With the acceleration of the general rural exodus, the capitals have grown and have come to shelter the major portion of these new states' populations.

In the 1980s and '90s, a more favorable political climate brought improved perspectives to indigenous communities. The process of identification of native lands, based upon the realization of numerous anthropological and historical studies, permitted some autochthonous populations to define their borders at the levels maintained prior to the rubber boom invasions. By the end of the 20th century, large areas which sheltered numerous populations were demarcated for the exclusive use of the Indians (with non-native resident populations indemnified and removed). This process occurred on the Yanomami and Ticuna lands, along the upper and middle Negro River, in the Javari Valley and Kayapó areas and others.

From the times of the original chroniclers, the Amazon and its populations have changed quite a bit. There are no longer 1,400 peoples, divided into 94 linguistic families, as Curt Nimuendaju's elaborate ethnographic map of the 1930s indicated. Today, the Amazon contains some 160 peoples, the majority of which have managed demarcate their lands, reserving for their descendants a section of Brazilian territory endowed with enough natural resources to provide for future generations. On the juridical-legal plane, the 1988 Constitution eliminated the institution of tutelage, affirming Indians' civil capacity and recognizing native cultures and languages as an integral and permanent part of the Brazilian nation. Today, the native peoples of the Amazon express their interests not through the official Indian Service, but through different representative organizations at various levels of the political scene, ranging from the local and ethnic on up to the regional and national political arenas. Today, such indigenous organizations as FOIRN, CIR, CIM, CGTT, CGTSM, UNI-Acre and CIVAJA (among many others) exist in order to make indigenous views and interests heard. There are over 200 of these organizations in the Amazon alone and their general coordination is undertaken by the COIAB, located in Manaus.

The existing cultural and linguistic diversity still represents a patrimony of inestimable value. If we do not hear of complex cultural forms such as those encountered by the first chroniclers and researched by today's archeologists, it must nevertheless be admitted that an impressive vitality has taken hold of contemporary native socio-cultural manifestations. This, in turn, creates greater challenges for the human sciences today than in the past.

According to the IBGE's 2001 census data, Brazil contains some 734,000 Indians—almost the same number as 800,000 "Indios bravos" once noted by Councilor Veloso at the dawn of independent Brazil. The annual growth rate of this native population over the last decade (10.8%) is superior to that of the Brazilian population in general (1.6%), and we can thus suppose that the Veloso population estimate is now being superseded at this very moment.

An evaluation of the demographic profile of today's indigenous peoples in the Amazon, based on data brought together by FUNAI and several NGOs during the 1990s, permits us to detect several significant changes. Medium-sized societies (between 200 and 2,000 members) are now in the majority (70 out of 136) and represent almost a third (28%) of the total indigenous population. Meanwhile, micro-societies represent only a small part of the total (3.3%) while large ethnic groups (with more than 2,000 members) account for 68.3% of the total indigenous population (Oliveira, 1999).

It has become necessary to incorporate new scales when thinking about contemporary indigenous peoples and cultures. Thousands of young Indians are currently concluding their high school degrees and dozens are studying in universities—this, too, is a new situation. An expressive part of today's native population also maintains some form of residence (fixed or provisional) in small interior cities or even in big urban areas.

Different from the recent past, indigenous identity is today a mark of high self-esteem, not only on the part of religious and political leaders, as an expression of a supposed traditionalism, but also on the part of the youth who are tied into contemporary processes of globalization. Indigenous identities are the result of a collective referencing of origins (always lived in various ways, in unique cultures) and these are important intellectual and emotional anchors in the current context.

The recovery of ancestral values and dignity is not just a possibility open only to those who have been born into autonomous social units, outside of indigenous posts and lands. The generations born on the reservations, like the descendants of the colonial Indians (*tapuios, caboclos,* and the Indians of the religious missions) demand that this possibility be open to them as well.

An important and characteristic phenomenon of the current conjuncture of Brazilian indigenous life is the rebirth of identitary affirmations by collectivities which have apparently already been assimilated (in other words, which have been considered to be assimilated by the authorities and non-indigenous peoples). To be an Indian no longer means to be an exemplary primitive, nor does it mean that a given symbol or custom—or even set of symbols and customs—need be maintained. Ethnic markers change, culture by culture, in different historical contexts. Given this, there is no single thing which can conclusively be said to represent "true Indianness" in Brazil today.

Final Considerations

In this chapter I have sought to utilize the instruments of history and anthropology to break with the idea which has historically been used to understand native peoples in Brazil: that they are inevitably slated to disappear, in spite of all the good will which could be directed towards them. This process does not exist—and never has existed—in a spontaneous, homogenous, rectilinear and inexorable form. The autochthonous populations of the Amazon were not primitive, simple, nor fated to disappear as soon as the Europeans arrived on the scene. These were, in fact, representations which were constructed about these populations and which have been historically presented as natural fact, perhaps so that the active desire of making natives disappear, camouflaged as prophecy, would have a greater chance of converting into reality. Here I have sought to explain how this belief originated, how individuals and social groups supported it, and what interests and contexts it has been linked to.

I have also sought to identify the concrete processes through which autochthonous populations became connected to the colonial context and, later, inserted into the formation of the Brazilian nation. In order to do this, I have shown how these processes have varied over time and across regions, identifying the different modalities of objectification which were projected upon native populations and pointing to parallel classificatory categories (both identitary and juridical) and the political structures which implemented them.

Four modes of being Indian were identified throughout history. These are: descent from missionary village collectivities, from the rubber extraction frontier, from SPI activities and, last but not least, from the dispersed families which today claim identity as remnant groups. These four modalities are the result of processes which regulated compulsory labor and forms of territorialization which, when situated in their contemporary contexts, are linked to differentiated political strategies and projects.

The indigenous condition should not be racialized nor idealized. It cannot be measured with DNA, nor with a greater or lesser adherence to a given social representation of "Indianness," no matter how circumstantially dominant it might be. Indians are all those who belong to collectivities which claim pre-Columbian American descent. The decisive factor for this identitary affirmation can be nothing more nor less than self-definition, and the only admissible counterproof that can be set against this is the observation of group practices. As Quixote reminds us, "men are the children of their works."

I have also tried to indicate the singular character of the long, hard road which the autochthonous populations of the Amazon have followed from the 16th century to the present date. Colonial visions of the Indians, articulated as these were with mechanisms of compulsory labor, gave legitimacy to their forced incorporation as Christians, and in function of this, their enslavement and extermination. Something similar seems to have occurred in Brazil's neighboring Hispanic nations. The principle of Manifest Destiny which has operated in the U.S. context may have also led to similar results, though these obviously possess different historical and religious roots. Both systems ultimately and contradictorily spread aid and taught the highest values while simultaneously distributing punishment and terror.

A particular way of thinking of state policies regarding autochthonous populations began in Brazil with independence, sustained by the argument that the Indians were the natural and primordial owners of the land. This led to the rejection of violence as a norm in the relationships forged between the Brazilian state and these peoples. This view became institutionalized in the formation of heterogeneous imperial administrative structures even as it consolidated its popularity through romanticism, with the Indian being adopted as a unique symbol of Brazilianess. It lost strength during the Republic—which saw itself as the introducer of modernity and the child of the West, an heir to Greco-Roman tradition— but was once again reborn in the saga of the modern *sertanistas*. This latter movement, in association with a key institution (the Army), maintained itself as a sort of permanent tutor of the country's destiny, blazing a trail through the backlands and guaranteeing national unity and ringing in the dawn of modern progress even while it pacified and protected the native populations of Brazil. These populations, in turn, unfortunately continue to be imagined as fragile, obsolete and lost in the distant jungles, almost as if they were living fossils, desperately in need of protection and tutelage. In this sense, the Indians continue to be seen as icons of a deeper Brazil, of conquered *sertões* and of *sertanistas'* values, protagonists, one and all, in the great narrative of national creation.

Notes

1. That legal dimension includes both administrative and juridical dispositions as well as the ideologies and the values which sustain them. In this sense, Catholicism and the language of catechism were integral parts of the official structure of the colonial period and the Empire.

2. Roberto Cardoso de Oliveira, *A Sociologia do Brasil Indígena* (Rio de Janeiro: Tempo Brasileiro, 1978). 2ª. Edição.

3. Otávio Guilherme Velho, *Frentes de Expansão e Estrutura Agrária* (Rio de Janeiro: Zahar, 1970); *Capitalismo Autoritário e Campesinato* (Rio de Janeiro: Zahar, 1976).

4. Darcy Ribeiro, *Os Índios e a civilização* (Rio de Janeiro: Editora Civilização Brasileira, 1970).

5. José de Souza Martins, *Capitalismo e Tradicionalismo* (Rio de Janeiro: Livraria Pioneira Editora, 1976).

6. João Pacheco de Oliveira, "O caboclo e o brabo: Notas sobre duas modalidades de força-de-trabalho na expansão da fronteira amazônica no século XIX," *Encontros com a Civilização Brasileira*, 11, 1978.

7. Herman Merivale, *Lectures on Colonisation and Colonies* (London: Frank Cass, 1967 [1861]).

8. G. Wakefield, "Colonização," *Revista de Imigração e Colonização*, 7 (3): 337–415, 1947.

9. Karl Marx – "L'accumulation primitive." In *Le Capital*. (Paris: Éditions Sociales, 1976).

10. Frederick Jackson Turner, "Social Forces in American History." In *The Turner*

Thesis Concerning the Role of the Frontier in American History, George Rogers Taylor (ed.) (Boston: D. C. Heath, 1967).

11. H. J. Nieboer, *Slavery as an Industrial System: Ethnological Researches* (New York: Burt Franklin, 1971. 3rd ed. [1910]).

12. Evsey Domar, "The Causes of Slavery and Serfdom: A Hypothesis," *The Journal of Economic History* 30 (1): 18–32, 1970.

13. Pierre Bourdieu, *A economia das trocas simbólicas* (São Paulo: Perspectiva, 1974).

14. Marc Bloch, *Apologie pour l'Histoire, ou Métier d' historien* (Paris: Armand Collin, 1993).

15. Alfred W. Crosby, *Imperialismo ecológico.* (São Paulo: Companhia das Letras, 1993).

16. Jules Verne, *La Jangada* (roman) (Paris, 1881).

17. José Maria Ferreira de Castro, *A Selva* (Lisboa: Guimarães 1981).

18. Agassiz quoted in the *Jornal do Commércio,* 18 May, 1865. Following the same line of thought, Tavares Bastos, ruminating on how to increase the flow of foreign settlers to the region, presented his definitive judgment on the region in the following way: "Manaus has an old reputation for fertility, beauty and an excellent climate. The margins of the Solimões or Upper Amazon Rivers are perfectly habitable" (*O Valle do Amazonas* [1866], São Paulo: Companhia Editora Nacional Brasiliana 106, 1937, 2ª. ed., p. 371).

19. "Le Brésil et la colonisation," *Revue des Deux Mondes,* 15/06/1862.

20. Said, Edward, *Cultura e Imperialismo* (São Paulo: Companhia das Letras, 1999).

21. This is not to say that these national elites didn't often use romanticized images of native peoples as diacritical marks which supposedly separated the "national spirits" of the new American peoples from their metropolitan antecedents. As we discuss above, across the Americas and especially in both the United States and Brazil, romantic Indianism became a popular literary trope which sought to express these new peoples' sense of socio-cultural uniqueness and, through this, to reinforce their pretensions to political independence. It is important to remember, however, that such constructed uses of *The Indian* had little if anything to do with the realities experienced by the actual native populations which these nations were in the process of conquering and/or absorbing.

22. This was the case of Von Martius' thesis, which was given a prize by the IHGB, as well as Varnhagen's historical investigations.

23. David Sweet, *A Rich Realm of Nature Destroyed: The Amazon Valley, 1640–1758* (Madison: University of Wisconsin Press, 1974).

24. Betty Meggers, *Amazônia: A ilusão de um paraís* (Rio de Janeiro: Paz e Terra, 1978).

25. Such as Michael Heckenberg and Eduardo Góis Neves.

26. Regarding a small village which the Spanish managed to take, Carvajal compares its inhabitants' earthenware with that of Málaga, observing that he had never before seen such beautiful and sophisticated pieces.

27. See also Mary Lucy Murray Del Priore, "Retrato da América quando jovem: Imagens e representações sobre o novo continente entre os séculos XVI e XVIII," *Estudos Históricos*, 5 (9), 1992.

28. Ronaldo Vainfas, *A Heresia dos Índios: catolicismo e rebeldia no Brasil Colonial* (São Paulo: Companhia das Letras, 1994).

29. Ronald Raminelli, *Imagens da colonização: a representação do índio de Caminha a Vieira* (Rio de Janeiro: Zahar, 1996).

30. Wars of extermination were directed against certain peoples such as the Tupinambás of Maranhão, the Mura, the Mundurucu and the Indians along the Negro River. The reasons for these wars were quite varied. The Tumpinambás were targeted for having been converted by French Capuchins and for having aided in the construction of their São Luis colony (i.e. for being allies of the French); the Negro River Indians were accused of having allied themselves with the Dutch. The other groups were held responsible for reducing trade and refusing evangelization.

31. See João Daniel (SJ), *O Tesouro descoberto do rio Amazonas*, 1710.

32. One source, based upon the chronicles of the time, estimates that in the five years between 1621 and 1626, just one *capitão-mor* of Pará had exterminated or captured 500,000 Indians (Oliveira 1988: 72).

33. The term sertão today designates a specific eco-system characterized by and arid climate and infertile soil. During the colonial period and the monarchy, however, it was indiscriminately applied to all the backland regions which were predominantly inhabited by Indians, which were unknown to the white man and were dangerous and difficult to colonize (see Amado, Janaína – "Região, Sertâo, Nação." *Estudos Históricos* 8 (15), 1995. The Amazon rainforest and the chaparral and savannas of Central Brazil as well as the western central wetlands were understood to be "sertão" according to this definition. The men who explored these regions, the so-called *bandeirantes*, were frequently understood to have a specialized kind of knowledge (that of understanding how to deal with the "índios bravos" or "wild Indians" who occupied these regions) and were often also known as *sertanistas*. "*Sertão*" and "*sertanista*" are such specific terms that they've been left in the original Portuguese. The first can be glossed in English as "backlands" and the second as "backwoodsman."

34. An image that was also used by the British historian John Hemming as the title of one of his principal studies, *Red Gold: The Conquest of Brazilian Indians* (Cambridge: Harvard University Press, 1978).

35. The villagers spoke a pidgin or general trade tongue known as the *lingua geral*

(the "general language" or *nheengatu*) which had been created by the missionaries and which was largely based upon Tupi, but which included European religious and political categories.

36. Rita Heloísa Almeida, *O Diretório dos Índios* (São Paulo: Editora da Universidade de Brasília, 1998).

37. Antonio Carlos da Fonseca Coutinho, *Notícias da voluntária redução de paz e amizade da feroz nação do gentio Mura nos anos de 1784, 1785 e 1786*.

38. Trans. note: A large native dwelling, roughly similar to a longhouse.

39. José Bonifácio Andrade e Silva, "Apontamentos para a civilização dos índios bravos do Império do Brazil [1823]," in *Legislação Indigenista no Século XIX: Uma compilação: 1808–1889,* Manuela Carneiro da Cunha (org) (São Paulo: Edusp., 1992), 347–360.

40. This expression is used by the historian K. Spalding in order to refer to those Peruvian Indians who were strongly integrated into colonial activities. It has been used on occasion in the Brazilian context as well.

41. See Maria Helena P. T. Machado, "Um mitógrafo no Império—a construção dos mitos da história nacionalista do século XIX," *Estudos Históricos,* 25, 2000, for an analysis of the Couto de Magalhâes.

42. These were the so-called *seringais de caboclos* (Oliveira 1979), who operated without northeastern laborers. They predominated in areas where rubber trees were less dense and/or where difficult terrain complicated the collection and transport of latex. Such circumstances made operating with local native labor more cost effective than importing workers from the Northeast. See Barbara Weinstein, *Prosperity without Development* (New Haven: Yale University Press, 1980).

43. Curiously enough, in the slang of the rubber circuits, recently arrived workers from the northeast were jocosely known as *brabos* (wild), while those who had adapted to the collection techniques and life along the circuits were known as *mansos* (tame). This indicates a possible association between the manner in which rubber tappers were mobilized and the characteristic process of training and repression which was utilized to incorporate the *wild Indian* into the colonial world.

44. There was strong resistance against accepting African and Asian immigrants.

45. Darcy Ribeiro, *Os Índios e a Civilização* (Rio de Janeiro: Editora Civilização Brasileira, 1970).

46. Sheldon H. Davis, *As vítimas do milagre* (Rio de Janeiro: Zahar, 1978).

5

Chile *Mestizo,* Chile *Indígena*

José Bengoa

> *Chile, distinguished and fertile province,*
> *in the famous Antarctic region*
> Ercilla. "La Araucana"

The Spanish *conquistadores* of the South American continent were obsessed with the south—*Terra Australis.* They advanced from the Caribbean, Mexico, and Panama, and the indigenous inhabitants told them that farther south were kingdoms full of gold, the mythical *El Dorado.* There was much truth to it: Peruvian gold was real. Once there, however, they were directed southward again. The richest Inca mines were at Marga Marga, in the central part of what is now Chile, where a Quechua colony of miners (*mitimae*) sent gold to Cuzco.

There are very close estimates for the amounts of gold produced when parts of Chile were within the limits of the Inca Empire. The Spanish intercepted a Quechua convoy transporting all of the gold mined in the last year during which the mines were independent, which was on its way to Cajamarca to pay the ransom for the Inca who was Pizarro's prisoner. The shipment had clearly been delayed already and in the end was seized by the conquerors. On the basis of that reference alone it has been possible to estimate the quite considerable levels of production, showing that the natives had not been lying to the Spaniards.

Pedro de Valdivia, *El Conquistador,* traveled from Extremadura in Spain to the battlefields of Flanders and the Italian peninsula, crossed the ocean to Panama, and marched on to Peru, where he petitioned the Crown for permission to conquer the south of America. He crossed the desert and arrived at what is now Santiago de Chile, in the Mapocho River valley.

After conquering, colonizing, and killing indigenous inhabitants, he prepared for his journey farther south, where not even the Inca's representatives had arrived. He founded settlements, built churches, set up gold-panning operations, and believed that he had conquered the territory. His passion was to arrive at the Straits of Magellan, and he sent his admiral,

Juan Bautista Pastene (an Italian like Columbus), in search of the end of the world, *fines terrae*. On a similar mission, a young Spaniard, Alonso de Monroy, crossed rainforests and mountains until he arrived at the Chiloé archipelago and took a look at the fjordlands of the planet's far south. It was said that there among the islands was the City of the Caesars, where golden towers glowed in the sunlight. For centuries, such fantasies sent expeditions to the south.

This image of the south of the world has been a constant part of Chile's history. It is said that on his deathbed in exile in Peru, Bernardo O'Higgins, founder of the Republic, had exclaimed "Magellan, Magellan!"—his final words calling out the Antarctic aspirations of the recently established nation.

Mestizo Chile in the Central Valley

History, nevertheless, has been complex, and the south has been characterized more often than not as distant and unconquerable.

Pedro de Valdivia and his followers traveled southward and tried to dominate the indigenous Araucanos. The indigenous population of the territory that is now central and southern Chile had different names, but they all spoke the same language. From a hundred kilometers north of Santiago to the islands of Chiloé people spoke "the tongue of the Earth" as it was called by the Spaniards, translating *mapu* as Earth, and *dungun* as word or tongue. The language was also called *Chilidugu* by the Jesuits. The Spanish called the native people *Araucanos* in order to have one generic name for all the groups. The name was later popularized with the publication of the epic poem by Alonso de Ercilla, "La Araucana" (Madrid, 1589–1590). Today the descendants of those indigenous groups refer to themselves as Mapuche; *che* means people, so, variously, "people of the Earth," "people of the land," "people of this place." Foreigners are called *huincas* or *winkas*, according to the orthographic preference of the speaker, which means outsider, thief, or white person, etcetera. It is possible that the term once referred to the Incas, *pu Inca*, who were the first organized foreigners to arrive in the area. Here I use the terms "Araucanos" and "Mapuche" indiscriminately, although the former is used more often when the reference is to the term preferred by the Spanish.

Don Pedro founded the city of Concepción and tried to make La Imperial the capital of the Kingdom of Chile.[1] This city was founded at the meeting of two navigable rivers. It was probably one of the most important ceremonial sites of Mapuche society in the south, densely inhabited and accessible by river from considerable distances. It was the only place where so many native people lived together in close proximity, with homes and croplands organized in a way that resembled Spanish towns.

Pedro de Valdivia failed in his endeavor, the only Spanish *conquistador* in Latin America who died at the hands of the natives during the early days of the colony. The southern lands were retaken by the Araucanos. A new contingent of *conquistadores* arrived under the command of the son of the Viceroy of Peru, Garcia Hurtado de Mendoza. It was an army commanded by the sons of the Spanish nobility. They slaughtered and tortured the population in a display of blood-letting that seemed to be guided by a long history of contempt for "commoners," such as Castilian peasantry, Moors and Gypsies, Jews and other minorities that had been harshly repressed on the Iberian peninsula. Once again the Spaniards founded settlements and cities in the conquered areas. The war between them and the Araucanos lasted from the mid-sixteenth century, when the first *conquistadores* arrived, until the end of that century, when the indigenous defenders again won a military victory. For a second time, a Governor was to die at the hands of the Mapuche warriors: Martin Garcia Oñez de Loyola, Governor of Chile, was killed at Curalava by the Araucanos led by Pelantaru.[2]

> Martin Garcia [Oñez] de Loyola, nephew of Ignacio de Loyola, arrived at Valparaiso with his wife, Doña Beatriz Clara Coya, daughter of Don Diego Lairitupaca, who was captured by Don Francisco de Toledo in the Andes and beheaded in Cuzco—the legitimate descendent of the great Guainacapac, last and most powerful monarch of Peru . . . From this marriage was born a daughter, whom he took to Spain from the city of Concepción and the king married her to Don Juan Henríques de Borja, gentleman of the house of Gandia, and granted her the title *Marquesa de Oropesa de Indias*. (Bengoa 2007)

The houses of Loyola and Borja, among the great families of Spain, were joined with the Coyas, of the old Peruvian monarchy. This history of intermarriage between the nobility of Spain and the native Americans has not begun to be told nor understood, and is undoubtedly one of the origins of Latin American *mestizaje*. There is a beautiful painting in the Church of the Company of Jesus in Cuzco that includes the likeness of Clara Coya, *Marquesa de Oropesa de Indias*. The noble title is significant: it carries the weight of the gold of Peru.

The Mapuche destroyed all of the cities south of the Bio Bio River and north of the Chacao Strait that separated Chiloé Island from the continent. The imaginary south of the world collided with reality. This clash strengthened the shape that the new nation was to take from then on.[3]

Chile's Central Valley as an Island

In 1600, the territory of Chile was divided in two: the Central Valley to the Bio Bio River, and the south. North of the Bio Bio, a *mestizo* Chile was being built; and south of the Bio Bio, indigenous Chile resisted.

The indigenous population was to disappear physically from the Central Valley, and vanish altogether from the national image. While general intermarriage would in fact take place in the central part of the country, the natives as such were to be "thrown out," "launched" as a collective image towards the frontiers: the Peruvian and Bolivian racial groups to the northern frontier, and the Mapuche or Araucanos to the southern borders.

For centuries Chile was to remain a small space, an island. To the north lies a desert, difficult to cross and one of the driest regions on earth. To the east are the Andes, outlining the territory like a giant natural wall. To the west, the Pacific Ocean, an enormous sea that, due to winds and currents, was navigable only along its coast; its seafarers might arrive with great difficulty at Callao (Peru) and Panama or, in the opposite direction, try to pass Cape Horn or the Straits of Magellan, one of the most difficult routes in the history of sailing. The southern border was protected by the Army of the Frontier, financed by the King of Spain with the famous *Real Situado*, sent every year in a fleet of ships. Colonial Chile was always subsidized, existing "at the pleasure of the King" and supported by the product of his wealthier colonies. It was a small territory, with a small population. Between the northernmost and southernmost cities, La Serena and Concepción, there are only 800 kilometers; between the mountains and the ocean, no more than 100. Not all of this territory was settled, and the few inhabitants that were there in colonial times lived in the small valleys.

Chilean society was born into this small space, perceived very early on as a Western, Spanish society, and therefore white, Roman Catholic, and with ties to the tradition of European thought. This was the Chilean identity for many, and many still think that it should be maintained. Given those original ethnic or racial identifications, not a few have an image of Chile as being at quite a distance from Latin America. The indigenous population in the central part of the country was effectively annihilated as a coherent entity, and those who remained united with the recent arrivals in a process of widespread intermarriage.

Generalized *Mestizaje*

Chileans of the Central Valley saw themselves as white and Roman Catholic, and thus far removed from the indigenous world. That society denied the mixed racial nature of the population from the very beginning. Yet the image that was thus created is undoubtedly contrary to the facts. Chile is a *mestizo* country. The Chileans who imagine themselves as not being indigenous are as *mestizo* as those Chileans who imagine themselves as indigenous. In biological terms, there was generalized crossbreeding through intermarriage, and in social terms, there was cultural fusion.

There is a double image of *mestizaje* in Chile. On the one hand, it shares the predominant character of the Catholic Spanish American culture and subordinates those elements that manifest the indigenous root. On the other hand, it is characterized by the dominant self-consciousness of belonging to the indigenous races, subordinating the elements that identify Chilean nationality and Western Christian culture. In reality generalized *mestizaje* began with the Conquest, and the resulting population issued from a brutal biological fusion. Testimony abounds:

> Things went from bad to worse, there being nothing but warfare and misfortune and much hunger and nakedness, and above all it should be considered that the oppression of the unfortunate Indians is a shameful calamity, the robbery of their cattle and crops and of the people themselves to be used and what is worse, the women [used] for worse things, with such luck that in just one place where there were soldiers recently arrived from Spain together with the others who depended on the Field Marshall, there were weeks when sixty Indian women gave birth from among those who were at his service but not that of God . . . and thus the Indians were so justifiably angered that there should be no frightful surprise at the fact that there were so many rebels.[4]

Los conquistadores arrived alone, with very few women, in contrast to the Anglo-Saxon arrivals in North America, but also in comparison with newcomers to other places in Spanish America more accessible to Spain, like Mexico and even Lima. The trip to Chile was very hard during the first centuries of the colony, and women arrived infrequently.[5]

Nor were there large indigenous populations. The first census records of the colonial period give evidence of the reduction of the indigenous population, which decreased from more than a million people at the time of the

Conquest (Bengoa 2007) to nearly one hundred and fifty thousand, a population that remained at this level until the early twentieth century. Conversely, the records show a persistent increase in the *mestizo* population. Even within the part of the population described as "indigenous"—referring to those who would not submit to the will of the Spanish—there was a growth of the *mestizo* population. The leaders of the revolts that occurred in the seventeenth and eighteenth centuries were identified as *mestizos*, although they were totally involved in Mapuche society and culture.

Prejudice against "crossbreeds" was widespread. The son of a Spanish father and a native mother was considered to be *mestizo*. That condition was known as "rightful *mestizaje*" according to the Spanish. "Reverse *mestizaje*" implied perversity.[6] A Spanish woman could not have children with native men, according to the beliefs and moral stereotypes of the times.

> More than six hundred Spanish women are the captives of those Indians, the daughters and wives of noblemen who died serving in the war . . . and the outrages that afflict their very blood . . . It is estimated that four hundred were taken captive when Valdivia was destroyed and, according to Father Ocaña, four hundred more were taken at Villarica.[7]

And Captain González de Nájera says:

> "Who would not feel wounded and indignant at the sight of their own Spanish women enslaved—so delicate, of such esteem and quality?"

Rape, in fact, occurred on both sides, but was acceptable when the father was Spanish and the mother a native, and was considered to be "rape" only when the father was indigenous and the mother either Spanish or of mixed race—*chilena*. Quiroga sets the moral code by stating that "although the rightful *mestizos* are bad, the backwards mestizos are undoubtedly worse."[8] Years later, a captain arrived at an indigenous settlement and remarked that "several girls came, the oldest not being more than twelve years old, so white and blonde and lovely that it was marvelous to see them, and they spoke only the natives' tongue."

The Whitening of the *Mestizo* Society

The fusing or blending that was commonplace during the Conquest had to be made more orderly. A classification system had to be established. During the seventeenth century, following the death of Governor Oñez de

Loyola and the destruction of the settlements in the south, the Kingdom of Chile became more organized in the Central Valley, with a southern frontier against the rebellious Indians. Slowly, the population of central Chile began to grow, and typical social segmentation processes became evident, with some becoming richer and others poorer, laying the socio-economic groundwork for the establishment of the lower classes as well as of the elites. Within this social differentiation, everyone had the same origin: mixed through intemarriage, or *mestizaje*. What, then, were the differences between the *criollos*, the *mestizos,* and the indigenous natives?

The first census taken in Chile is known as the Jáuregui Census of 1778. It was done in the Diocese of Santiago, covering the inhabited area known today as the Central Valley. The census determined that:

> The population of the Diocese of Santiago had 259,646 inhabitants distributed as follows: 190,919 whites or 'more or less pure blooded European descendants,' 20,651 *mestizos* or individuals of mixed race, 22,568 Indians and 25,508 blacks.[9]

In the colonial period, the mixed-race Chileans already imagined themselves as white "descendants of a more or less pure European race." The "whites" are classified as *peninsulares*, or those born in Spain. At the end of the colonial period there were no more than 15,000 *peninsulares* and their immediate family members.[10] The *criollos* are defined as "people of the white race and more or less pure European origin." And the *mestizos* were classified as "those individuals who because of the color of their skin or other physical accidents seemed to have been born of parents from different castes or, more specifically, of Spanish and Indians."[11] An imaginary line of social classification separated the *criollos* from the *mestizos*.

> It was hard to distinguish the *criollos*, sons of 'pure' Spaniards, from the *mestizos*, descendants of Spanish men and Indian women. Apparently the census of the Santiago Diocese in 1778 overcame the difficulty by including as 'whites' all those individuals who were believed to have the physical characteristics of the Spanish race and by creating a very reduced group of *mestizos*, whereas it could be truly said that the latter made up the large majority of the lower classes in the city and the countryside in Chile.[12]

Chile also was a country assumed to be without a significant black (African slave) population. At the end of the colonial era, however, there were no less than ten thousand slaves, and twice as many free blacks and *mulatos* as appear in the census. This population disappeared from the *criollo* conception of itself in the Central Valley, and thus was erased from social reality, blending, too, into the generalized *mestizaje*. The indigenous population accounted for by the colonial census referred to people who submitted to the regime of "Indian settlements," the old *encomiendas*, territories committed to a Spanish colonist or grants of land authorized by the King, located at the margins of the lands belonging to the *criollos* themselves in the Central Valley. About 95,500 such people are included in the estimate made for the region south of the Bio Bio by Governor Ambrosio O'Higgins in 1791 and 1796. They were "friendly Indians," allied by means of the "parliaments" held occasionally, but living outside the system established by the colonial classsifiers.

The Jáuregui Census classification is the product of an imagined self-image—Chile as a white nation—that was to persist throughout the history of Chile. Wishful thinking overcame reality. The black population in the center of the country became invisible and "disappeared" in the process of *mestizaje*. The indigenous population in that part of Chile was reduced by the colonial census, then made to disappear definitely in the nineteenth century, "bred out of existence" by the same homogenizing process. Popular rural society was to be a combination of all these origins, but the dominant sector of the population saw itself as white. Such is the power of historical classification systems.

In 1813, at the outset of the Republic, Don Juan Egaña ordered a census that obtained information on about 586,848 inhabitants. The classification system consisted of Spanish Europeans, Spanish Americans, Spanish Asians, Canary Islanders and Africans, Indians, *mestizos, mulatos,* and blacks. The final four groups were the so-called "castes" (see Bengoa 2007). The *criollos*, the majority of the population, considered themselves to be Spanish Americans rather than Spanish Europeans.[13]

Since the founding of the independent nation, Chileans held to a self-image of "European Americans." The categories of *mestizo*, black, and *mulato* were lost in nineteenth-century censuses, and references to Indians were restricted to those who lived on reservations created between 1881 and 1927.

These elements of social and ethnic identity-building, and the usual processes of differentiation and segregation begun after settlement, are fundamental to an understanding of the creation of the Chilean Republic, its movement towards independence, and the organization of the state. As the saying goes, "As we see ourselves, so shall we be seen." The Republic was to be the "*criollo* Fatherland," to use the concept coined by Severo Martínez Peláez. At the end of the colonial era, this idea of the *criollo* was constructed from the elite's ethno-cultural adherence to European thought and custom, particularly to the ideas of the Enlightenment that the Bourbons tried to impose in Spain at the end of the eighteenth century. The socio-cultural spread of the *criollo* elements in the central region of Chile will also be the key to understanding interethnic relations in the nineteenth century.

Indigenous Chile in the South

After the Mapuche insurrection of 1598, all the Spanish cities south of the Bio Bio River were destroyed. Some of these settlements, such as Valdivia, were large and had substantial population; the city of Imperial had even been considered as the site for the capital of Chile. The territory was dismembered and eventually a frontier was established at the Bio Bio River, and guarded by numerous forts built by the Spanish. In 1641, fifty years later, the Governor of the Kingdom of Chile, Marqués de Baydes, signed a peace agreement between the Spanish and the Araucanos at the Parliament of Quilín.[14] That was one of the most significant victories that any indigenous group won during the Spanish colonial period in Latin America.

The peace achieved at the parliaments meant a very long period of independence for the Mapuche. From 1598 until 1881 they would live without being dominated by an outside government, subject only to their own norms and laws. Their territory extended from the Bio Bio River to the River Maullín, which was roughly the northern limit of the settlements within the Diocese of Chiloé. The movement of the Araucanos across the Argentine *pampas* led them to increase control over an area that extended to the Atlantic Ocean.[15]

Peace brought great changes to indigenous society. Former gardeners and farmers became horsemen and herdsmen.[16] They took horses from the Spanish and soon became an equestrian society; in this case as in various others, this indigenous culture rapidly adopted a European import and improved on it. The natives lightened the weight of saddles and learned to raise the animals, and the horse became central to their new life and culture. They used them for warfare and that, perhaps, was the principal factor that allowed them to fight the Spanish on an equal basis in the early years. During the period of declared war, at the end of the sixteenth and the first half of the seventeenth century, it seems that the natives created specialized military units that formed a permanent militia. When the peace agreements were formalized, these militias sought new outlets for their activities other than settle for the peaceful lives of farmers, and began to roam the *pampas* on the eastern side of the Andes in what is now Argentina.

A huge number of wild cattle and horses had grown on the broad plains of the Atlantic side of the mountains. According to some historians, they were the offspring of the animals that escaped the first destruction of Buenos Aires (1541). The old indigenous cavalry became active cattle traders, moving animals to the markets established on the northern frontier of Indian territory and on the southern border near Valdivia. Often the animals were slaughtered and processed as jerky, dried beef and horse meat known by the Quechua term *charqui* among the *criollo* traders,[17] a staple of the growing commercial activity in the Pacific region. Bales of that dried meat were shipped to California in the nineteenth century.[18] The beautiful Mapuche or Araucano silver ornaments and artifacts produced during that period attest to the level of prosperity attained by the natives during the time of their greatest affluence and cultural splendor—the second half of the eighteenth and first half of the nineteenth centuries.

In 1810, Chile's declaration of independence from Spain did not cause great repercussions in the indigenous society of the south. After the war of independence, however, there was a period of guerilla warfare during which the majority of the Mapuche fought on the side of the royalist elements, because they had established formal peace treaties with the King of Spain, as defined at their parliaments, and therefore felt that it was their duty to honor those commitments.

During much of the republican period, life in the society established south of the Bio Bio was wholly different from the *criollo* society of the Central Valley. The Chilean state did not have sovereignty in those territories. At the beginning of republican period, Chilean territory reached a limit at some four hundred kilometers south of Santiago. There was a fort on the coast at Valdivia and a group of peasant farmers left over from the Jesuit missions in Chiloé, both completely isolated from the center of the country. Towards Antarctica, an unknown land called Trapananda was a realm of dreams and utopias.

Nonetheless, interest in the southern lands was constant. From the middle of the country, from the capital in Santiago, eyes were on the south, fearfully gazing at the savagery of barbarians, but also looking at the opportunities and wealth that lay there—it was said—for the taking. Many attempts at colonizing the Straits of Magellan were made in the period of President Bulnes, 1840 to 1850,[19] and, beginning in that first decade of the second half of the century, immigrants from Germany were invited to colonize what is now Valdivia.

During the nineteenth century, the Chilean elite, like others in the western hemisphere, was convinced that immigrants from Europe were the source of civilization and progress necessary for our young nation. Consequently, and considering the area to be "empty lands" in the south, the state promoted a pro-immigration policy. A commission traveled to Germany and contracted numerous colonists. In a few years, an enclave society came into existence to the south of the Mapuche communities of La Araucanía, in the area known today as the lakes region. For sixty years or more, until well into the twentieth century, there was limited direct communication with the center of the country. A prosperous industrial society was built up: the first modern smelting ovens were established to produce steel for the nation, shipyards for large vessels were constructed, and infrastructure for processing agricultural products was created. German was spoken in the schools and in daily life.[20]

The Mapuche were left to occupy a median strip between the Bio Bio and Valdivia rivers (Río Cruces), hence between the *mestizo* Chilean society to the north, in central Chile, and the new German enclave. The government at the time began to debate the policies to be applied in those lands, where it had no effective jurisdiction as they were in the hands of the Indians. In Santiago, there was a general lack of knowledge about those distant places, hence numerous and often contradictory opinions about the region. With regard to the size of the indigenous population, the majority of Chileans believed that the lands were practically uninhabited and that the Indians had all but disappeared.

Many circumstances explain the occupation processes that occurred during the second half of the nineteenth century. There was rapid population growth in the *zona central*, the Central Valley, which created pressure on the territory, forcing expansion both north and south. A structure of *haciendas*, or large estates, dominated the agricultural system in the central region, and with it a system of servitude that gave the laboring classes no opportunity to improve their economic condition, and none at all to obtain a parcel of land upon which to begin an independent life.

The discovery of gold in California in the middle of the nineteenth century carried thousands of peasant farmers and poor Chileans to seek their fortune in those distant latitudes. Later, the construction of railroads in Chile as well as in Peru allowed thousands of workers to flee the countryside. Demographic pressure led to territorial expansion because the Central Valley was dominated by the iron hand of the landowning oligarchy. If there had been no possibility for expansion, there would probably have been a general insurrection or revolution in Chile late in the nineteenth century, just as it broke out in Mexico at the beginning of the twentieth. Many individuals in various social sectors, and even political leaders of the time, predicted and expected it.

The second half of the nineteenth century was a period of territorial expansion also on an international level. The explosive development of industrial capitalism drove great masses of Europeans to move to America and elsewhere in the world where there were spaces thought to be empty, *terra nullius*, no-man's-land. A progressive intellectual environment contributed to the local elites' approval of this process. In Chile, the subject of European immigration was to dominate all debate during the period.

It was not by chance that, during the same period, social evolutionist ideas began to appear. In indigenous southern Chile, the role played by positivist evolutionist ideologies was a determining factor. Studying the history of that period today leaves no doubt at all that those ideas, current to the epoch and considered "scientific," became the doctrinaire, moral, and even "historical" justification for invasions of indigenous territories. In that period too the historian Diego Barros Arana was writing the *Historia General de Chile*, the first great, modern history of the country. That author, enthusiastic social evolutionist cognizant of all the more noteworthy authors of that intellectual current of the times, illustrated the life of Indians with the most degrading imagery. His postulation of an antithesis between a civilized world and primitive and barbarian societies was decisive in carrying out the concentration (*reducción*) of the indigenous population into small areas.

Economic reasons may also explain the occupation of indigenous territories in the second half of the nineteenth century. The growth of the international wheat market reached a peak in that period. Chile became active in wheat export by opening Pacific trade with California. Changes in the means of transport—the Clipper Ships—allowed Chilean wheat to arrive as far as England. Voices arose throughout the country about the "unoccupied lands" in the south, spoken of as "the granary of Chile" in those days. For the European colonists, this image projected a bright future, with lands good for growing wheat and secure European markets in which to sell it.

One of the most influential incidents of this period was the story of "Joven Daniel," a passenger ship that went aground on the coast at Puaucho, today Puerto Saavedra, and was boarded by the coastal Indians. Among the passengers was a young upper-class girl who apparently died, but according to the rumors circulating in Santiago was taken prisoner by the Indians, with all of the imaginable consequences of abuse, rape, and whatever stereotype of barbarism could be called upon. Monvoisin, a renowned French painter passing through Santiago at the time, produced a dramatic illustration of how the girl, Elisa, was subdued. The public response in the capital was horror, not of the actual deeds, for there were no witnesses, but rather to images generated by that public itself. The result was the breach of relations between the *criollo* elites and the natives. Until 1859 there had been bridges, above all between the regional elite in the Concepción area, *the* frontier city in the south, and the Mapuche who joined the revolutionary wars on its side. In the decades following the incident the ties were broken, and accusations of barbarism prevailed. Even the Roman Catholic Church, which until the 1860s stood for protecting the Indians, kept quiet. The Italian missionaries, who had been active defenders of the indigenous population, left the field open for the occupation of the territory.

These territorial occupations were among the first "global operations" to occur in the modern world. Antonio Varas, a member of President Manuel Montt's Cabinet (1850–1860) and one of the best known personages on the Chilean political and cultural scene of the nineteenth century, traveled to the United States in order to study the policies there regarding migration, territorial occupation, and dealings with the Indians. Upon his return, he wrote what was to be a decisive report that provided a plan for the territorial expansion process. The newspapers of the time gave detailed information about the French expansion into Algiers and the system of settling colonists in those areas. Finally, the Chilean and Argentine armies were going to coordinate their actions in detail, synchronizing the Argentines' "Conquest of the Desert" across the pampas with the Chileans' "Pacification of the Araucanía," as it was called. A high-ranking Argentine officer, Oloascoaga, was detailed as the liaison officer with Chilean army, and would be in constant contact with General Julio Argentino Roca, commander of the Army of the South, moving southward at the same moment, arriving eventually in San Carlos de Bariloche.

The second half of the nineteenth century was also the time when almost all national borders worldwide were established. It was the time of "putting in order" (*acomodando*) the old colonial frontiers, the occupation of what was considered to be "unoccupied territory," and the formal constitution of nation-states. The Chilean elite was not alien to this process.

In 1866, an attempt was made to move the frontier from the Bio Bio River fifty kilometers southward to the Malleco River, resulting in a very bloody period of warfare between the Chilean Army of the Frontier and the Indians. The same tactics were applied as in the wars of many years ago: the army moved into "enemy territory" during the summer, burning houses and rounding up cattle in an attempt to destroy the economic base of the indigenous society.

The period between 1866 and 1881 was one of intense frontier warfare, with military incursions from the Chilean as well as the Argentine sides. Following contemporary policies (those applied in the United States and elsewhere), the strategy was to build frontier outposts in the form of small occupied forts, which, in this area, separated the central region of the country from the south and separated the German enclave farther south from the indigenous territory.[21]

This period in the history of indigenous peoples is both dramatic and interesting. On both sides of the Andes, the Mapuche formed extensive defensive alliances and organized powerful military detachments. While maintaining trading activities on both sides of the mountains, they also moved from one side to the other to do battle with both invading armies. Given a certain parity of military technology, it was not easy for the Chilean Army of the Frontier to win a decisive victory over the Indians, who moved on horseback and often had better mounts and greater warrior skills. The Indians used the tactic of surprise to great advantage and even though they had not fully adopted the use of firearms, were not easily taken by surprise by the Chilean army.

Military technology also changed dramatically in the decades of the sixties and seventies in the nineteenth century, with the development of the breech-loading rifle and the rapid-fire cavalry carbine that were among the winning factors for the final military occupation of the Indian territories. The invention of the telegraph was another factor; more than one high-ranking military officer of the time said that it was the equivalent of adding another regiment to his command. And, in addition, the railroad reset the frontier at but a few hours from Santiago, the nation's capital.

Thus 1879 marked the beginning of the expansion of the frontiers of what had been Chilean territory since the colonial period, with movements towards the north, the south, and into the Pacific. In the same year the War of the Pacific began between Chile and the joint forces of Bolivia and Peru, lasting until 1883, when the Treaty of Ancón was signed with Peru.[22] On February 24, 1881, a defensive settlement or fort was established at Temuco, in the center of Araucanía, and on January 1, 1883, the city of Villarica was resettled, three centuries after its destruction by the Mapuche.[23] The same troops that had gone to fight in the north were transferred to the south for the military occupation of Araucanía—that is, the region between the Malleco and Toltén Rivers.

During the same period, on September 9, 1888, an Agreement of Intent was signed by Ariki Aramu Tekena, chieftain of the Rapa Nui people on Easter Island, and Captain Policarpo Toro of the Chilean Navy, leading to the incorporation of that remote island in the middle of the Pacific Ocean into the national territory and under the sovereignty of Chile. At that time, too, the establishment of cattle ranches in Patagonia and on the island of Tierra del Fuego was to have disastrous effects on the indigenous populations that lived there, the Aónikenk and Selk'nam, who were completely eliminated. The first land grant to the cattle companies was made in 1885.[24]

In sum, the reality of the Chilean state in the nineteenth century was quite different from the situation in the twentieth century. Most of the "unoccupied" lands were inhabited by indigenous groups. The state's effort to expand in those years was considerable. There was movement towards the north, the south, and into the Pacific, but no policy for the protection of indigenous peoples during those campaigns. Indeed, there was a sort of extermination policy that in the north was known as "chilenization," and the Aymara Indians subject to it sought survival through silence.[25] In the far south, the result was total extermination. It was genocide. On Easter Island the indigenous population was reduced to nearly one hundred people, and they fell prey to leprosy. And in the central southern region, a policy of establishing reservations was implemented for the Mapuche, following international policies of the time.

In these years too the nation's self-portrait would be completed. The Central Valley had always romanticized its "Magellanic vocation." The dream of being the country of the "famous Antarctic region" was to be fulfilled. Expansion northward and southward was seen by the elites of the middle of the country as a civilizing process.[26]

As a consequence, the remaining Indians were subordinated and concentrated on reservations. It was a period of physical and cultural extermination. Central Chile expanded from Santiago to every corner of the newly conquered territory, without any change to its cultural, social, and institutional character that sought to eliminate or hide ethnic differences and even regional idiosyncrasies.[27] Consequently, most impartial observers and foreign visitors at the beginning of the twentieth century assumed that the Mapuche had disappeared with the annexation of their territories by the Chilean and Argentine states.[28]

The Origin of the Ethnic Conflict in Chile

How many Mapuche were there at the beginning of the twentieth century? How many were settled on reservations, which is to say, how many were given land on reservations? How much land was given to each family?

Despite popular assumptions of very small numbers, scholars have found different answers to these questions.[29] The National Population Census of 1907 included a special census of indigenous people, supervised by the Capuchin missionary congregation. Father Jerónimo de Amberga, a thoughtful German, said that many Indians refused to answer because they were afraid, and that the census takers did not reach all of the places being polled. Nonetheless, it's possible to estimate even the approximate size of the indigenous population at the moment when they lost their independence. The 1907 Census of the Araucano Indians, which gives details of the provinces and municipalities of the period, documented 101,118 Araucanos, as the Mapuche were called then.[30]

The census surprised the Chileans, who believed that the Indians no longer existed and, above all, that the lands in the south were uninhabited. By contrast, numerous scholars or local officials point out that the number of Indians should have been even greater. Many knowledgeable contemporaries, such as Tomás Guevara, who was then the director of the high school in the recently founded city of Temuco, believed that there were more than 150,000.

The lands that had been conquered were parceled out according to several classifications. The Indians were to be settled on reservations. The remaining lands were considered property of the state, public lands that would be auctioned to colonists, especially foreigners.[31] An Indian Settlement Commission was created by the national government to carry out this complex operation of territorial allotment.

Land granted as reservations comprised 536,000 hectares under *títulos de merced*,[32] or formal land grants, meaning that the average amount of land per person would have been less than five hectares (one hectare is equal to 2.471 acres). Nevertheless, as often occurs, information about the resettling of the Indians is inconsistent. The official figure used as a reference is that the average allotment of the formal grants was 6.4 hectares per person, but that is an uncertain figure at best. The Interamerican Committee for Agricultural Development (CIDA, *Comité Interamericano de Desarrollo Agrícola*), one of the most authoritative sources, reports the following figures:

Table 1. Information about Indian Settlement in Chile

	Títulos de merced	Hectares	People
Arauco	66	7,116	1,912
Bío Bío	6	659	112
Malleco	350	83,512	11,512
Cautín	2,102	317,112	56,938
Valdivia and Osorno	552	66,711	7,261
Llanquihue	2	84	16
TOTAL	3,087	475,423	77,751

As commonly occurs, more precise information is difficult to confirm.[33] But we can be certain that the state delivered at least 3,078 deeds of land, which, according to the measurement techniques of the time, were equivalent to 475,423 hectares and benefited 77,751 Indians. The 1907 Census thus confirms that many were left without land, illustrating the origin of the *minifundio indígena*, or the tiny farms of the Mapuche.[34]

The state delivered 6.1 hectares per person. The families grew and in 1963, 36 years later, the average plot had become 1.8 hectare per person. Today our studies show that that there is an average of 3.6 hectares per family, and also demonstrate that the size of the average Mapuche family is larger than the national average; the national average was 3.4 in 1990, compared to the average Mapuche family, 6.3 in 1995 (see Bengoa 1996). According to the 1992 census, 235,000 Mapuche lived in rural communities, and if the land comprises an area of nearly five hundred thousand hectares, the division yields less than two hectares per person. Much of that land has also suffered physically in terms of the soil quality.

The allotment of land—*reducciones* or indigenous communities—ended in 1927.[35] Many communities parceled their lands among family members and legally, though not in practice, they were dissolved. This happened most noticeably in the provinces of Malleco and Arauco, closer as they were to the northern frontier. Numerous questionable sales of land, including outright seizures, brought an avalanche of documents that filled the land registrars' offices in charge of recording property transactions and deeds.

The origin of the present land conflicts lies in this period between 1927 and 1973, when 168 communities disappeared completely and their lands were seized. That land later passed on to private individuals, colonists, or corporations, and the indigenous owners had to emigrate. Consequently, 2,134 settlements remained within the common property regime established by the system of *títulos de merced* and 784 were parceled into individual family properties. In 1970, the lawyers of the government

Department of Indian Affairs (DASIN), Jorge Osses and Hugo Ormeño, estimated that the Mapuche had lost 131,000 hectares of the area granted by those original deeds, meaning that only about four hundred thousand hectares remained.[36]

What follows is relatively well known. In 1941, when the Popular Front governed Chile, the Interamerican Indigenous Conference was held at Pátzcuaro, Michoacán, Mexico, convened by that country's President Lázaro Cárdenas. Chile was represented by a young Indian leader, Don Venancio Coñoepán Huenchual, who became one of the principal indigenous leaders of the twentieth century. His was a generation of young Mapuche men, mostly the sons of the old chiefs, *caciques* or *lonkos*, who, during the period of independence, believed that it was possible to integrate with Chilean society appropriately and without discrimination. They formed a large movement called the Araucana Corporation, elected congressmen, made demands for schools and roads, confronted cases of abuse, and dreamed of a harmonious relationship with Chilean *mestizo* society. Don Venancio Coñoepán served in the national Parliament for several terms as representative of several political parties, winding up in the Conservative Party, the party of the Right that represented the *criollo* land owners, the oligarchy, the upper class itself. That strange situation is hard to understand and interpret. But the utilitarian manner of Mapuche participation in national political activity has been and remains evident. They felt in those days that an alliance with the Right was the most direct way to achieve their interests, and so they worked within it. Nevertheless, Coñoepán and his movement were made invisible. Only during a brief period in the 1950s, under the semi-populist government of General Carlos Ibáñez del Campo, was there any apparent progress in indigenous affairs when Coñoepán was named Cabinet Minister, but with little practical consequence.

The "integration" policies, as they were called, did not obtain the results desired; to the contrary, they led to an increase in the differences, indeed contradictions, between the indigenous society and the rest of the nation. Urban migration increased during the post-World War II period, as did the levels of poverty among the communities and families who remained in the Indian territories. Not only was there no integration or progress, but social distancing, discrimination, and marginalization continued and grew. By the mid-1960s the policies of integration had failed, and the indigenous movements began to make more radical demands.

The hopes placed in Salvador Allende's government, and the protests of indigenous organizations and peasant farmers that took place in the period of the *Unidad Popular*, or Popular Unity coalition of 1970–1973, ended sadly with much violence, a large number of "disappeared" detainees, and Mapuche leaders gone into exile. The Indians thus had not better luck than the rest of the popular sectors in Chile at the time.

Until that time, the Mapuche were the only indigenous group formally recognized as such in the country. They generally understood politics according to the theory and ideology of the Latin American and Chilean Left. Many Indians were actively involved in Chilean political parties and joined those that formed the Leftist Popular Unity coalition. During the period 1970–1973 their protests were framed by the demands for *Reforma Agraria* (Agrarian Reform), when a revolutionary ideology of land redistribution dominated expressed concerns. At that time affirmation of ethnic identity was not their first priority. The self-image, as was the case throughout Latin America, was class-oriented and defined by peasant farmers, *el campesinado*.

After the *golpe de estado* (military coup) in 1973, a variety of Mapuche organizations confronted the military dictatorship, with the support of the Roman Catholic Church. Given its eagerness to privatize everything, the Pinochet government decreed that the land of the indigenous communities should be divided into small properties for individual families, and between 1979 and 1990 all of the *títulos de merced* allotted by the state fifty years earlier were legally voided. The ownership of land in the reservations was no longer collective, but became family-owned properties and remains so to this day. That does not mean that the communities that live on the reservations have disappeared in any social or political and especially not in any religious-cultural sense. But the consequences of this internal division of land and individualization of ownership have been profound and prejudicial. On the one hand, land was assigned only to those who lived in the countryside, leaving aside those family members who had migrated to the cities. They were paid for their portion of the land in money, but the property values were extremely deflated and those payments were merely symbolic. The transformation of the reservations into private property led to considerable pressure to sell the land that now belonged to individual families; non-Indian investors placed the greatest pressure, particularly in areas near the lakes, rivers, and other places that were attractive as tourist destinations. Numerous fraudulent methods were used to buy the land, such as the system of "99-year rental contracts" that reduced even further the territory that belonged to the indigenous population.

It was not until the 1980s and 1990s that Chile began to ask itself some of the new Indian questions of ethnicity, identity and participation that were shaking Latin America,[37] and, with it, a long period of conflict began. The subject of the Mapuche is one of the most complex political and social issues in the contemporary Chilean political situation. Their indigenous movement is perhaps the only social movement that disputes the political successes of economic growth and the development model adopted by Chile.[38] The first government of the "democratic transition" under President Patricio Aylwin promulgated an Indigenous Law, or *Ley Indígena*, in 1993 that set limits on the purchase and sale of land. This opened the way to new land purchases that could benefit the communities by establishing a *Fondo de Tierras*, or Land Purchase Fund. The Law called for scholarships and other affirmative-action measures, bilingual intercultural education, and legal recognition to the communities. That legislation passed during a new period of capitalist expansion in Chile, highlighted by rapid economic growth. And this expansion created pressure once again on the Indian lands and land in general, provoking numerous conflicts with logging companies, tourist enterprises, public works such as hydroelectric projects, and roads.

Mestizo Chile of the Central Valley expanded into *Indígena* Chile in the south in the late nineteenth century. But that process of expansion was filled with contradictory behavior and policies, as shown in this brief historical account. A society that still looks upon itself as white, Roman Catholic/Christian, and Western European while belittling its indigenous inhabitants does not demonstrate much capacity for integrating its diversity. Chile has united its national territory—and thus "fulfilled its destiny" to reach the fabled far south—but has done so by suppressing the indigenous peoples in the south, and has thus created a conflict that lasts to this day.[39]

Notes

1. See José Bengoa. *Historia de los antiguos mapuches del sur* (Santiago: Editorial Catalonia, 2004; 2nd ed., 2007).

2. This long story is told in detail in ibid.

3. Mario Góngora, perhaps one of the most important Chilean historians, has argued the hypothesis of the central importance of "the southern war" in the formative process of the centralized Chilean state. He also points out relationships between that experience and the evolution of types of urban structures and the character of the population. See Mario Góngora, *La idea de Estado en Chile* (Santiago: Editorial Universitaria, 1982). The winner of the National Prize in History, Don Alvaro Jara, has developed a similar thesis, although from a different point of view, underlining the importance of the war in the south in the early configuration of the country in its central

regions, often harassed by fears of the barbarians. See Alvaro Jara, *Chile: War and Society* (Santiago: Editorial Universitaria, 1972).

4. Mariño de Lobera, *Crónica del Reyno de Chile* (Madrid: 1960), 520.

5. This is not meant to be an erudite historical production, but we have researched this subject in the Indies Archives in Seville, looking through the tomes titled "Travelers to the Indies," where the names of the passengers of each of the ships that sailed to the Americas were registered. The number of women is very small and those bound for the south in the early periods were rare exceptions.

6. Translator's Note: There is a play on words here, because "*al derecho*" can mean "straight forward" or "straight ahead," while "*derecho*" means "law" or "right." "*Al derecho y al revés*" means "forwards and backwards" or "right and wrong." When one is new to Spanish and receives the instructions "*a la derecha*" and "*sigue derecho*"—"to the right" or "keep going straight"—it is often confusing.

7. Padre Gabriel Guarda, "Los cautivos de la Guerra de Arauco" (Santiago: *Boletín de la Academia chilena de la Historia* 98: 93, 1987).

8. Jerónimo de Quiroga, *Crónica del Reyno de Chile* (Santiago: Editorial Andrés Bello, 1978), 232.

9. Diego Barros Arana, *Historia General de Chile.* Rafael Jover's ed., vol. 6 (Santiago: 1886), 374.

10. This number is exaggerated, although there really was an important arrival of *peninsulares* in Chile towards the end of the colonial period. In Mexico City in 1790 there were only 2,300 European Spaniards among 59,000 people defined as being of the "white race." There the arrivals from Spain were called *gachupines,* or "men who wear pointed shoes that pretend to be spurs," and in Chile, as throughout the rest of America, *chapetones,* which, according to Vicuña Mackena, refers to the word *chape,* or the braid of hair that was the fashion of those early Spanish colonists.

11. Reference is from Barros Arana, *Historia General de Chile,* bk. 7, pt. V, ch. 26, p. 56.

12. Barros Arana, *Historia General,* 447.

13. National Archives of Chile. *Censo de 1813,* made by Don Juan Egaña by order of the governing *Junta* made up of *señores* Pérez, Infante and Eyzaguirre (Santiago: Imprenta Chile, 1953).

14. This affair was dealt with in detail in my *Historia de los antiguos mapuches del sur.* I will soon publish a book with copies of the texts of treaties that I have researched in the Indies Archives in Spain. It is the only Spanish American treaty with the Indians published in the Collection of Treaties of the King of Spain, a collection of numerous volumes containing all the peace treaties and records of other dealings that the Kings of Spain made with kings, princes

and so on, primarily in Europe and around the world of that time. It is a very important book, in which is included the Peace Treaty of Quilín between the Governor of Chile and the Araucano *caciques*, or chiefs.

15. There were certainly many periods of warfare and violence, although peace agreements were predominant throughout this long period of history, 1641–1881. In the seventeenth century there were frequent Indian wars and rebellions, above all in the south where peace agreements had not been established, among the so-called *Cunco* Indians, today known as the Huilliche, or southern Mapuche. In the eighteenth century there were two large general insurrections, and in the nineteenth century the first guerilla war took place between the pro-independence faction and the Spanish, with the aid of the Indians, known as the War to the Death, following the final battles for Chile's independence from Spain. In 1850 and 1859 there were two regional revolutions that involved the southern Mapuche who aided the regional forces at Concepción. And, finally, beginning in 1866 and until 1881 there was a final period of warfare that concluded in the so-called Pacification of Araucanía, or the Occupation of Arauco.

16. This process of changes and the characteristics of the herding society are described in my *Historia del Pueblo Mapuche* 6th ed. (Santiago: Ediciones Lom, 2006).

17. Translator's note: *ch'arki* is a Quechua term.

18. Translator's note: there was considerable trade of wheat and lumber from southern Chile to California during the Gold Rush period.

19. Once again the south dealt a bad hand to the Chileans. When Fort Bulnes was founded near what is today Punta Arenas, the military contingent left there died of hunger. The location is still called *Puerto de Hambre*.

20. We have detailed the history of that region in J. Bengoa, *The Social History of Chilean Agriculture* (*Historia social de la agricultura chilena*, 2 vols.), vol. II (Santiago: Ediciones Sur, 1991).

21. The first line of forts was known as the Malleco Line, following the course of that river, and the second was the Tolten Line for the same reason. Between those two rivers there was a band of close to 300 kilometers of Indian territory that divided the continent from ocean to ocean, crossing Chile through the Andes and across Argentina, where another line of forts "protected" the Province of Buenos Aires from the threat of Indian attack.

22. Said treaty left the geopolitical situation of the cities of Arica and Tacna subject to a plebiscite to have been held in 1893, but the vote never happened. The uncertain situation continued until 1929, when Tacna reincorporated with Peru and Arica was placed under Chilean sovereignty.

23. We have gone into the details of these historical processes in several books. A collective report, result of the efforts of the Commission for Historical Truth and a New Deal (*Comisión de Verdad Histórica y Nuevo Trato*), is published in

the book compiled by J. Bengoa, *La Memoria Olvidada. Historia de los Pueblos Indígenas de Chile* (Santiago: Editorial del Bicentenario, 2004).

24. That refers to the Sociedad Werhahn y Cía. that was granted 123,000 hectares on Tierra del Fuego, then inhabited by the Selk'nam. See that story in Bengoa, *La Memoria Olvidada.*

25. See the book by Sergio Gonzalez, *El Dios Cautivo. La chilenización del Norte Grande* (Santiago: Ediciones Lom, 2005), and *La Memoria Olvidada.*

26. The most important book written during the period about these affairs is *The History of the Civilization of Araucanía* (Historia de la civilización de la Araucanía) by Tomás Guevara, later President of the Chilean Historical and Geographical Society, a scientific association modeled after those created at the same time in Europe and the United States.

27. The Germans in the south would, themselves, be quickly "*chilenizados.*" As we have explained in other publications, the arrival of the railroad connected the German cities to central Chile, whereby they submitted to national institutional and cultural structures. As a result they lost much of their industrial dynamic, and many of the region's industries disappeared during the following decades. The 1960 earthquake buried what had remained of that enclave. See J. Bengoa, *The Social History of Chilean Agriculture.*

28. At the beginning of the twentieth century, Tomás Guevara wrote *The Last Araucano Families* (*Las últimas familias araucanas*), because he wanted to leave this testimony to the last survivors.

29. See J. Bengoa, *Historia de un conflicto,* 2nd ed. (Santiago: Editorial Planeta, 2002 and 2004), and the already cited *Historia del Pueblo Mapuche.*

30. In Arauco there were 4,706 people; in Malleco, 12,259; in Cautín, 46,781; in Valdivia, 26,134; and in Osorno and Carelmapu, 11,358. The inhabitants of the archipelago of Chiloé were not registered.

31. As was true in many other countries, permission to settle was granted to companies or private businessmen. These enterprises promised to contract colonists in Europe and take them to their destinations. The companies kept part of the land. There were considerable conflicts because most of these enterprises did not fulfill their contractual obligations with the state nor with the colonists.

32. *Títulos de merced* is the name given to deeds of property ownership given free of charge by the Chilean state to the Mapuche for their reservations. Those deeds were delivered beginning in 1884 and the process continued until 1927. They were collective deeds made out in the name of the chief of a multifamily group, position of leadership that is called *lonko* in *mapudungu*, meaning "head" (*cabeza*) or *cacique* in its incorrect Spanish translation.

33. The numbers vary. According to the General Archive of Indian Affairs, today in the hands of the National Commission for Indigenous Peoples' Development

(CONADI, *Comisión Nacional de Desarrollo Indígena*), organized by the Department of Indian Affairs/National Agricultural Development Institute (DASIN-INDAP) in the 1980s, only 2,919 "reservations" or communities were really assigned, which means a difference of 168. These could have been lost or simply disappeared at the time. The land measurements made during the 1980s, when the deeded lands were subdivided, gave a figure of 510,768 hectares as *títulos de merced*. This was due to the differences produced by modern surveying equipment. In the communities located in the mountains, the old deeds gave very imprecise figures. When their areas were recalculated with modern equipment, the number of hectares increased, but their real size—in terms of landmark references—stayed the same.

34. The Indian Settlement Commission was created to take charge of the definition of the boundaries and the allotment of the reservations. Over the past years, many studies have focused on that process that is the origin of present day conflicts. "The proceedings of the Settlement Commission were slow, complicated and arbitrary. For example, the Commission resolved that the lands occupied by Indians would be assigned '*en Merced*' or 'by the grace of' their authority, although the beneficiaries had to prove that they really and continuously had dominion of said lands for at least a year, meaning, among other things, that the grazing lands were left out. The labor of the Commission was extremely slow, such that when they arrived at a given area, much of the Mapuche land had already been taken hold of by private citizens, making proof of real possession impossible. On many occasions land was given to private individuals where Mapuche families had already been settled, meaning that part or all of a *título de merced* designated for the Indians was given to whites or Europeans. The colonists' ambitions gave way, bit by bit, to their moving the fences that defined the property lines and the progressive invasion of the Deeded Indigenous Lands." Report of the Commission for Historical Truth and a New Deal," in J. Bengoa, *La Memoria Olvidada*, Introduction.

35. It is very important to note that the policies applied to the indigenous population during this period (1881–1931) were debated in the National Congress and legislated into law; they were not the simple results of adventurers, spontaneous agents or situations that were beyond control. Though such influences did exist, they were always subject to the law of the Nation and the powers of the State. See J. Bengoa, *La Memoria Olvidada*, and also by this author, *Historia de la Legislación Indígena en Chile* (Santiago: CEPI, 1992), also published in the journal *América Indígena* (Santiago: Instituto Indigenista Interamericana, 1996).

36. After the government had allotted the *títulos de merced,* the state continued to cede land to the Mapuche by various means, for, as we have seen, many had not been settled. For example, in some cases where the Mapuche continued living on their traditional sites, without any deed or title, they were granted a *título gratuito de dominio,* or a "free deed of domain." There have also been

transfers of public lands. It has been estimated that 661 free deeds were designated and given to Indians during the twentieth century by the Ministry of Land and Colonization and other government agencies, and one hundred deeds were authorized by judicial authorities in Concepción. Furthermore, we have to add the so-called *Títulos de Comisario* used in the Province of Osorno, particularly in San Juan de la Costa. Those would have designated some five hundred thousand hectares but were not recognized legally. The Huilliche, or the Mapuche who lived to the south of Valdivia, received portions of those deeded lands to the degree that they still inhabited them, and that process has continued until the present democratic governments have transferred the last agricultural properties.

37. J. Bengoa, *La emergencia indígena en América Latina* (Mexico: Fondo de Cultura Económica, 2003). For the 99-year contracts, see *Informe de la Comisión de Verdad Histórica y Nuevo Trato, La Nación,* 28 de octubre, 2003.

38. The Mapuche affair is the only case of charges of human rights violations in Chile that is currently on the docket at an international level. In April 2006, the Special *chargé* for the Rights of Indigenous Peoples at the United Nations, Rudolph Stavenhagen, sent a letter to the Chilean government calling its attention to a number of complaints about human rights violations in the south of Chile, especially in the prisons.

39. Translation <richard.dodge@gmail.com>, November 2007.

6

National Expansion and Native Peoples of the United States and Canada

Roger L. Nichols

In July 1845, New York editor of the *Democratic Review,* John L. O'Sullivan, tried to justify American expansion when he wrote that it was "our manifest destiny to overspread the continent allotted by Providence for the free development of our yearly multiplying population" (Nye 1974: 15). While clearly not original, his ideas described the intellectual basis for American and, to a lesser extent, Canadian actions toward Indians and First Nations (in Canada there is a difference) peoples from the earliest inter-racial contacts to the near present. Nevertheless, until the mid-1860s, the policies and actions of the two countries varied widely. Many of the differences resulted directly from early British oversight in Canada, differing chronologies of national development, varieties of physical geography, and the size of both native and invading populations in the two nations. Until the mid-1860s the respective ideas about territorial expansion and how to deal with the native peoples within their boundaries differed substantially. Only after that decade did the native policies and their results in the two countries gradually became similar.

When Europeans began their explorations of other parts of the world in the late fifteenth century, Pope Alexander VI sought to direct their actions. For example, both the 1492 "Privileges and Prerogatives" issued to Columbus by Ferdinand and Isabella and the 1493 "Inter Caetera" (written by the pope) included the assumption that the Catholic Church had the authority to control the overseas actions of the secular rulers. Accordingly, Alexander wrote that valid "discoveries" could occur only where the lands were not ruled by "any Christian king or prince . . . or people" (Thorpe 1909: I, 39–42; Commager 1949: 2–3). A year later, in the 1494 Treaty of Tordesillas between Portugal and Spain, the rulers asked permission from "his Holiness . . . to confirm and approve" the agreement and to issue new bulls that would censure "those who shall violate or oppose" their pact (Commager 1949: 4).

Although the willingness to accept papal claims of authority to direct international explorations faded quickly, the doctrine that explorations and "discoveries" had to be limited to regions inhabited by non-Christians remained. In 1496 King Henry VII of England signed letters patent giving John Cabot and his sons authority to explore the "provinces of the heathen and infidels" throughout the world, though without any reference to church authority (ibid.: 5). Other monarchs followed suit, if somewhat hesitantly, as each ruler seemed to assume that under his divine right powers he could proceed without the pope's blessing. Yet the explorers continued to link church and state as did Jacques Cartier in 1534, when he ordered his men to erect a large cross with a shield bearing a fleur-de-lis and a plaque that stated "Long Live the King of France" near the seacoast before his return to Europe. The Indians objected to the cross and plaque, but Cartier ignored their complaints (Biggar 1924: 64–65).

A half century later the English expressed similar attitudes in Queen Elizabeth's 1584 charter to Sir Walter Raleigh for his Roanoke colony, and again in 1606, when King James I issued the first charter to the Virginia Company (Thorpe 1909: 53–57; Poore 1877: II, 1379–82). Later in the seventeenth century both England and France restated their disregard for any tribal titles or claims to much of present Canada. In 1670 Charles II issued a charter to the Company of Adventurers of England trading into Hudson's Bay, usually known as the Hudson's Bay Company, granting it authority over the entire region drained by that body of water. Within a year Quebec officials met Indians near Montreal and asserted French national claims to all of Canada. Through this action, as in their *prises de possession,* the French aimed their claims at other Europeans and gave no serious thought to any possibility that the native people might actually own the land or its resources (Eccles 1969:108–110; Jaenen 1984:29).

By the time the English won the French and Indian War and ousted the French officials and troops a century later, patterns for dealing with native people had been set for generations. With their new dominance in much of eastern North America, British officials in what became the United States and Canada implemented policies for managing relations with their tribal neighbors under the Proclamation of 1763. This acknowledged an Indian Country closed to European settlement within which the native people held a possessory claim to the soil. Under that English plan, to get land, the colonists had to obtain it from the Indians through cession, purchase, or warfare (Jensen 1955: 640–64). In theory, that legal requirement led to policies and actions that often appear similar in the native-new-comer relations of the two nations. In fact, however, it applied mostly to the American colonies because settlement in Quebec already extended well beyond the Proclamation line.

Despite this apparent similar legal framework, the two developing nations would experience sharply differing histories. While the United States became independent in 1783, the colonies that became Canada took until 1867 to acquire anything like national status. Because they shared few experiences related to territorial growth or nation building until the last third of the nineteenth century, the two British North American societies often saw those two issues play out differently. In the United States a burgeoning population demanded land and resources that could only come from their foreign or tribal neighbors, while American governmental leaders from George Washington on publicly favored national territorial expansion. The Canadian story bore little resemblance to this. Rather than leading a united people in an aggressive push for new lands, spokesmen for the various English colonies faced an entirely different situation. First, they remained subjects of the British. Then, they quarreled repeatedly with each other and with the French in Quebec over unification and ideas of nationhood.

Historians' Views

As territorial expansion and its impact on native peoples occurred differently on each side of the international border, scholarship on these issues differs as well. Led by Albert K. Weinberg, U.S. scholars examined nationalism, expansionism, a sense of mission, as well as specific wars and diplomatic issues. Much of this writing stressed ideas of American exceptionalism as illustrated by the term "Manifest Destiny" (Weinberg 1935; Parish 1943; Erkirch 1944; Pratt 1950; Burns 1957; Alstyne 1960; Merk 1963).

Reflecting a substantially different historical experience, Canadian scholars expended far less effort analyzing their nineteenth-century territorial growth or Indian relations. When they did, the story that emerged bore little similarity to that south of the border: rarely did anything resembling a Canadian version of American "uniqueness" appear in these analyses (Denison 1909; Galbraith 1957; Morton 1964; Creighton 1965; Creighton 1970).

Nationalism and the desire for territorial expansion operated more openly and continuously in American scholarship than it did among Canadians. In fact, my survey of hundreds of articles and books on Canadian history and Indian policies located only one specific use of these related ideas, and that spoke of "an Ontarian sense of Manifest Destiny" rather than a national one (Miller 1989: 153; Nichols 1998:349–67). General

Canadian histories written before the 1980s barely mention Indians when discussing the period after the eighteenth century. In U.S. historiography, conversely, for much of the last half century, Indians and territorial expansion received continuing or at least frequent attention from historians of American diplomacy, expansion, and settlement.

In its drive to expand, the United States came to regard its European and tribal neighbors as either dangerous or savage. Canada, on the other hand, retained its status of separate British colonies on either side of Quebec for nearly another century. During most of that time the Hudson's Bay Company's Rupert's Land holding of the entire north and west blocked potential expansion. In addition Canadian leaders lacked the authority or any clear popular support for acquiring western lands. At the time Canadian territorial growth appears more reactive than that of the United States because American expansionism threatened Canada, not the other way around.

The small, scattered Canadian colonies had few reasons to think in national terms. Not many economic, social or political ties bound the English maritime colonies of New Brunswick, Prince Edward Island, and Nova Scotia to each other or to Quebec and Ontario later. Occasionally, politicians in the maritime colonies talked of uniting their own region, but their efforts attracted little popular support. Well into the middle of the nineteenth century British policy makers oversaw many governmental activities in their remaining North American colonies.

Canadian historians tend to stress the divisions among the various colonies and the reasons their leaders failed to think in terms of a continental nation. Donald Creighton, a leading scholar of Canadian national development, points out that nation-building and territorial expansion in Canada came as responses to outside pressures rather than from strong internal demands for land. He cites British desires to back away from their North American colonies and the perceived threat of possible invasion by the United States as the chief motivations for the 1867 Confederation of Canada (Creighton 1970: 15).

Not all scholarship supports that idea. For example, in *Promise of Eden,* Doug Owram contends that by the 1850s a small, vocal group of men holding influential business and government positions had become avid expansionists. Their ideas, most often expressed by George Brown, editor of the *Toronto Globe,* pushed for an end to the Hudson's Bay Company monopoly over the northwest. As early as 1849 Thomas Keefer, a railroad engineer, had written that "as a people we may as well . . . attempt to live without books or newspapers, as without Railroads" (Owram 1980: 42). A strong economy during the 1850s boosted frontier settlement, and by 1855 the *Globe* pointed out that settlers had purchased the last farm lands available to them in Canada west. Clearly, the early nationalists thought that a shortage of western agricultural lands might inhibit continuing immigration and economic growth (ibid.: 38–43).

For the Toronto-based expansionists, western lands offered somewhat different attractions than they did to leaders in the United States. True, they saw the acquisition of new territory and resources as beneficial to encourage continued immigration, but their efforts stemmed from a desire to strengthen existing communities rather than to populate distant frontiers. So the West appealed to them more as an area that would stimulate economic development in the already settled regions than as a place for expanded settlements. So instead of proposing their version of the Homestead Act to lure pioneers westward as the United States would do, they dreamt first of building a transcontinental railroad system that would tie what became Ontario to the Pacific coast. Unlike the situation south of the border, where the overnight settlement of California brought strident demands for a railroad connection with the East, from the start Canadian expansionists linked their ideas about railroads to the potential benefits of trade with Asia. To achieve that goal before the Americans, George Brown told his readers that the best route for a transcontinental railroad lay "through British Territory" (Owram: 49). To him and his fellow nationalists that meant extending Canadian authority westward to the Pacific. In their public discussions of expansion and their attacks on the Hudson's Bay Company fur-trade monopoly, almost no thought seems to have been given to the native people. If territorial growth occurred in anything like the manner in which these expansionists hoped, it would threaten the Indians' way of life. Ignoring that issue, the expansionists claimed that once the Hudson's Bay Company lost its monopoly, the Indians would benefit because they would have more trade options. However, these men had little knowledge of the trade and knew even less about the Indians. Their claim that the Hudson's Bay Company monopoly hindered possible western development was true. At the same time, Company policies kept most potential settlers out of the region, thus protecting the tribal people there (ibid.: 51–52).

While these debates continued in Canada, the American Civil War to the south helped stimulate an effort to establish a political union of the maritime colonies with the United Canadas—present Quebec and Ontario. This foundered over efforts to build an intercolonial railway connecting Halifax on the east coast with Quebec and Montreal. The rejection of the

British funding terms as too harsh by Canadian negotiators outraged the maritime officials. The Halifax *Morning Chronicle* reported that "the union of the British American Colonies, as a group, is no longer a project which men of the present generation can hope to see accomplished." It went on to urge its readers to turn their attention to other projects (Creighton 1965: 25). Clearly not all eastern Canadians shared this disappointment, because even after Confederation became a reality in 1867, voters in Nova Scotia overwhelmingly rejected being forced into the new union. Both the British and leaders of the new Canadian government ignored their wishes.

At the end of the American Civil War the federal government demanded huge reparations from Britain for damages done to American shipping by Confederate cruisers built in British shipyards. U.S. negotiators blamed the British government for these losses, and the continuing dispute caused some Canadian leaders to fear that the issue might cost the newly established Confederation parts of what became the Prairie Provinces. Then the 1867 U.S. purchase of Alaska from the Russians reinforced the idea that the United States might try to seize all of British North America beyond the borders of the new Dominion of Canada. Canadian efforts to control the West surely grew out of such concerns. In January 1870, Conservative Prime Minister John A. MacDonald wrote that "it is quite evident to me . . . that the United States government [is] resolved to do all [it] can, short of war, to get possession of our western country, and we must take immediate action and vigorous steps to counteract them" (Creighton 1970: 15). "Defensive expansionism" proponents took little notice of tribal groups or claims on their land.

To some extent, scholars who study American Indian and First Nations issues reflect these differing patterns. U.S. historians stress the continual hunger for tribal land and resources, while those studying Canada say far less about those topics. For example, almost all scholarship on American western expansion assumes that at least into the 1880s Indian affairs remained an important issue. At the time, federal officials faced repeated demands to investigate corruption and failed Indian polices, but leaders north of the border heard few such calls. In fact, other than drawing some minor complaints about the early results of their actions from missionaries, parliamentary Indian policies drew little public attention. As a result, Canadian leaders congratulated themselves on their peaceful dealings with tribal groups. Thus in 1877 Prime Minister Alexander Mackenzie reported to Parliament that, unlike the policies of the Americans south of the border, Canadian plans were inexpensive and "above all, a humane, just and Christian" way to deal with the tribes (Canada, *Debates*, 8 Feb. 1877: 3).

While American authorities treated tribal people as enemies or at least obstacles to national growth and development, early Canadian leaders considered First Nations people as military and diplomatic allies. During the treaty talks at Ghent at the end of the War of 1812, one British negotiator, perhaps trying to make his U.S. opponents look bad, reported that "I had till I came here no idea of the fixed determination which prevails in the breast of every American to extirpate the Indians and appropriate their territory" (Nichols 1998: 141–43; Parsons 1973: 340). Apparently, the British oversight of Indian affairs in Canada until 1867 moderated similar frontier views if they existed there. When that country received Confederation status and its leaders took control of dealing with tribal groups, few abrupt changes occurred immediately. However, as continental expansion became a central force, Canadian Indian policies came to resemble those of the Americans more closely than they had done previously.

Early Approaches

In the United States, even some of the founding fathers already exhibited a strong sense of national mission. John Adams, the second president, announced that the new country was "destined beyond a doubt to be the greatest nation on earth" (Burns 1957: 65). A year later, in 1786, Thomas Jefferson, the third president, expressed a similar idea when he wrote that the United States "must be viewed as the nest from which all America, North and South, is to be peopled" (Boyd 1954: 9–218). A generation later John Quincy Adams added the influence of the Almighty to this idea. Writing to his father, he said that "the whole continent of North America appears to be destined by Divine Providence to be peopled by one *nation*" (Bemis 1949: 182).

While it made no references to divinity, the Supreme Court of the United States outlined tribal rights and land claims in several early nineteenth century decisions. The 1823 *Johnson and Graham's Lessee v. William McIntosh* ruling, although rarely quoted, stated the bases for American legal claims on Indian lands. The Court stated "that discovery gave [the federal government] an exclusive right to extinguish the Indian title of occupancy, either by purchase or conquest" and that "the Indian occupants are to be considered merely as occupants" (Prucha 2000: 35, 37). This based national claims on doctrines that stretched back to the Proclamation of 1763 and beyond, to the late 1490s.

Later in the 1820s, Secretary of War John Eaton, speaking for the Jackson administration, claimed that no one considered existing treaties with the Indians to be permanent agreements. Shortly after this, a spokesman for the House of Representatives Committee on Indian Affairs lent support to that idea when he wrote that Indian treaty-making was little more than an "empty gesture" made to appease the "vanity of tribal leaders." If that were not clear enough, the committee document went on to say that existing treaties were little more than a "stately form of intercourse" used to keep peace and to acquire Indian land (Cave 2003: 6).

North of the border, meanwhile, religious, linguistic, and national differences divided French and English-speaking population, while intense localism separated the Maritime Provinces from those of the interior. For a while these problems led to rejections of efforts to unite Quebec, Upper Canada, Nova Scotia, and New Brunswick under a single legislature (Reid 1964: 84–87). They also diverted attention from territorial expansion and kept Indian affairs far from the center of political debate. Nevertheless, during the 1864 discussions about continental union, George Cartier, one of the Quebec delegates, noted that "We all desire that these provinces should be as great as possible." While hardly a ringing endorsement of militant nationalism, this suggested at least a limited interest in political expansion (Creighton 1965: 140).

Often that same apparent nonchalance carried over into native affairs as early as the late eighteenth century. At the time officials in Canada seem to have paid only sporadic attention to nearby tribal groups, except as economic partners and the source of occasional land cessions. That is demonstrated clearly by the treatment of Indians who had sided with the British during the Revolutionary War. When their allies, the Mohawks and other Iroquois, learned that the 1783 Treaty of Paris had ignored their contributions and in fact overlooked them entirely, they denounced the British bitterly. Not only had they fought alongside them against the colonists, but they suffered major loses in battle and experienced devastating invasions of their land with destruction of crops and villages. Responding to their complaints, officials in Canada offered refuge to tribal groups wanting to flee the new United States. This persuaded the Mohawk Joseph Brant to lead nearly 1800 Loyalist Indians into present Ontario, where they founded what became Brantford, and where the Six Nations people still occupy a reserve (Stanley 1950: 148–210; Johnson 1963: 267–82).

At the same time as the British welcomed Indians into their land, leaders in the newly independent United States looked upon tribes that had been neutral or fought for the British allies during the war as defeated enemies. Placing the tribes into this category, American negotiators imposed three harsh treaties (Ft. Stanwix, 1784; Ft. Ft McIntosh, 1785; and Ft. Finney, 1786) that took land from tribes living in western New

York and the upper Ohio River Valley. These one-sided land grabs demonstrated that the new national leaders believed they had conquered the tribes in that region. The Indians objected, asserting that they had not been defeated and that even though the British may have lost the war, they had no right to cede tribal land to the United States. Continuing raids along the upper Ohio River convinced American leaders to impose their demands with military force. So in late 1790 Josiah Harmar led nearly 1,500 men into Ohio, only to be defeated decisively by the Miami and Shawnee they encountered. When Arthur St. Clair led another frontier army against these tribes the next year, the Indians crushed his troops in one of the worst military defeats in American history. In 1794, however, General Anthony won a decisive victory at Fallen Timbers that ended the fighting south of the Great Lakes for nearly a generation (Hurt 1965: 104–14).

New Approaches North and South

During the decade 1780–90, while Canada sought to assist its tribal partners, costly warfare forced American leaders to shift their thinking about Indian policy. Certainly they did not change their fundamental goals—getting tribal lands and resources—but the nearly bankrupt Confederation Congress came to recognize that continuing violence and frontier warfare had brought the government to the brink of collapse. As a result, when crafting the Ordinance of 1787 that created the Northwest Territory, the legislators inserted Article III which promised that the United States would treat tribes "with the utmost good faith." With the coming of the new government under the Constitution, a few leaders looked for ways to reconcile national expansion with just treatment of the Indians.

Initially, Secretary of War Henry Knox thought that honesty and national honor were at stake and that the government had little choice but to carry out such an effort. He feared that if the United States destroyed the Indians, "the disinterested part of mankind and posterity will be apt to class the effects of our Conduct and that of the Spaniards in Mexico and Peru together" (Horsman 1968: 132). Expressing ideas that came to be associated with Jeffersonian agrarianism, he called for the nation to give the tribes "all the blessings of civilized life." It should work to wean them from the chase, teach them American-style sedentary agriculture, and provide them with churches and schools.

Thomas Jefferson echoed and expanded these ideas. He too assumed that the nation had to incorporate Indians within its population and economy. Certainly as much an expansionist as anyone of his generation, during his presidency he pursued these ideas continually while hoping that Indians could be persuaded to become settled farmers. That would open more land for settlement by white pioneers. Then the native farmers could learn from their neighbors, and gradually racial and ethnic differences might disappear. Jefferson actually took this thinking a step farther by suggesting that Indians be incorporated into the general society through intermarriage. He seemed disappointed and angry when few tribal people took those steps. In the summer of 1812 he commented that Indians who rejected the benefits of American society "will relapse into barbarism and misery." Once that happened, rather than welcome the tribes into the body politic, the expanding United States "shall be obliged to drive them, with the beasts of the forest into the Stony Mountains" (Horsman 1968: 133–34).

While American pioneers demanded that their leaders open tribal lands for settlement, the situation in Canada remained less volatile. During the 1780s and 1790s the leaders welcomed both white and Indian refugees from the United States. When American negotiators browbeat tribal leaders into accepting large land cessions, Canadian officers encouraged Indians to resist American demands. Until 1796 British troops remained stationed at the so-called Northwest Posts, military garrisons within the United States. From there Canadian fur traders moved among the disaffected villages, keeping economic and diplomatic ties strong and doing whatever they could to weaken or disrupt American influence on the scene.

The beginnings of a basic shift in Canadian-Indian relations began during the years following the American Revolution. At the same time that British authorities welcomed migrations of tribal groups into present Ontario, they accepted another 100,000 or more refugees—United Empire Loyalists—from the United States. Many of these people settled near or even among Indians in central Ontario, sowing seeds for later difficulties there. To get land for the newcomers the government negotiated treaties with local Ojibwa bands, promising that the immigrants would be helpful to them. That did not occur. Instead, Mississauga leaders grumbled that "when we camp on the shore they drive us off & shoot our Dogs and never give us any assistance" (Smith 1987: 27). Others remembered that at first the whites had asked for only "a small piece of land" but later "continued to ask, or have obtained by force or frauds, the fairest portions of our territory" (Nichols 1998: 145).

Because many of the pioneers had come from the United States, they often harbored bitter anti-Indian feelings that spread discord and violence to frontier regions in Canada at the time. In one ugly incident in August 1796, three white men killed the local Mississauga chief Wabakinine when he tried to protect his sister from them. They beat the chief severely and attacked his wife too. When other Indians heard the noise the attackers fled, leaving both the chief and his wife to die within the next two days. At that point the tribal people comprised most of the local population, so the authorities held the attackers for trial to calm the scene. Officials asked for witnesses to testify, but none came forward so eventually the murderers went free. At the same time local leaders worked feverishly to prevent further violence, and although the Indians were outraged, British negotiators worked to isolate them and discourage any retaliation (Nichols 1998). In cases of this sort British officials established a pattern that at least partly describes long-term Canadian dealings with the First Nations groups: they did as little as they had too until circumstances persuaded them to take some action.

By 1800 a small but steady stream of settlers flowed into Canada from Europe and the United States. That migration led to renewed efforts by leaders there to negotiate new land cessions with the local Mississauga hunting bands. For a time that approach seemed to cause few difficulties because the native people surrendering the land were not agriculturalists. Yet continuing settler abuses of the scattered villagers north of Lake Erie brought Indian complaints about pioneer intrusions "on our hunting ground, which is our farm." Friction at traditional Indian fishing sites also brought bitter denunciations of the whites. "When white people sees anything that they like they never quit us untill they have it. . . . The taking or stealing from us is nothing, for we are only Massessagoes" (Smith 1987: 32). By 1805 when British authorities sought more land cessions, chiefs Golden Eagle and Wahbanosay realized that the earlier agreements had gone far beyond their understanding of having surrendered only the use of the areas in question. As a result they limited new sales to coastal land only, while retaining most of their hunting territory.

Growing Anti-Indian Attitudes

In this period British officials gave little apparent thought to what role the native peoples would play in the developing Canadian society. Yet this became an increasingly thorny issue as settlement increased and the frontier population demanded access to tribal lands and resources. Some pioneers saw Indian lands as a vacant wilderness and the people as "idle, drunken [and] dirty." Others denounced their tribal neighbors because they refused to work and did little more than "infest the barber shops" (Smith 1987: 32; Nichols 1998: 167). It is unclear how many Canadians held these views, but they did not encourage officials there to consider rapid territorial expansion. By that time the British sought to keep peace with the tribes. Clearly this set their policies apart from those operating in the United States, where bitter wars in the Ohio River Valley and contentious relations with the Cherokee in Tennessee kept the government off balance much of the time.

Throughout most of the nineteenth century Americans, including many of their leaders, characterized Indians negatively more often than did Canadians. The pressures caused by an expanding population, and the rapid creation of new states and territories indirectly created support for the idea that Indians could not rise to the level the white citizens. Hence they came to be viewed as obstacles to national growth. In 1824 Georgia Governor George Troup rejected efforts to incorporate tribal groups into American society. He described them in racial terms, as a people who stood between whites and blacks and could never rise to the level of the whites. The next year Missouri Senator Thomas Hart Benton denounced Indians as "a parcel of miserable barbarians" (Horsman 1968: 135–36). Only a few months later, in a Cabinet meeting, Henry Clay of Kentucky attacked efforts to bring education and religion to the tribal people. "It was impossible to civilize Indians," he told his shocked colleagues (ibid.: 32).

These sentiments demonstrated the strong influence that growing expansionism in American society had on ideas about how to treat Indians. By the 1820s many national leaders publicly rejected the ideas expressed by Knox and Jefferson almost a generation earlier. The so-called civilization program that had been in operation among some groups for several decades was thought to have failed. In its place calls for moving the eastern tribes beyond the Mississippi River could be heard. Tied directly to the recognition of growing American numbers and strength, what came to be called the Removal Policy changed the face of Native America by forcing most tribes west beyond the Mississippi River.

In obvious rejection of the earlier civilization program, President Andrew Jackson led the chorus to enact a new policy. Taking advantage of the settlement and economic development that had swept across most of the cis-Mississippi region, he called on Congress to enact legislation allowing the federal government to push the tribes westward. This move triggered a national debate over the place of Indians in the American future, bitter political infighting in Congress, and eventually the forced relocation of thousands of tribal people beyond the Mississippi that led to a variety of tribal actions, most of which proved ineffective in defeating or avoiding this policy (Prucha 1984; Satz 1975).

In 1827 the Cherokee Nation declared that they were an independent nation and adopted a constitution patterned on that of the United States. In response Georgia state officials passed anti-Cherokee laws and encouraged state residents to invade tribal territory and to seize the Cherokees' property. Tribal leaders turned to the federal courts for their defense. That tactic failed, but their suit resulted in the famous 1831 *Cherokee v. Georgia* decision written by Chief Justice John Marshall. In that ruling Marshall rejected Cherokee claims of sovereignty, and labeled the tribes "domestic dependent nations." Much like the 1763 Royal Proclamation which set out the concept of an Indian Country, this decision proclaimed that the tribes lacked independent status. It strengthened the authority of the federal government to dictate what actions Indian groups could take, laid the legal foundations for most of government-tribal relations to the present, and allowed the government to push Indians out of the path of an expanding Anglo-American society (Prucha 1984; Satz 1975).

Although lacking similar motivations, at least one Canadian leader responded in a like manner by proposing a removal program during the early middle decades of the nineteenth century. In 1836 Sir Francis Bond Head, the lieutenant-governor of Upper Canada, present Ontario, denounced the treatment of Indians by pioneers there as "the most sinful story in the history of the human race" (Dickason 1992: 226; Nichols 1998: 190). Echoing the comments of American humanitarians who supported removal in the United States, he noted that "Whenever and Wherever the Two Races come into contact with each other it is sure to prove fatal to the Red Man." Criticizing the ongoing attempts to acculturate the tribal people as total failures, he proposed a modest removal program to separate Indians from all contacts with the whites. If the plan proved successful, he assumed that it would end the Indian problem and open more good land for Canadian pioneers. Bond Head personally traveled to Manitoulin Island near the north shore of Lake Huron and Georgian Bay and persuaded the Ottawa and Ojibwas people there to allow the bands he sought to move to settle on a part of the island.

The Indians who were to be moved objected immediately. There was little question that some wanted to gain the promised isolation from the whites, but the land in question offered little else. Chief Joseph Sawyer pointed out that while his people now "raise our own corn, potatoes, and wheat . . . if we go to Maneetoolin, we could not live; soon we would be extinct as a people" (Smith 1987: 162–63). As in the United States at the time, missionary groups like the Wesleyan Methodist Conference protested against the removal plan because it "had single-handedly disrupted their school and mission activities" (Nichols 1988: 191–92). Eventually the governor's plan moved a few hundred tribal people north and opened almost three million acres of nearly unoccupied land in exchange for the dubious benefit of northern isolation for the tribes. Several motivations distinguished the two removal programs. In the United States immense political pressure from states with large numbers of Indians occupying valuable land proved central. That certainly was not a factor in Canada, where Governor Bond Head's rhetoric suggested strong humanitarian reasons for his actions. The scope of the two efforts differed as well. In the United States tens of thousands of people from almost all of the eastern tribes experienced forced relocations. By contrast, Canadian removal affected only a few small bands with several hundred members, only a tiny portion of the total native population (Nichols 1988: 191–92).

Issues at Mid-nineteenth Century

With removal in full swing, many tribes living in the upper Midwest looked north to Canada as an escape from forced migration. Having fought alongside the British during the War of 1812, some had continued to make nearly annual visits to Canadian trading posts after that conflict ended. Rejecting the unwanted removal across the Mississippi, they chose to accept the long-standing promises of Canadian officials and to migrate north. Between 1833 and the mid-1840s, about 2,500 Ottawa, Potawatomi, and Ojibwa immigrated into present western Ontario. There they filtered into lightly occupied regions, often joining tribal relatives. When a new Chief Superintendent of the Indian Department chided the frontier agents for encouraging this migration, they responded that these tribes had been promised sanctuary during and after the War of 1812. In addition they cited an 1841 order that bid them to continue welcoming the refugees from the United States (Clifton 1975: 34–90). Clearly at this point the two societies acted in almost totally dissimilar manner.

Removal during the 1830s highlights another significant difference in tribal experiences in the two nations. Not all tribes in the United States accepted forced relocation. Some tried to use the federal courts to seek redress. Some fled to Canada, and in the end several groups took up arms to fight it. During the summer of 1832, the so-called British Band of Sauks and Mesquakies stumbled into the Black Hawk War. Rejecting earlier treaties under which they had ceded their Illinois and Wisconsin lands, they returned from Iowa, setting off a panic in the frontier communities.

When the summer violence ended, well over 1,000 Indians had died. From 1835 to 1842, the Seminoles in Florida fought a bitter and expensive conflict with the U.S. forces as they rejected efforts to force them out of their traditional homes (Nichols 1992; Mahon 1967). In Canada at the same time, while a few minor incidents between pioneers and Indians occurred, no open warfare broke out between the government and the tribes.

No sooner had the removed tribes gone westward than the entire situation there changed, as the nation surged to the Pacific Coast acquiring the western third of its territory. The government annexed Texas in 1845 and settled its dispute with Great Britain over the Oregon Country boundary a year later. Then in 1848 Mexico signed the Treaty of Guadalupe Hidalgo, surrendering the southwest and California. By this time Manifest Destiny had become an accepted idea, and territorial expansion had produced a continental nation. It would be almost another two decades before the British North America Act laid the foundation for any rapid expansion to occur in Canada, and even then there is little evidence to suggest that Canadians had their own variety of the rabid nationalism that existed in the United States at the time. Instead, bitter religious divisions between Protestants and Catholics as well as the fears of the strong French minority in Quebec worked to inhibit the development of nationalism. Therefore, despite repeated efforts to create a self-conscious Canadian identity, that did not occur until after 1949, when Newfoundland finally agreed to become a part of Canada.

Territorial expansion to the Pacific brought violence to the plains in both nations. Repeated Indian wars disrupted the process of pioneer settlement, corporate investment, and resource development efforts. Between 1850 and 1890, virtually no present Western state avoided inter-racial violence as the independent and formidable tribes of the plains, mountains, and deserts sought to maintain their independence and to retain their honor and homelands. For a long generation American commissioners sought to negotiate peaceful agreements in order to protect advancing pioneers, but they had little success. The frontier population had accepted the Manifest Destiny ideal almost entirely, while local editors called for the extermination of troublesome Indians. By that term they meant any tribal groups that refused to halt their raids, surrender their land and its resources, and accept the bleak reservations then being designed for their use. In 1865 a Nevada newspaper demanded the "total extermination of every redskin from the British [Canadian] to the Mexican frontier" (Gold Hill *Daily News,* Feb. 11, 1865). Eleven years later, when the Lakota Sioux and Cheyenne destroyed George A. Custer and much of the Seventh Cavalry at the Battle of the Little Big Horn, the Laramie (Wyoming) *Daily Sentinel* noted that "a bounty [be] placed on Indian Scalps so that it pay better to prospect for them than for gold or silver" (July 7, 1876).

Reformers, often referred to as the "friends of the Indian," sought a return to the formerly discredited civilization program of the Jeffersonian era. In 1867, hoping to end plains violence, the Indian Peace Commission trekked west, extracting treaties at Fort Laramie in the North and Medicine Lodge Creek farther south. The negotiators bribed and browbeat tribal leaders to sign the treaties committing themselves to gradual movement onto newly created reservations. Once that happened, American reformers and officials alike assumed that in a few short years the Indians would be acculturated and assimilated, thus ending the Indian problem that had plagued the nation since its independence. At the same time, the Congress ended the treaty system, so that any new agreements that might be negotiated went to the executive branch rather than the Senate for approval (Prucha 1994: 289–310). So the rapid territorial acquisition of the 1840s and the continuing tide of settlement in the West brought the era of real, tribal independence to a close. By late in the nineteenth century a combination of soldiers, treaties, pioneers, railroads, and mining corporations combined to overwhelm the western tribes.

Métis and Western Issues

In Canada the long-term and large-scale fur trade operating from Montreal and at Hudson's Bay had created a situation that seems to have had no counterpart in the United States. Over the generations a large population of *Métis,* the descendents of French traders or of English-speaking Hudson's Bay Company employees and Indian women, developed in the West. Unlike the United States, where the government considered such people to be members of their tribal heritage, in Canada many of them lived in communities separate from the local tribes along the Red River Valley in present Manitoba. Canadian officials farther east barely recognized their existence, so after 1812 tensions and minor incidents occurred frequently for decades. The Red River *Métis* practiced large-scale hunting to supply fur to the trade companies and carried out modest agriculture on their riverfront lands. A decade or more of bitter trade competition ended in 1821 when the Northwest Company and the Hudson's Bay Company combined. That merger shifted the major trade routes from Montreal north to HBC posts and reduced the fur brigades' needs for foodstuffs the *Métis* had supplied (Dickason 1992: 262–65).

Despite their distinct non-Indian character, in many ways the Red River and later Saskatchewan communities experienced the same treatment as did the tribal groups. As the government talked about encouraging settlement in the West, *Métis* self-identification as a distinct people grew. By the 1840s they petitioned Alexander Christie, Governor of Red River and Assiniboia, to clarify their status and to accept their rights based on native blood. To their dismay he rejected their claims to land or for any special treatment, and said that they had only the rights of all British subjects. By the 1850s continuing *Métis* demands for local control ran into the growing movement to annex the Red River region to Canada. Despite requests for local control, in 1858, when the British government took British Columbia from Hudson's Bay Company control and made it a new colony, the Red River settlement failed to get the same treatment. Colonial Secretary Herman Merivale rejected such a move (Dickason 1992: 265). That left *Métis* and Indians alike outside of the process of nation-building, but also without any protections from it.

At the time, the Canadian Confederation sought to create new provinces and to connect British Columbia with eastern Canada via a national railroad. To accomplish this, the Ottawa-based leadership needed to extinguish Indian title to the land needed for a right-of-way, and that need led to negotiating treaties for tribal lands just at the time the U.S. government had ended its treaty-making approach. In the Canadian case, some of the negotiations resulted from Indian demands that surveyors, soldiers, and settlers keep off their land until the tribes received government promises to protect their interests. Prior to Confederation British officials had negotiated some 123 treaties with First Nations groups in the eastern half of the country. Now, between 1871 and 1877, negotiators signed the first of the seven numbered treaty agreements with Cree and Ojibwa groups from northwest of Lake Superior west into southern Alberta. During the next several decades the Ottawa government drew up dozens of small reserves for the First Nations groups on the plains (Miller 1989: 207–24).

By the 1870s the native-newcomer situations on both sides of the border still differed somewhat, though the policies each nation adopted had come to resemble each other. In both countries Indians had been asked, bribed, or forced onto reservations or reserves. Frequently in the United States the government had to use troops to push reluctant hunters onto the reservations, so that battles and wars marked the process. In Canada, by the time railroad construction crews and a smattering of settlers reached the central plains, the traditional economic bases of the fur trade and buffalo hunting had virtually ended. So rather than having to be forced onto the new reserves, native people there looked to the treaty agreements as government promises that offered hope and support. Aside from the 1869 *Métis* resistance in the Red River country and the 1885 *Métis* and Indian uprising, the Canadian record featured little violence, particularly when contrasted to what was happening at the same time in the United States (Miller 1989: 225). It is possible that Canadian officials managed to avoid violence by sending the North West Mounted Police west in early 1873, ahead of opening much of the region for settlement. More likely, the central reason why western Canada had fewer violent confrontations with tribal peoples than did the United States was simple demographics. North of the border very few people occupied small parts of an enormous area, so at least for a generation there was neither much contact between the races nor much debate over using the resources.

American officials had no such luxury. Miners seeking gold and silver combed the mountain valleys for ore. Homesteaders seeking free farms surged onto the plains by the tens of thousands. Hunters working to supply the transcontinental railroad construction crews slaughtered tens of thousands of buffalo from the ever-dwindling herds, and wagon trains carried thousands more settlers to many parts of the West. Often these people trespassed directly on the lands used or claimed by the powerful and sometimes aggressive mounted tribes of the plains. This led to repeated minor incidents and frequent panicked calls for military intervention that brought the army and the tribesmen into open conflict. Once the troops defeated or rounded up a particular tribe or band, they forced the Indians onto a reservation and often remained nearby to ensure that the tribal people stayed there (Utley 1984).

Forcing Acculturation

Having taken much of the Indians' land, nationalists in each country turned to their next task, that of "civilizing" the native people so that they would disappear as a foreign element in each of the two societies. Because now there was no place else for Indians to go, the acculturative ideas and practices that dated to earlier generations finally could be employed. Beginning in earnest with President Ulysses Grant's peace policy during the late 1860s, federal agents, schoolteachers, Christian missionaries, model farmers, and others moved onto the American reservations to begin their work of uplift. The same thing took place on Canadian reserves within the next decade. Hoping to disrupt tribal practices of passing cultural ideas from one generation to another, both governments established local day schools and distant boarding schools. There they forbade tribal languages and forced the children to discard their native clothing, accept white man's names, and eat non-Indian foods.

Designed to transform Indians into farmers, reservations in both nations failed because the difficult environment, lack of funds, and cultural resistance limited the acculturation programs. Several decades earlier, in 1857, Canada had tried to encourage tribal people to enter the general society through what it called enfranchisement. This process sought to wean individual tribal members from their communities "in exchange for" full citizenship. To achieve that goal, the native person had to persuade a review board that he was educated, debt-free, and of good moral character. At that point the man would receive twenty hectares of land from the tribal holdings. All of this was supposed to occur as a result of the efforts of Christian missionaries, teachers in residential schools, and model farmers working on the reserves. This policy failed utterly, and between 1857 and 1920 only 250 individuals surrendered their Indian status to become Canadian citizens (Miller 1989: 255).

When enfranchisement proved ineffective in breaking up tribal groups, the Department of Indian Affairs launched repeated efforts to achieve that goal in other ways. It sought to control tribal councils, depose chiefs and other leaders who chose not to cooperate, and force First Nations people to conform to the white man's standards, all with but modest success. This effort had little chance to succeed because it ignored what First Nations people told the officials repeatedly a decade before the first efforts at enfranchisement. While as individuals they accepted some education, they rejected all efforts to dismember their communal land holdings, one of the central goals of the enfranchisement program (Miller 1989: 106–107).

In the United States too the authorities soon came to realize that their programs for bringing Indians into their society lagged far behind their expectations. So the government listened to the continuing demands of reformers who still thought in terms that Thomas Jefferson would have recognized. As the Canadians had tried with enfranchisement, American officials determined that the tribes had to be dismembered. In the reformers' view, the communal nature of Indian society stood in the way of progress and civilization. So for at least a generation they pushed for a program to break up tribal landholdings. This effort culminated in 1887, with the passage of the General Allotment Act. Under that legislation tribal communal land holdings ended. Each family received a specific allotment of land. The government sold most of the remaining land. After a few years, the reformers expected reservation dwellers to thrive on their individual farms, and in doing so to accept the other aspects of "real" American civilization (Prucha 1984: 659–86).

The allotment of a particular plot of ground to each family or single individual was somehow supposed to bring about a magical transformation. The savage hunter would become a settled farmer who then could be assimilated easily into American society. This myopic view ignored reservation locations far from markets, difficult physical environments, lack of equipment, credit, or experience, and cultural objections by the Indians. The greed of white farmers and ranchers who swarmed onto tribal lands during allotment and Indians' willingness to lease their farms to nearby settlers also helped to undermine the allotment program. Its only real success was in removing nearly two thirds of Indian land and making it available to others by the 1930s, when the program finally ended. In Canada the seven numbered treaties signed between 1871 and 1877 reduced the tribal land base even more rapidly than allotment south of the border.

Conclusion

Even a brief glance at North American history since the 1760s finds obvious similarities in what became the United States and Canada. Native people in both countries faced invasions, epidemic disease, loss of most of their lands and resources, religious persecution, forced removals, and unwelcome acculturation programs. For a variety of reasons, whenever possible the governments in both nations used treaty negotiations rather than warfare to deal with the Indians. Usually talk proved more effective and much less expensive than guns. In the United States reform groups demanded honest and peaceful dealings with the tribes. Canadians had the luxury of ignoring the native people much of the time. As a result, by 1902 the Canadians had negotiated 483 such agreements. Figures for the United States are less clear. It signed 371 treaties, but nearly another hundred other "agreements" of various kinds were written too (Indian Treaties 1891–1912; Kappler 1904; Deloria and DeMallie 1999). During the twentieth century many Indians left the reservations or reserves to live among the general society in the cities and towns of the two countries. Yet many of those remaining on tribal lands are undereducated, unemployed, and unhealthy. To describe them another way, they include the very old, very young, very sick, and very poor (Deloria 1969; Cardinal 1969).

Throughout much of the nineteenth century self-conscious nationalism and a sense of mission played more immediate roles in the United States than they did in Canada. Nevertheless both British North American nations enacted policies and took actions that resulted from or partially caused demands for territorial expansion. Their efforts brought them into repeated contact and occasional conflict with the native peoples in each country. From the era of American Independence to the 1860s, Indian relations varied widely. In the United States tribes occupied land, blocked access to valuable resources, and occasionally proved dangerous neighbors. Canada, with few people and plenty of space, encountered few such difficulties. While both societies became continental nations by the end of the century, physical territorial expansion occurred in different periods and at different speeds in the two nations. As a result, specific policies regarding native people and how those should be implemented differed frequently.

At the time Canadians and Americans, if they thought about Indians at all, held similar views of the native peoples' status in society and how to get them to accept it. Starting with their claims to have the sole right to extinguish Indian title to the land, they assumed their own continuing superiority in all aspects of life. In their view this enabled them to justify land grabbing, forced virtual imprisonment on isolated reservations, open attacks on tribal cultures, the disruption or destruction of tribal governments, the kidnapping of children for educational purposes, and the transformation of group economic systems. Blinded by ethnocentrism, motivated by nationalism and greed, and ever certain that God was on their side, by 1900 Americans and Canadians alike employed nearly identical policies as they sought to accomplish their national destinies in the hemisphere.

Yet that obscures the clear and substantial national differences in motivation and actions that had existed previously. In the United States, the federal government utilized conscious desires for land and territory to justify its actions toward the French, British, Mexicans, and the tribal peoples. At the same time, unable or unwilling to restrain the pioneers, officials responded to their repeated demands for access to the lands and resources held by Indian tribes. These twin motivations resulted in forced removals, repeated warfare, enormous expense and bitter political fights with the so-called Friends of the Indian throughout the nineteenth century. Canadian leaders, in contrast, lacked the burning sense of nationalism or of a mission to extend their society outward that so permeated American thought. Without a clear sense of Canadians' existence outside of the British Empire, nationalism and territorial expansion came slowly. By the 1860s a few officials came to fear U.S. expansion. They saw their own lack of unity as an open invitation for land-grabbing by their southern neighbor. Thus their central motivation for creating a territorial union and for land acquisition often stemmed more from outside rather than inside pressures. As a result, they devoted much less time and attention to native affairs than did

U.S. policy-makers most of the time. In fact, because of their generally peaceful dealings with First Nations groups prior to the 1860s, they seemed to have assumed that issues related to Indian affairs required little attention or expense. Despite many specific similarities in policies and implementations, the attitudes toward, and motivations for, territorial expansion and nation-building differed substantially across the border throughout most of the nineteenth century.

Yet it remains true that the less obviously aggressive implementation of native policies in Canada did little to change the long-term results for First Nations people there. Their boarding-school system produced similar mediocre results, and brought much higher levels of anger and resentment than expressed in the United States. Repeated reports of physical and sexual abuse at the church-run schools in Canada led eventually to the establishment of a Truth and Reconciliation Commission (2008) and a system of financial reparations to individuals reaching nearly two billion dollars. This issue presents one of the few sharp contrasts in terms of the present conditions of native people in the two nations. If one considers matters of poverty, physical and psychological problems, lack of educational achievement, unemployment, and a host of other personal and social measures, the situation in both societies appear distressingly similar. So despite generations of differences in motivation and policies, one must conclude that their implementation brought few present differences for native groups in the neighboring countries.

References

Bemis, Samuel Flagg. 1949. *John Quincy Adams and the Foundations of American Foreign Policy.* New York: Knopf.

Biggar, Henry P., ed. 1924. *Voyages of Cartier.* Ottawa: Acland.

Boyd, Julian P., ed. 1954. *Papers of Thomas Jefferson*, v. 9. Princeton: Princeton University Press.

Burns, Edward McNall. 1957. *The American Idea of Mission: Concepts of National Purpose and Destiny.* New Brunswick, NJ: Rutgers University Press.

Canada. 1877. Debates of the House of Commons 1877.

Cardinal, Harold. 1969. *The Unjust Society: The Tragedy of Canada's Indians.* Edmonton, Alberta: Hurtig.

Cave, Alfred A. 2003. "Abuse of Power: Andrew Jackson and the Indian Removal Act of 1830." *The Historian* 65 (6): 1330–1353.

Clifton, James A. 1975. *A Place of Refuge for All Time: The Migration of the Potawatomi into Upper Canada, 1835–1845.* Mercury Series. Ottawa: National Museum of Man.

Commager, Henry Steele, ed. 1949. *Documents of American History*, 5th ed. New York: Appleton-Century-Crofts.

Creighton, Donald. 1970. *Canada's First Century, 1867–1967.* Toronto: Macmillan of Canada.

———. 1965. *The Road to Confederation. The Emergence of Canada: 1863–1867.* Boston: Houghton Mifflin.

Deloria, Vine, Jr. 1969. *Custer Died for Your Sins.* New York: Macmillan.

Deloria, Vine, Jr. and Raymond J. DeMaillie. 1999. *Documents of American Indian Diplomacy: Treaties, Agreements, and Conventions.* 2 vols. Norman: University of Oklahoma Press.

Denison, George T. 1909. *The Struggle for Imperial Unity.* New York: Macmillan.

Dickason, Patricia Olive. 1992. *Canada's First Nations: A History of Founding Peoples from Earliest Times.* Norman: University of Oklahoma Press.

Eccles, William J. 1969. *The Canadian Frontier, 1534–1670.* New York: Hold, Rinehart and Winston.

Ekirch, Arthur R. 1944. *The Idea of Progress in America, 1815–1860.* New York: Columbia University Press.

Galbraith, John S. 1957. *The Hudson's Bay Company as an Imperial Factor, 1821–1869.* Berkeley: University of California Press.

Horsman, Reginald. 1968. "American Indian Policy and the Origins of Manifest Destiny." *University of Birmingham Historical Journal* 11 (2): 128–140.

———. 1967. *Expansion and American Indian Policy, 1783–1812.* East Lansing: Michigan State University Press.

———. 1981. *Race and Manifest Destiny: The Origins of American Racial Anglo-Saxonism.* Cambridge, MA: Harvard University Press.

Hurt, R. Douglas. 1965. reprint, 2002. *The Indian Frontier, 1763–1846.* Albuquerque: University of New Mexico Press.

Jaenen, Cornelius J. 1984. *The French Relationship with the Native Peoples of New France and Acadia.* Ottawa: Research Branch, Indian and Northern Affairs.

Jensen, Merrill. 1955. *English Historical Documents: Vol. IX American Colonial Documents to 1776.* New York: Oxford University Press.

Johnson, Charles M. 1962. "An Outline of Early Settlement in the Grand River Valley." *Ontario History* 54 (1): 43–67.

———. 1963. "Joseph Brant, the Grand River Lands and the Northwest Crisis." *Ontario History* 55: 267–82.

Kappler, Charles J. 1903–41. *Indian Affairs: Laws and Treaties.* 2 vols. Washington: Government Printing Office.

Mahon, John K. 1967. *History of the Second Seminole War.* Gainesville: University of Florida Press.

McNab, David T. 1983. "Herman Merivale and Colonial Office Indian Policy in the Mid-Nineteenth Century." In Ian A. L. Getty and Antoine S. Lussier, eds., *As Long as the Sun Shines and Water Flows.* Vancouver: University of British Columbia Press, pp. 85–103.

Merk, Frederick. 1963. *Manifest Destiny and Mission in American History: A Reinterpretation.* New York: Knopf.

Miller, James R. 1989. *Skyscrapers Hide the Heavens: A History of Indian-White Relations in Canada.* Toronto: University of Toronto Press.

Morton, William L. 1964. *The Critical Years: The Union of British North America, 1857–1873.* London: Oxford University Press.

Nichols, Roger L. 1992. *Black Hawk and the Warrior's Path.* Arlington Heights, IL: Harlan Davidson.

———. 1998. *Indians in the United States and Canada: A Comparative History.* Lincoln: University of Nebraska Press.

Nye, Russel B. 1974. *Society and Culture in America, 1830–1860.* New York: Harper and Row.

Owram, Doug. 1980. *Promise of Eden: The Canadian Expansionist Movement and the Idea of the West, 1856–1900.* Toronto: University of Toronto Press.

Parish, John Carl. 1943. "The Emergence of the Idea of Manifest Destiny." In Parish, *The Persistence of the Westward Movement and Other Essays.* Berkeley: University of California Press, pp. 47–77.

Poore, Benjamin P. 1877. *The Federal and State Constitutions, Colonial Charters, and Other Organic Laws of the United States.* 2 vols. Washington, D.C.: Government Printing Office.

Pratt, Julius W. 1950. *America's Colonial Experiment: How the United States Gained, Governed, and in Part Gave Away a Colonial Empire.* New York: Prentice Hall.

Prucha, Francis P. 1984. *The Great Father: The United States Government and the American Indians.* 2 vols. Lincoln: University of Nebraska Press.

———. 1994. *American Indian Treaties: The History of a Political Anomaly.* Berkeley: University of California Press.

Prucha, Francis P., ed. 2000. *Documents of United States Indian Policy.* 3rd ed. Lincoln: University of Nebraska Press.

Reid, J. H., Stewart, Kenneth McNaught, and Harry S. Crowe, eds. 1964. *A Sourcebook of Canadian History.* Toronto: Longmans Canada.

St. Germain, Jill. 2001. *Indian Treaty-Making Policy in the United States and Canada, 1867–1877.* Lincoln: University of Nebraska Press.

Satz, Ronald. 1975. *American Indian Policy in the Jacksonian Era.* Lincoln: University of Nebraska Press.

Schellie, Don. 1968. *Vast Domain of Blood: The Story of the Camp Grant Massacre.* Los Angeles: Westernlore Press.

Smith, Donald B. 1987. *Sacred Feathers: The Reverend Peter Jones (Kahkewaquon-aby) and the Mississauga Indians*. Lincoln: University of Nebraska Press.

Stanley, George F. G. 1950. "The First Indian 'Reserves' in Canada." *Revue d'Historie d'Amerique française* 4: 148–210.

Thorpe, Francis N. 1909. *Federal and State Constitutions, Colonial Charters, and Other Organic Laws of the States, Territories, and Colonies Now or Heretofore Forming the United States of America*. 7 vols. Washington, D.C.: Government Printing Office.

Utley, Robert M. 1984. *The Indian Frontier of the American West, 1846–1890*. Albuquerque: University of New Mexico Press.

Van Alstyne, Richard W. 1960. *The Rising American Empire*. New York: Oxford University Press.

Weinberg, Albert K. 1935. *Manifest Destiny: A Study of Nationalist Expansion in American History*. Baltimore: The Johns Hopkins Press.

7

Homeland and Frontier

J. Edward Chamberlin

In the Americas, no less than in Asia and Africa and Europe, the frontier has always been ambivalent. It has been a gateway to new opportunities and old challenges, a threshold offering spiritual as well as material transformation, a door to both peril and possibility for wanderers and settlers alike, and a guard post between the barbaric and the civilized. The frontier opens out to the future and into the past, inviting us both forward and backward. Not surprisingly, this ambivalence has informed frontier attitudes and administrative policies, and has led to the confusions and the conflicts that have so often resulted from them.

The idea of home, and of homeland, also has its contradictions. Home is where we hang our hat, or where our heart is . . . which may be the same place, or maybe not. Home is where we choose to live . . . or where we belong whether we like it or not. It may be the place we came from, five or fifty or five hundred years ago, the place we are going to when our time is done, or the place we still haven't found but are looking for. And home is always border country, a place that separates and connects us.

The popular cowboy song "Home on the Range" catches the connection between homeland and frontier. It was composed over 125 years ago, but to many of us it is as familiar as a member of the family. "Oh give me a home where the buffalo roam." The rhymes in those opening lines, "home" and "roam," bound together by similar sounds, still pull in completely opposite directions, settling down and wandering. It's hard to imagine a more basic human opposition, or a more fundamental condition in the Americas. We remember these lines not because they tell one truth but because they tell two contradictory ones.

So perhaps the frontier should be imagined as a hinge rather than a door, bringing together all that we think of as contradictory, and constantly questioning our categories. This would make the frontier our ultimate trickster.[1]

The idea of Manifest Destiny catches something of this, with its determinisms and its freedoms, its interweaving of heredity and environment, its conflation of nature and nurture, its combination of the mechanism of beginnings and the teleology of endings, its confusion of inevitability and ingenuity. In Canada, perhaps because its beginnings were evolutionary rather than revolutionary, there has been a more explicit embrace of these contradictions with regard to its aboriginal peoples, as the apparatuses of separation—survey and settlement policies, Indian reserves and the Indian Act—went hand in hand with the agencies of assimilation—farms and schools, churches and courts, and various other instruments of order and good government. This has given Canada's history a more confused—some would say compromised (or more kindly, compromising)—character.

I want to address homeland and frontier from several perspectives. Liberals and conservatives, socialists and capitalists, nationalists and imperialists, regionalists and advocates for individual human rights, have all been involved in the dislocation, dispossession, and destruction of aboriginal peoples . . . and five hundred years later, people on all sides are still trying to figure out what happened and who is to blame. Good people have done bad things; and sometimes (whether by accident or design) bad people have done good things. And throughout it all the state—our so-called civil society—has wreaked just as much havoc as the scoundrels and scumbags who have flocked to the various frontiers.

Some of the reasons for this history are simple: fear and loathing; greed; ideologies of superiority; the "final solution," whether by termination (of tribal identity) or extermination. The holocaust of the Second World War and the horrors of slavery are indeed analogous to the deliberate campaigns against aboriginal people that have been carefully designed to obliterate them from the face of the earth, educate them into servitude, or turn them into white folks. Ethnic cleansing, of course, has often been the regional approach, and (as in the United States' Georgia removals) it worked as long as there was another place to send people to. Now, the streets and skid rows of our cities may be the new frontier for many Indians. And we must not forget the educational strategies that have been developed to remove aboriginal people from their languages, their livelihoods, and their lands.

Over thirty years ago, I tried to explain some of this in a book titled *The Harrowing of Eden: White Attitude Towards Native Americans* (1975). One of the questions many of us asked back then is caught in the title of this essay, "Homeland and Frontier." This was also the title of the 1977 report of the Mackenzie Valley Pipeline Inquiry. I want to bring this experience together with some ideas that have been part of my work more recently, to see whether they may cast some light on the subject.

Several themes come to the fore. The first has to do with the way in which we define aboriginal identity: by blood or by membership in a group. Related to this is the way in which we conceive societies: as organic entities to which we belong willy-nilly (like the family); or as communities organized along deliberate lines to which we choose to belong (like a neighborhood). Nations, at least as they have emerged in the modern consciousness, fall somewhere in between . . . and that in-between can be dangerous ground, no-man's-land in a war between one vision of society and another. Just like the frontier, in fact. Notions of citizenship are implicated in this, as are concepts of land title. Religious ideologies also get caught up in the confusion, along with questions about individual and collective relationships to greater powers, and the old tension between a spiritualism—or sometimes a materialism—of mediation (with its inevitable institutional paraphernalia) and of possession (with its overwhelming energies). Finally, there is that durable duo "separation" and "assimilation," which has defined the poles of aboriginal policy in the Americas, and has an unnervingly familiar counterpart in the dynamics of segregation and integration.

I have chosen two ideas to illustrate these themes. The first has to do with the definition of aboriginal identity, with specific reference to differences between Canadian and American historical practices, and with some suggestions about how this divergence may have shaped relations between settlers and indigenous people.[2] My second story is about "idle" land and "illiterate" people. Much has been written about idle land and its more extravagant imperial expression in the doctrine of *terra nullius* and other legal and philosophical justifications for the development of aboriginal lands, but the example I turn to takes the conditions of the Depression, the New Deal, and the Second World War as a more or less contemporary context for considering the ways in which our categories of development have corrupted our relationships with indigenous peoples. Put differently, we have proceeded in the Americas, and in some sad circumstances we continue to proceed, in a manner not unlike that described by the Guyanese sociologist Walter Rodney, writing in 1973 about *How Europe Underdeveloped Africa*.

"The radical principle underlying [the Canadian] policy of Indian management is to keep the Indian community attached to the land, at the same time giving the greatest freedom to individuals to secure their livelihood far and wide by any honest endeavour."[3]

This was the description given in 1914 by Duncan Campbell Scott, recently appointed Deputy Superintendent General of Indian Affairs in Canada, to Frederick Abbott, who was conducting a study of the Administration of Indian Affairs in Canada on behalf of the United States Board of Indian Commissioners, of which Abbott was Secretary. The Board had been established in 1869 (under President Grant's Indian "peace policy") to advise the United States government of needed changes in Indian policy and to oversee Indian appropriations and the conduct of Indian agencies. Various religious denominations nominated the members of the Board; and initially they exercised joint control with the U.S. Secretary of the Interior over two million dollars which Congress had appropriated, also in 1869, for "keeping the Indians at peace and promoting self-sustaining habits among them."[4] By the first decade of the twentieth century, however, the Board had lost much of its influence, but was nonetheless trying to demonstrate its commitment to the disinterested analysis of the state of Indian affairs. Things seemed to be going better in that line in Canada, so Abbott was directed to take stock of the situation, and to reflect on any lessons to be learned.

It was no accident that Scott's description emphasized the principle of maintaining the attachment of the Indian community to the land. The increasing—and increasingly obvious—shortcomings in Indian affairs in the United States seemed to be the product of a failure to maintain just that attachment. And conversely, Indian administrators in Canada seemed to offer some comparative advantages that flowed from a more consistent history of commitment to the inseparability of the native group and the land, with the matter of livelihood unmistakably part of the scheme but less specifically defined. Scott was knowledgeable about the history of Indian affairs in Canada; he had just written a series of essays on Indian policy from 1763 to 1912 for the volumes entitled *Canada and Its Provinces*, edited by Adam Shortt and Arthur G. Doughty and published between 1913 and 1914[5]; these articles provided then, and still provide, the most informed analysis of Indian affairs from the time of the Royal Proclamation. In a sense, they constituted Scott's preparation for his magisterial role over the next twenty years, from 1913 until 1932, as Deputy Superintendent General of Indian Affairs and the custodian of policy for the Department.

What Scott knew well was that from the beginning, Indian land and Indian identity were inseparable notions, in which both symbolic and substantial elements were incorporated. "One of the first recorded instructions to British colonial governors, issued by Charles II in 1670, declares that justice is to be shown to the Indians, and directs that persons be employed to learn their language and that their property be protected," noted Scott in his essay on "Indian Affairs, 1763–1841." "These words were merely the enunciation of a former policy," he continued, "for earlier in the seventeenth century lands had been ceded with due formalities and for definite considerations, and treaties and agreements had defined the civil relation of the aborigines and the ruler. It was the British policy to acknowledge the Indian title to his vast and idle domain, and to treat for it with much gravity, as if with a sovereign power."[6] Later, while discussing Sir Francis Bond Head's counsel (in 1836) to remove and separate the Indian population from contact with white settlers, he notes that it was "foredoomed to failure by the nature of the Indians, whose attachment to ancestral localities is strong and constant."[7]

The definition and protection of Indian lands was always a central tenet of British administration. This definition was a limiting exercise, as all definitions are, involving the translation of the notion of use and occupancy into that of proprietary interest, and the identification of specific lands reserved for the benefit of Indian bands out of the vast territory which had been their home. This took some time, and considerable ingenuity. As late as 1842, when Sir Charles Bagot appointed a royal commission to advise on Indian matters in Upper and Lower Canada, the registration and entitlement of reserved lands was indefinite and therefore vulnerable. It is easy to deplore the limited and convenient character of the diminished definition of Indian lands by an overbearing sovereign power. But a definition was needed; and in due course (and after much, often admirable, controversy) one was provided. In the matter of civil rights as well, the legal position of the Indian "developed" from the indeterminate to the definite.

But there was nothing indeterminate about the responsibility to protect Indian lands once they were defined by some form of commercial transaction such as surrender or a treaty. The British government established a clear tradition of accepting this responsibility, and of deploring any neglect or abuse. In 1850, two Acts were passed to protect Indian lands, one "An Act for the better protection of the Lands and Property of the Indians in Lower Canada," and the other "An Act for the protection of the Indians in Upper Canada from imposition, and the property occupied or enjoyed by them from trespass and injury." Prior to this, there had been no statutory authority to protect Indian lands from encroachment, though it had been a matter of policy to do so. After 1867 (the year of Confederation), Canada assumed this responsibility, often using its (admittedly intermittent and often selective) exercise of it as a mark of its British loyalist difference from the United States.

Having provided for the definition and protection of Indian lands, it was obviously necessary to define Indians in order to protect them. These two Acts therefore provided the first legal definition of Indian status in British North America. The most specific phrasing was in the Act for Lower Canada, defining Indians as "all persons of Indian blood, reported to belong to the particular Body or Tribe of Indians interested in such lands and their descendants" and delineating the circumstances of lineage or residence which would further qualify an individual. The definition was controversial and was amended a year later to exclude non-Indian men married to Indian women, and to prohibit whites from living on Indian lands. The Upper Canada Act introduced the principle that certain civil responsibilities (such as being liable for indebtedness) should be contingent upon possession of a minimum value of real estate held in fee simple (as distinct from entitlement as a member of a band in reserve lands); this would later become one of the key qualifications for enfranchisement (or full Canadian citizenship, with the consequent loss of Indian citizenship).

The most significant feature of this legislation for the future of Indian administration in Canada over the next hundred years was its premise that Indian status be contingent upon membership in a band or tribe, and that interest in Indian lands be considered a group interest. Indeed, in the language of the legislation, the definition of an Indian flowed from the band or tribal interest in the land designated as Indian lands, rather than the other way around; that is, being an Indian in terms of the legislation depended upon the collective interest in Indian lands.

In 1860, during the decade preceding confederation and independence, control of Indian affairs was transferred by the British government to the Crown Lands department of the United Province of Canada, in "An Act respecting the management of the Indian lands and property." This was appropriate on purely practical grounds, since Indian lands were the most economically valuable asset to be administered, and one of the worrisome features of this beginning of Canadian home rule was how to pay for the costs of supervising the real estate. But it was also appropriate in more general terms, since what was already well known as "the Indian question" essentially focused on the anomalous character of Indian lands and the attachment of the Indian community to these lands. From the beginning, Indian lands were both demonstrations of sovereignty (whether British, American, or Canadian), in the sense that their definition and protection were specifically reserved as a responsibility of the imperial or federal governments; and they were also challenges to that sovereignty, in that they implied a de facto acknowledgment of another form of sovereignty in the native community whose interests in the land were being recognized: "treating for the Indian title as with a sovereign power" was Scott's phrase to describe the process.[8]

Whichever way the issue was viewed, Indians and lands reserved for Indians—to use the language of Section 91 (24) of the British North America Act—were like warp and woof in the fabric of federal responsibility for Indian affairs that was being woven during these years. More important than anything else, and in the tradition of British imperial policy that the new Dominion of Canada inherited, was the principle that the policy embodied in this fabric—and the responsibilities that it implied— would be uniform in all parts of the country, and for all Indians and Indian lands.

This responsibility implied much more than managing the estate, of course. As he took over the effective superintendency of Indian Affairs in 1913, Scott looked back and described the pattern.

The year 1830 [when Sir George Murray, Secretary of State for the colonies, ended the military supervision of Indian affairs by creating two civil administrative departments for Upper and Lower Canada] may be fixed as the limit of the first regime in Indian affairs. Before that date a purely military administration prevailed, the duty of the government being restricted to maintaining the loyalty of the Indian nations to the crown, with almost the sole object of preventing their hostility and of conserving their assistance as allies. About 1830 the government, with the disappearance of the anxieties of the first period, began to perceive the larger humane duties which had arisen with the gradual settlement and pacification of the country. [Murray described it as a "settled purpose of gradually reclaiming the Indians from a state of barbarism, and introducing amongst them the industrious and peaceful habits of civilized life."] The civilization of the Indian became the ideal; the menace of the tomahawk and the firebrand having disappeared, the apparent duty was to raise him from the debased condition into which he had fallen owing to the loose and pampering policy of former days. Protection from vices which were not his own, and instruction in peaceful occupations, foreign to his natural bent, were to be substituted for necessary generosity.[9]

With this, we have Scott's enunciation of the ideals of protection and advancement, the modern alternatives (in Indian affairs, at least) to separation and assimilation, which in turn had informed the considerations of the special commissioner appointed in 1856 to report on "the best means of securing the future progress and civilization of the Indian Tribes in Canada, and the best mode of so managing the Indian property as to secure its full benefit to the Indians, without impeding the settlement of the country." The commissioner determined that the "course to be adopted in Canada must partake both of the separatist system, and also that in which the Indians are located with the white population. Which of these elements will predominate must depend upon the locality of the band."[10] Separation and assimilation were not accepted as mutually exclusive alternatives—as they were, for example, during certain periods in the United States—but as necessary and complementary components to accommodate the variety of situations of Indians and Indian lands. This was both a promising embrace of a contradiction at the heart of all civil (and in our times, openly multicultural) societies, aboriginal as well as non-aboriginal, and a fundamental problem, for the subtle but stubborn reason that contradictions are anathema when cultural traditions are in competition. That said, pluralism became an increasingly important part of Canadian political and cultural life, with constitutional protection for parallel regimes in religion (Protestant and Catholic), language (French and English), and law (French civil code and British common law).

By the time of Scott's superintendency, the terms had shifted from the awkward, contradictory "separation and assimilation" to the seemingly more congenial continuities of "protection and advancement," and these two words became the consistent touchstones in Canada during the period following confederation. At a major conference on The North American Indian Today held in Toronto from September 4–16, 1939, T. R. L. MacInnes, Secretary of the Indian Affairs Branch, described how "two distinct but complementary principles have guided Canadian Indian policy—protection and advancement."[11]

Although protection came first, advancement offered a more positive storyline, always appealing to politicians. In the words of W. E. Harris, Minister of the Department of Citizenship and Immigration (which had taken over responsibility for Indian Affairs in January 1950 from the Department of Mines and Resources), "full citizenship with the same rights and responsibilities as those enjoyed by other members of the community" and "the integration of the Indians into the general life and economy of the country" constituted "the ultimate goal of our Indian policy."[12] The word "assimilation" was used less often during these years, though at the time of the Special Joint Committee of the Senate and the House of

Commons, which sat from 1946 until 1948 to consider revisions to the Indian Act, it was routinely noted that the goal of the department was the eventual assimilation of the Indian population. As one witness remarked, "We are reminded constantly by our Director [at the time, Robert A. Hoey] to have that in mind."[13]

But since the instrument of advancement was always assumed to be Indian lands, protection of these lands was still necessary at all stages of the process until full enfranchisement. As David J. Allan, Superintendent of Reserves and Trusts from 1938 to 1952, confirmed during these Special Joint Committee hearings in 1946, the government strategy was "to use the Indian reserves and the resources pertaining thereto to make of Indians self-reliant Canadian citizens."[14] The emphasis on increased self-reliance is one of the continual refrains of Canadian Indian policy, and Allan's comment is entirely consistent with MacInnes' closing statement in his address to the 1939 Conference. "While complete enfranchisement is visualized as the ultimate goal of Indian policy, the more immediate object of administration is to make the Indians self-supporting on their reserves under the varying degrees of supervision that local conditions may demand."[15]

In his opening remarks at that Conference (at which very few Indians were present), Co-chairman Charles Loram spoke of some of the characteristics of the administration of Indian affairs in North America.

The Indians in America differ from other minority groups in Canada and the United States in that by treaty and public sentiment they have been definitely accepted as national responsibilities by the two governments . . . In the United States there is much more publicity regarding the present condition of the American Indians than in Canada. This may be due to a difference of tradition, for in the United States we seem to be more prone to wash our linen, clean or unclean, in public. Perhaps because of our restlessness, our willingness to experiment, our besetting sin in so often mistaking change for progress, our systems of education, all in the United States . . . have 'views' on the Indian question which we are allowed and even encouraged to make public. In Canada, so it seems to me, the British traditions of reticence, of letting well alone, of hushing up scandals, of trusting officials, are stronger, so that there is apparently not so much interest on the part of the public in the so-called Indian Question.

There were four more specific reasons for this difference, Loram suggested.

The first is the much stricter and more just observance of Indian treaties in Canada. The second is the existence in the United States of such organizations as the Indian Rights Association, the American Association of Indian Affairs, and other groups of public-spirited citizens who, in season and out of season, agitate for the improvement of Indian conditions. The third reason springs from the publication in 1928 of the remarkable report on *The Problem of Indian Administration* [the *Meriam Report*] which sounded the clarion call for reform, and which is still our best authority and guide. The fourth reason for the greater public knowledge of, and increased interest in, Indian Affairs in the United States, is the skill and vigor with which the present Commissioner of Indian Affairs has launched and directed his program of "A New Deal for the American Indian."[16]

The Commissioner was John Collier, who had been an advocate for the *Meriam Report* and an architect of the Indian Reorganization Act (1934), which gave legislative expression to the "definite Indian policy and program" that Loram spoke about. Its New Deal ideology was complemented by the anthropologists whom Collier brought into the Indian Service, or used as advisers, from the Bureau of American Ethnology (a division of the Smithsonian Institution) and from the universities. It was at first not an easy alliance, for many of the leading American anthropologists saw American Indians as a vanishing species, degenerate versions of pure aboriginal societies. But even so, their documentation of the cultural devastation caused by the policies of the past was useful in promoting reform, and there were enough social scientists who either shared Collier's interest in ascertaining the basic structures and materials of Indian cultural stability, or who were fascinated by the dynamics of acculturation, to provide a core of allies for Collier's reform enthusiasms. It was, of course, an awkward time for anthropology and race relations alike, as the natural and the social sciences were only just beginning to disentangle the confused logic of racial strains on the one hand and evolutionary forces and processes on the other, including complex questions of hereditary and environmental influence. The focus was on the reservation as the locus of coherent tribal life, a kind of social, psychological, economic, and political microcosm of either ethnic inertia or ethnic change.[17]

The anthropologists brought in to assist in the New Deal reforms were at first coordinated by Duncan Strong, from the Bureau of American Ethnology; in 1936 an Applied Anthropology division was established in the

Bureau of Indian Affairs. This unit was disbanded a couple of years later because of budget restrictions, but many of the anthropologists continued to work within the Bureau. Even with the changes that took place in Indian administration in the United States during the late 1940s and 1950s, it is notable that the tradition of anthropological direction continued, if somewhat intermittently. In 1958, for instance, the anthropologist Philleo Nash was appointed Commissioner of Indian Affairs.

The involvement of social scientists in the Indian Bureau in the United States was initially to assist the lawyers in developing specific tribal constitutions provided for under the Indian Reorganization Act, so that the constitutions drawn up would be congruent with actual social structures; and more broadly, to develop strategies for using tribal and other indigenous cultural institutions as instruments for social change.

This undertaking involved, among other things, social and psychological (or "personality") studies on particular reservations, and in due course included work on new Indian educational and medical programs. The use of applied social science in the administration of U.S. Indian affairs during this period was profoundly important, and extended to the legal functionalism of Felix S. Cohen, a lawyer with the Department of the Interior who had been active in the drafting of the Indian Reorganization Act. In 1942, the first *Handbook of Federal Indian Law* appeared, under Cohen's hand. Harold Ickes, the Secretary of the Interior, described its purpose: to "give to Indians useful weapons in the continual struggle that every minority must wage to maintain its liberty"; and Cohen spoke of his belief "that understanding of the law, in Indian fields as elsewhere, requires more than textual exegesis, requires appreciation of history and understanding of economic, political, social and moral problems."[18]

In all of this the Indian Rights Association and the American Association of Indian Affairs played an important role. There was no counterpart north of the border—though some of the anthropologists who were involved in Canada, such as Diamond Jenness, had great influence. Jenness shared with many of his American counterparts a conviction that as "the old order passeth, yielding place to new," so must the Indians. He had spent a good part of his life in the Arctic homeland of the Inuit (Eskimo) peoples of Canada, and became convinced that since their way of life was changing (from nomadic hunting to serviced settlements) and the land could not support sufficient agricultural or industrial activities to sustain them, they would eventually have to move south to survive. Protection of their traditional northern livelihood was no longer possible; and therefore southern advancement was both the only alternative and (according to the principles informing aboriginal administration) the unavoidable responsibility of the government.[19] Some acculturation was taking place, Jenness recognized; and he could see no other choice. That said, I think Jenness would have been deeply disturbed by the way in which any evidence of acculturation, any adoption of new technologies, was later used—during the Mackenzie Valley Pipeline Inquiry, for example—to promote the rapid exploitation of aboriginal lands and resources. It was the domino argument turned on its head; once any change in traditional practices had taken place, the proponents of progress argued, there was no turning back for aboriginal people. Indeed, government and industry had an obligation to help them complete the transition from primitive to modern livelihoods. Projects should go ahead, and aboriginal people should get with the program or get out of the way.

There was nothing corresponding to the *Meriam Report* in Canada; but there was a small number of commentators drawing attention to conditions on Indian reserves and in the north (where there were no reserves, because there were no treaties) that were not unlike those chronicled by Lewis Meriam and his colleagues. There was also what Loram referred to as "the much stricter and more just observance of Indian treaties," and a history of Indian policy less given to the kinds of erratic shifts that had characterized Indian affairs in the United States, and less inclined to ideological extremes. This was cause for celebration, and comparisons to the sorry American legacy of wastage and war in what Helen Hunt Jackson called (in 1881) *A Century of Dishonour* were amplified by the devastations of the general allotment policy chronicled in the *Meriam Report*. This gave considerable (albeit often unwarranted) satisfaction to Canadian politicians and administrators, who were always ready to celebrate their British practice of keeping their word, even when they were in the process of breaking it. But many of them really seemed to believe their rhetoric. Many also believed that the combination of a general historical (rather than a specific ideological) imperative, within a tradition of pragmatic rather than doctrinaire adherence to principles, put an added burden of responsibility on the custodians of that history and those principles . . . which was to say, on the Department of Indian Affairs. Furthermore, as Loram pointed out, the Department had a particular responsibility not only to the Indians but to the public.

The *Meriam Report* had focused on government responsibility over and over again, in a way that was especially compelling to Canadian administrators because the more frequent recourse to the courts in the United States provided a check which was not effectively present in Canada. In a section on "The Government as Guardian and Trustee of Indian Property," the *Report* noted that

> emphasis must constantly be placed on the fact that in the conduct of the legal affairs of the Indians the national government is in the position of a trustee of the highest type. Before the advancing wave of Anglo-Saxon civilization the Indian has gradually relinquished his vast inheritance, until now, located in a few scattered places in our western country, he has but a remnant of his former possessions left to him. The national government has assumed to act as trustee of this estate, and it goes without saying that its duty is to conserve and develop it . . . The constituted conservators of the Indian wealth are inevitably tempted to compromise and to assume the role of the arbiter rather than of the advocate of Indian claims. Surrender to this temptation offers an enticing escape from political and legal entanglements.[20]

Felix Cohen described this in the legal terms which have since provided the basis for a number of court actions brought against federal governments in both countries. "There is a tendency of non-lawyers to confuse two very different legal relationships: trusteeship and guardianship. Guardianship is a relation that limits the personal rights of the ward. Trusteeship is a relation that limits the property rights of a trustee and makes the trustee the servant of the trust beneficiary."[21]

This ideal informs what Duncan Campbell Scott referred to as the "radical principle underlying Indian policy." But governments deal with realities, and the conflicting interests they present; and from early days even the most scrupulous public servants found themselves working alongside unscrupulous politicians and private interests to conflate guardianship and trusteeship and interpret treaties and other solemn undertakings in ways that diminished the land base and destroyed the livelihoods and languages of Indian people. Cohen's stern reminder was written in 1953, in the shadow of land surrenders in Canada which dislocated and dispossessed another generation of treaty Indians in order to make room for a new kind of settlement, the settlement of soldiers returning from the Second World War. And who could argue with their right to some land? Especially if it wasn't really being used by the wandering Indians.

In his address to the 1939 Conference, John Collier elaborated on the complex mixture of motives and mechanisms that shaped Indian policy in the United States. His focus is of course on the United States and the use of the allotment policy as an agent of advancement.

During the years when the rivalries of England, France, and Spain on the continent gave the various Indian tribes positions of strategic power, negotiations with these tribes were carried on by the colonies and later by the United States on the basis of international treaties. These treaties acknowledged the sovereignty of Indian tribes and implied the acknowledgement of a possessory right in the soil that the tribes occupied. After the cession of Louisiana by France in 1803, the termination of the war with Great Britain in 1814, and the cession of Florida by Spain in 1819, there developed an increasing tendency to deny the sovereignty of Indian tribes and to deal with them by force of arms. This tendency was marked by the establishment of an Indian Office as part of the War Department, in 1824. The United States continued for a time to make treaties with Indian tribes, but these treaties were generally made at the conclusion of a war or under a threat of military force . . . In literally hundreds of cases, however, white land-seekers persuaded Congress or the Indian Service to violate these treaties, to ignore Indian land titles, and to dispossess the Indians of those fragments of land and resources guaranteed to them by treaty. Finally, in 1871, Congress prohibited the making of treaties with the Indians . . .

Popular resentment against the economic waste and cruelty of the government's military policy led to the substitution of a more subtle and on the whole less honest method of dispossession, the allotment policy, which was instituted in the 1850s and made general in 1887. Under this policy the objective of transferring land to the whites was pursued through the mechanism of individualizing land ownership and abolishing tribal control over land tenure. The allotment policy contemplated voluntary sales of land by individual Indians and forced sales of tribal land. Humanitarian aspects of the policy involved education of the Indian in agricultural and urban occupations, health and educational services, and increased governmental support for missionary work.

On its face a purely economic measure, the allotment law actually was a weapon for cultural destruction as well. While treaties and wars had served to dispossess the Indian of his land, they nevertheless failed to break down the internal organization and culture of the

Indian tribes. The allotment law, on the other hand, by individualizing the land, destroyed community and family ownership, and by
scattering the Indians onto their individual (never family) allotments,
completely disrupted community and family life. In an effort to "civilize" and assimilate, Indian languages were systematically suppressed
in the Indian schools; the religious ceremonies, the poetry, music, and
traditions were discouraged or suppressed; the arts and crafts were
allowed to decline and in many cases completely to disappear. The
destruction of everything Indian penetrated to and affected the deepest spiritual strata of Indian culture.[22]

Collier was of course hardly a disinterested witness, since it was his own
agitation against the Dawes Act and other iniquities during the 1920s that
helped awaken public opinion and generate the reforms of the early 1930s,
and that provided Meriam and his colleagues with many of their most
telling arguments. But Collier's description was accurate, in the main; and
the Indian Reorganization Act which he helped bring into being was
notable for its reaffirmation of the integral character of the government's
responsibility for both Indians and Indian lands.

Charles Camsell, the Canadian Deputy Minister of the Department of
Mines and Resources (and responsible for Indian affairs since a merger
with the Departments of Mines, Interior and Immigration in 1936), was
not there to hear Collier in September of 1939. But all of the senior offi-
cials of the Indian Branch were at the Conference: the Director, Harold W.
McGill; the Superintendent of Lands and Trusts, David J. Allan; the Super-
intendent of Welfare and Training, Robert A. Hoey; the Superintendent of
Medical Services, E. L. Stone; the Secretary, T. R. L. MacInnes; and Mindy
Christianson, the General Superintendent of Indian Agencies. On the
American side, the senior Indian Affairs officials were all present.

David Allan was paired with Harper at the Conference, and each discussed "Indian Land Problems." "The time is not far distant when the 'surrender' of land will be a relic of the past. . . . With a definitely increasing
Indian population every acre of (Indian land) is important to the future welfare of Canada's Indians,"[23] proclaimed Allan, proceeding to give an account
(similar to Collier's) of the policy of individual allotments and pointing out
the irony that among the proponents of the policy were "the sincerest and
least self-interested of the Indians' friends. They saw in allotment a means of
stopping the white man's utter disregard of the tribal titles by giving the
Indian the kind of title [fee simple title] which would be respected."

For his part, Harper knew more about Indian lands in the United States than anyone else in or out of the Indian Service. He had participated in the extensive study of *Indian Land Tenure, Economic Status and Population Trends* which had been part of a Report of the Land Planning Committee of the National Resources Board, and shortly after this 1939 Conference he was appointed Senior Field Representative for the United States Indian Service. In the mid 1930s, he was Executive Secretary of the American Indian Defense Association, later to become the Association of American Indian Affairs.

Activist non-native organizations supporting Indian rights had been an important part of American Indian affairs since the nineteenth century, but the formation of these groups in the 1920s was prompted by a specific legislative initiative called the Bursum bill. It was introduced by Senator Holm Bursum of New Mexico, and would have confirmed non-Indian rights to Pueblo lands upon demonstration of possession of the lands over a period of years, placing any adverse burden of proof of title onto the Indians. The Pueblo lands had been under dispute for some time, and the issue had become politically focused since New Mexico became a state in 1912; but only to those locally interested in white settlement or the exploitation of natural resources was there anything substantially uncertain about the entitlement of the Pueblo to the lands reserved for them. Bursum's bill constituted an attempt to resolve the issue by dispossessing the Pueblo. It had the support of the Secretary of the Interior, Albert B. Fall, who proposed to open "such portions of [Indian] reservations as are being used to the detriment of our people."[24] "Our people," from Fall's perspective, were white people.

The successful campaign to ensure the defeat of the Bursum bill crystallized the movement for a reform of Indian affairs in the United States, with the focus on Indian lands. One of the products of the defeat of the Bursum bill was the establishment of a Pueblo Lands Board to deal with the disputed claims; it was the forerunner of, and the model for, the United States Indian Claims Commission (eventually established in 1946), and of the Canadian Commissioner for Indian Claims, established in 1969 and the forerunner of the land claims negotiations which have been an important part of native affairs in Canada since 1973.

There was another issue which, almost as much as the Bursum bill, drew attention to Indian lands during this period. Since the U.S. Congress had abolished the treaty system, public domain lands had from time to time been withdrawn for the creation of Indian reservations by an executive order of the president. The legal status of these executive-order reservations was not always clear, and they proved to be vulnerable to encroachment and to restoration to the public domain. As petroleum and natural gas development became an issue in the southwest, the ability to obtain permission to explore and develop petroleum and natural gas resources on Indian lands was increasingly urgent. Fall ruled that executive-order Indian reservations (distinct from the treaty reservations) could be developed under the General Leasing Act of 1920, a ruling that eliminated the need to obtain Indian consent and substantially excluded the Indians from development royalties. This action was justified on the grounds of expediency— there were about 22 million acres of executive-order lands, located mainly in Arizona and New Mexico, which (on the advice of both the Commissioner of the General Land Office in the Department of the Interior and by the Department's own solicitor) could not be considered part of the public domain.[25] The situation was further complicated by the fact that even on treaty reservations, exploration and development leases had to be approved by the authority of the tribal council speaking for the Indians involved— but groups such as the Navajo had no tribal council. So of course one was created to secure the sale of leases.

The petroleum and natural gas issue took five years of strenuous and often bitter dispute to resolve and culminated in the Indian Oil Act of 1927, effectively equating Indian title to executive-order and treaty reservations, and providing for the leasing of rights.

The American officials who participated in the 1939 Conference were veterans of these wars on behalf of Indian rights; specifically, they were convinced that the most serious jeopardy in which Indians were continually placed was the jeopardy of losing their lands, or of losing control of the development on their lands. It was no wonder, in the context of this kind of confusion over entitlement in the United States that many of them looked with admiration on the statutory precision and comprehensiveness of the Canadian Indian Act, and on the clearly defined status of lands reserved for Indians under the provisions of the treaties, especially those signed since 1871 (the year in which the United States Congress had prohibited the signing of any more treaties with its Indian nations).

The Indian Reorganization Act had much wrong with it—among other things, it was autocratic in some of its prescriptions, and offended many Indian groups as yet another policy imposed from without. And many critics in the United States objected to its advocacy of collective as distinct from individual enterprise among Indians, for it was resolutely committed to establishing tribal authority and to communal land tenure. But there was no mistaking the crisis out of which it arose, nor that it had focused attention on the matter of Indian lands and on the urgency of finding ways of ensuring the attachment of each Indian community to its land. The notion of Indian advancement informing the Act was perhaps debatable—though it certainly was consistent with what David Allan described as the Canadian objective of making the Indian "a good Indian rather than a third- or fourth-rate imitation of a white man"[26]; but its central commitment to the protection of Indian lands for the use and benefit of the Indians was consistently acknowledged.

Allan Harper had been part of all this, and his familiarity with Indian affairs in Canada led him to write, in 1946, a series of articles on "Canada's Indian Administration." Together they constitute the most comprehensive analysis of Indian affairs in Canada since Scott's historical work published 30 years earlier. Harper's articles appeared in *America Indígena*, a journal of the Inter-American Indian Institute. The Institute was another of the products of John Collier's relentless energy, in this case directed towards reviving Indian nationalism throughout the western hemisphere and maintaining contacts among the Americas on matters affecting Indians. The Institute was an offshoot of the First Inter-American Conference on Indian Life held at Patzcuaro, Mexico, in the spring of 1940. Fifty-six official delegates from nineteen American republics met with forty-seven Indians representing various tribes and seventy-one social scientists to discuss and cooperate in dealing with the problems of the 30 million Indians in the western hemisphere. Interestingly, only two countries did not send official delegates: Paraguay and Canada.[27] On Canada's part this may have been an expression of its belief that its Indian policy, like its British legacy, was *sui generis*. It may also have been because it was fighting a war in Europe at that time, a different embrace of that very same British legacy.

Harper's articles outlined the principles informing Canadian Indian policies and the legislative and administration arrangements which had been established to put these principles into practice. He found much to admire in Canadian practice, and much of comparative interest. Remarking on Indian status under the Indian Act, he noted that "an interesting feature of this definition is its insistence upon the criterion of group association. It is virtually impossible to be an 'Indian' apart from some recognized group of Indians. . . . In the language of the Act, a group of Indians is always called a 'band,'" of which there are three types, most Indians belonging to bands "who own or are interested in a reserve or in Indian lands in common, of which legal title is in the Crown." The defining characteristic of reserves as "for the use and benefit of the Indian band" therefore makes the reserve, as Harper implies throughout his discussion, the locus of Indianness under the Act.

"The surrender of Indian land for disposition to whites presents one of the really critical tests of government guardianship," Harper continued. "And it is only fair to add that the danger of irreparably injuring the Indians' total welfare and future by excessive cession of reserve land may arise not only from a government's compliance with white pressures, but also from the willingness of Indians themselves to turn their capital inheritance into more immediately expendable assets. A wise law must protect both government and Indians from short-sighted decisions." In concluding his account, Harper reemphasized a contradiction that has long been at the center of Canadian Indian policy: "Reliance is placed upon the geographically segregated and administratively supervised land reserve as the principal instrumentality for controlling and directing the Indian's cultural transformation."[28]

————

My second story has to do with the trinity of writing, speech, and language . . . the Father, Son, and Holy Ghost of cultural categorization. Right away, this puts us into the business of categorization, of classifying. But for now, I want to start at the headwaters of a river, and see where it takes us.

The continent's rivers—the St. Lawrence, the Mississippi, the Rio Grande, the Ohio, the Mackenzie, the Yukon, the Colorado, the Columbia—have determined the history as well as the geography of North America. They have shaped the social, economic, and political development of the continent and figure prominently in the songs and the stories that illuminate its history. Of these, perhaps none compares to the Columbia—the legendary "river of the west" that inspired Spanish and British explorers in the late seventeenth century, until it was finally "discovered" in 1792 by a newly minted American from Boston, Robert Gray and named after his ship. With this, the United States laid claim to the entire Columbia watershed, a claim that was reinforced twelve years later by Meriwether Lewis and William Clark, journeying to the west coast along the Snake River and down the Columbia. By 1811, the trader and geographer David Thompson had explored and mapped the length of the Columbia, given a sense of its extraordinary scale, and (with his British fur-trading partners) complicated the American interest in the region.

Starting high in the Rockies, the Columbia is the largest river flowing into the Pacific, with a mean flow at its mouth eight times that of the Colorado at Yuma. Its length is over 1,200 miles, and its drainage area over a quarter of a million square miles. It provides the only deep water harbor between San Francisco and Cape Flattery, and along with its tributaries it has rapids and waterfalls, as well as canyons, valleys, and plains, that rival any in the world.

Early development of the social and economic potential of the river, beginning in the nineteenth century, focused on navigation and irrigation. In the entry on the Columbia River in the *Encyclopedia Britannica* edition of 1957 both these preoccupations are obvious. In its opening sentence another central theme is established, with the river described as "one of the world's great hydroelectric streams. More than 30% of the potential hydro power of the United States is located within its watershed." The article then goes on to chronicle the projects that engineers and construction companies had undertaken to harness that diverse potential, especially the Yakima and Vale-Owyhee irrigation schemes, and the Bonneville and Grand Coulee dams—projects which, in the words of Woody Guthrie (from a song called "Roll On, Columbia"), were destined "to run the great factories and water the land." In their own way, these projects represented the potential of the entire northwest, a place unlike any other on the continent.

Guthrie's song was one of 26 that he wrote under the sponsorship of the Department of the Interior (which had sponsored the *Meriam Report*) and the Bonneville Power Authority. He came to the northwest with a deep sense of the plight of the dislocated and the dispossessed. If he ignored the situation of native Americans—and he surely did—he did so from within the same ambivalent ideology of oppression and opportunity that was also being used to further their cause, and with a sense that institutions, not individuals, are the major agents of dispossession and dislocation yet will provide the main remedy. This, of course, was also the principle underlying treaty-making. The conflicts that sometimes emerge these days between semi-institutionalized environmental activism and aboriginal communities had their counterpart in the institutional conflicts between progressive political agendas and indigenous priorities in the 1930s, 40s, and 50s.

Guthrie's rousing songs were sung by the most progressive people in the land. He rang the changes on the theme of developing the potential of the Columbia River for the benefit of the region. New industries will bring new jobs. "Shiploads of plenty will steam past the docks," he observed, bringing the trade on the coast into the interior. And "rich farms will come from hot desert sand." All of this would come about because of the river and the energetic development of its potential.

Guthrie's songs were sung, in his own words, "at all sorts and sizes of meetings where people bought bonds to bring the power lines over the fields and hills to their own little places. Electricity to milk the cows, kiss the maid, shoe the old mare, light up the saloon, the chili joint window, the schools and churches along the way, to run the factories turning out manganese, chrome, bauxite aluminum and steel."

This kind of development was on the agenda for the entire United States during this period, and a little later in Canada, with projects such as the James Bay Hydro and the Mackenzie Valley Pipeline providing a counterpart in the 1970s and 1980s. The Alaska Native Claims Settlement Act provided both a model for the settlement of Cree land claims in Quebec, and an illustration of another strategy for fulfilling Manifest Destiny. And whether wearing the cloak of sovereignty or sustainability, it is still on the agenda, on both sides of the border.

Rural electrification programs across the United States began in earnest in 1936, substantially advanced through the Rural Electrification Administration's funding of local and regional cooperatives. Federal water developments for navigation, irrigation, and flood control included the development of hydroelectric power not only to bring electricity to the farms but also to fund other development initiatives in the years following the Depression and the Second World War. All of this converged with the growing determination of the United States—and in due course, Canada—not just to be active in stimulating agricultural and industrial development but to be proactive in securing energy and power resources, a determination that got its second wind in the past few years. The Tennessee Valley Authority (established in 1933), with its complex strategies of regional co-option in the furthering of development initiatives, provided one of the most comprehensive peacetime models of institutional intervention in this arena.

But all of this took a unique form in the northwest. In a song called "Grand Coulee Dam," Guthrie caught something of the attitudes that shaped settler myths about the Columbia, with their complex mixture of the natural and the man-made, of wilderness and civilization, and of what another poet (the northern Irishman Seamus Heaney) once called territorial piety and imperial power.

Well, the world has seven wonder that the travelers always tell,
Some gardens and some towers, I guess you know them well;

But now the greatest wonder in Uncle Sam's fair land,
It's the King Columbia River and the big Grand Coulee Dam . . .

She winds down the granite canyon and the bends across the lea,
Like a prancing, dancing stallion down her seaway to the sea;
Cast your eyes upon the biggest thing yet built by human hands.
On the King Columbia River, it's the big Grand Coulee Dam.

In the misty crystal glitter of that wild and windward spray,
Men have fought the pounding waters and have met a watery grave.
Yes, it tore their boats to splinters, but it gave men dreams to dream
Of the day that Coulee dam would cross that wild and wasted stream.

Uncle Sam he took the challenge in the year of 'thirty-three,
For the farmer and the factory and for all of you and me.
He said "Roll along, Columbia, you can ramble to the sea,
But river, while you're rambling, you can do some work for me."

Now in Washington and Oregon you can hear the factories hum,
Making chrome and making manganese and light aluminum,
And the roaring flying fortress wings her way for Uncle Sam,
Spawned upon the King Columbia by the big Grand Coulee Dam.[29]

It doesn't take a literary critic to recognize in this song the insignia of naturalness, sovereignty, and independence associated with the river; and of ingenuity, inspiration, and industry correspondingly identified with the government. The power of the Columbia, mighty and majestic, is not so much controlled as it is "harnessed," the way one might harness horses, for example (which become, like the river, no less themselves for being made useful to humans), and, more particularly, put to the cultivation of the land, which was the criterion of civilization according to the familiar European discourse that was part of the invention of America (the only argument being whether Christianity should come first).

In this scheme, the Columbia becomes a useful river, like the Nile; but it remains a great river, also like the Nile, along which many civilizations too have prospered. It is a "modern" river, but one that retains the ancient aura of the wilderness—a frontier wilderness that had been announced as closed by Frederick Jackson Turner and the Census Bureau in the 1890s, but which remained wide open in the American imagination and in the northwest. In this region of the imagination, the river is both wild and civilized, both a part of nature and a part of us. This catches the contradiction at the heart of Indian policy as well, with its programs for Indians who are expected to remain Indian and to become white, to retain their traditional values and to replace them with those of the settler society.

Like Indians too, the Columbia River was in many respects wonderfully resistant to classification. It flows first, and for a long distance, directly north; and then directly south for an even longer stretch; and finally west to the sea. Its headwaters, in Columbia Lake and the Finlay Creek glacier fields, are within 50 yards of the Kootenay River, which runs in exactly the opposite direction. It flows through a wide range of ecologies, from the semi-desert highland and lowland plains to mountain and coastal rain-forests, and almost everything in between. And it "belongs" to two power-ful nations—or to about twenty, depending on how you count—to all of whom the secular as well as the sacred politics of water are central.

A powerful iconography comes into play here, wherein some rivers, like the Columbia, have a larger-than-life status ultimately beyond human control, and beyond human capriciousness. "As long as the rivers flow," goes the promise of many of the Indian treaties. Stop the rivers, and some-thing unthinkable will happen, because something both unnatural and unholy has been done.

But the importance of rivers goes to another longstanding theme, and illuminates a basic tenet of Manifest Destiny and frontier development. One of the venerable parables of European settlement in the Americas has to do with turning a wasteland—sometimes construed as a wilderness—into a garden, or making the desert bloom. There is a powerful Judeo-Christian rhetoric at work here, in which the land that brings forth plenty is deemed to be blessed by God, while the land that does not is cursed. This marker of divine disfavor finds its secular counterpart in the Victorian virtues of industry and thrift, which were routinely invoked as a contrast to Indian habits of idleness and improvidence. Indeed, for a century they had been used to justify the taking of idle land by an international legal argument according to which "nations cannot exclusively appropriate to themselves more land than they have occasion for, and which they are unable to settle and cultivate." This was the logic of the eighteenth-century Swiss jurist Emmerich de Vattel, whose *Law of Nations* was routinely invoked to justify dispossession.[30]

In fact the strategy was often much less ideological. What tended to happen was that the dynamics of cumulative encroachment—a railway line or road through Indian lands, some livestock grazing, a few scattered white settlers, and then perhaps a small settlement—generated a pattern of use and a climate of expectation that very often resulted in the retreat of the Indian people for whose benefit and use the land had originally been set aside. Indian homelands were only possible on the frontier; and as the frontier moved, so did the homelands. "The Indian will ever retreat as our Settlements advance upon them," said George Washington in writing to a Congressional Committee in 1783. "They will be as ready to sell as we are to buy. That is the cheapest as well as the least distressing way of dealing with them." He added that "the gradual extension of our Settlements will as certainly cause the Savage as the Wolf to retire; both being beasts of prey tho' they differ in shape. In a word there is nothing to be obtained by an Indian War but the soil they live on and this can be had by purchase at less expense."[31]

It was a pernicious strategy, operating under a veneer of commercial respectability: destroy the market for the product, and then buy it out in an apparently free transaction. In contrast, the treaty and reserve policy which the British established and the Canadians inherited was designed to secure Indian homelands, however diminished, from further encroachment once settlement reached the frontier, and to protect the Indians from just this kind of commercial sleight-of-hand. The overriding precedent for this policy, which the treaties and reserves translated into the *realpolitik* of nineteenth- and twentieth-century national life, was the Royal Proclamation of 1763, which set aside "all the lands and territories lying to the westward of the sources of the rivers which fall into the sea from the west and north-west" as Indian Country, and forbade "on pain of Our Displeasure, all Our Subjects from making any Purchase or Settlements whatever, or taking Possession of any of the lands reserved to the Several Nations of Indians, with whom We are connected, and who live under Our Protection without Our special leave for that Purpose first obtained."[32]

This language was just the sort of thing to infuriate the rebellious colonies, of course; but men like Washington recognized the military instinct and commercial genius informing the British instructions. So the new republic's land-use planning strategy to allow for orderly settlement combined British experience with American enterprise, incorporating an insidious (and irresponsible) Washingtonian pragmatism as when Timothy Pickering argued (in 1785) against acquiring more land from Indians at that time.

"The purchase will be as easy made at any future period as at this time. Indians having no ideas of wealth, and their numbers always lessening in the neighbourhood of our Settlements, their claims for compensation will likewise be diminished; and besides that, fewer will remain to be gratified, the game will be greatly reduced, and lands destitute of game will, by hunters, be lightly esteemed."[33]

—·—

Hopes of civilized and well-irrigated abundance on "a vast and tawny plain" resonate 150 years later in the last stanza of the poem by Irene Welch Grissom, an Idaho poet writing around 1930:

. . . . .
He did not see the arid land
Of drifting dust and desert sand,
The scanty grass and prickly-pear
That fought to hold a footing there.
He caught the flashing silver stream
Of ripples dancing on a stream,
Now gayly winding all about
Through fields of green, then in and out
Of nodding grain, and everywhere
The water went the earth was fair
With growing things—the embers died—
The silent plain was dark and wide.[34]

What we don't have are the voices of the Nez Perce, the Shuswap, the Kootenai, and the other aboriginal peoples whose world was about to be washed away, literally as well as figuratively.

This is where the damming of the Columbia and its tributaries comes into perspective. Within two decades, the hydroelectric projects along the river had brought light to the darkness and water to the desert, had eliminated the menace of both drought and flood, and had transformed what one contemporary called the "arid, desolate sagebrush lands" of the Snake River plains into Idaho's most prosperous agricultural region, while the river remained in the minds and myths of the region as more or less wild—witness Guthrie's description of the Columbia as a "prancing, dancing stallion." And the Indians, here and elsewhere, all but disappeared from their former homelands, retreating to the jails and refugee camps that went by the name of reservations (the Cree word for reserve translates as "all that is left when the rest has been given away"). Later, the Indians reappeared in the slums of our cities.

Exorcizing the specter of the Great Depression renewed a fundamental conflict once again having to do with land. This was the period in which restoring native American tribal autonomy and revitalizing native American economies was high on the agenda, stimulated in large measure by the *Meriam Report* of 1928 and the Indian Reorganization (Wheeler-Howard) Act of 1934. These regional and national ambitions also involved new strategies for bringing land back into production—specifically, by the radical management of water resources, and by equally radical herd and crop management initiatives. The federal government, stimulated by New Deal energy and idealism, found the most obvious testing grounds for this environmental engineering and behavioral modification on Indian land.

In this connection, let me add a few words about how the admirable determination of John Collier to bring about the reestablishment of tribal governments came into conflict with his equally admirably determination to conserve and develop the dry land territory of the Navajo.

The Navajo had been farming for generations, planting crops and raising stock. They first came from the northern plains and tundra lands, and the region where they live at present is very dry, with grasslands vulnerable to drought and overgrazing. When they arrived from the north, about 500 years ago, they brought some of their own ways and adopted some new ones: land cultivation patterns, the arts of weaving, and some religious rituals from the Pueblo; the keeping of sheep and the crafts of silver and turquoise from the Zuni and the Spanish; and horses probably also from the Spanish. Horses have long been important to the Navajo, in ways that go well beyond their practical necessity: they work the land, pull the wagons, carry the men and women, and herd the stock, but they also graze wild on the grasslands, signify prestige and power and a kind of irrational, transcendent defiance of the pressures of survival. They represent a kind of covenant, linking Navajo subsistence with Navajo sovereignty.

The Navajo were first forced off their lands by Kit Carson, operating under instructions from the United States government. But a few years later, after a terrible time in captivity in a place called Bosque Redondo, they were allowed to move back. The next threat to the Navajo came not from frontier greed and corruption and the apparently boundless violence of American law and order, but from their supposedly enlightened friends.

Towards the end of the nineteenth century, after the trauma of the Civil War, attention in the United States turned to the Indian question. Even the most dedicated friends of the Indians saw tribal allegiance as the root of the problem, for it interfered with their acceptance of individualism and property ownership. The solution—which John Collier scathingly condemned—was to break up that allegiance by severing each community's attachment to its homeland, or to the reserves to which many had been moved. During the 1880s, the Americans passed the General Allotment

Act, which abolished tribal control over land tenure and opened up these lands for individual ownership—first of all by Indians, and in short order by unscrupulous whites. This Act was one of so-called Homestead acts that were intended to provide nineteenth-century settlers with an opportunity for advancement independent of class.

For the Indian people, the Allotment Act provided nothing. It was appreciatively referred to by President Theodore Roosevelt, around the turn of the century, as "a mighty pulverizing engine to break up the tribal mass." And it did its job, dispersing about 90 million acres of land formerly reserved for tribes, and leasing much of the remaining lands for grazing by white ranchers. Accompanied by the suppression of Indian languages, traditions, and ceremonies, it also broke the spirit of many Indians and undermined the structure of many tribal governments. But fifty years later, the tribes were still there, though often in wretched circumstances. In 1928, concerned over this destitution and dispossession and by the appalling health conditions, severe educational limitations, and grotesque administrative arrangements prevailing in many Indian communities, the American government commissioned Lewis Meriam to conduct his survey.

The *Meriam Report* ran to nearly 900 pages of remarkably thorough description and analysis. It was harsh in its criticism of the land allotment policy, recommending the reestablishment of tribal governments with control over land and resources. It was eloquent in its celebration of the values of community and of place, and of the interdependence of spiritual and material values in both native and non-native society. But it forgot about the importance of horses. Or more precisely, dismissed them in one paragraph titled "Worthless Horses."

The Indian Reorganization Act (1934) sought to revitalize tribal councils and develop local economies. This meant, among other things, new grazing practices to reverse fifty years of white leaseholders' abuse and to sustain the sheep and the goats that were a staple of Navajo life. Accordingly, the Navajo tribal government was asked to implement the livestock reduction program designed by the government. The reduction was to be based on what were called "sheep units," which represented the quantitative consumption of grass by dependent animals. Everything was measured in sheep units. People were henceforth to order their lives in sheep units. Even horses were measured in sheep units—they eat as much grass as five sheep—and the federal government directed the Navajo to round up their five sheep-unit, economically worthless, horses and sell or destroy them. The Navajo said no.

Ultimately their refusal to cooperate inevitably put both the Navajo nation and the livelihood of its people in jeopardy, for they were still dependent on the United States government in a variety of ways. Subsistence and sovereignty came into conflict with a narrow utilitarianism and a misplaced morality of progress. The reasons for this stand-off are often blamed on ignorant, idealistic officials. If only they had known more about the Navajo, or about tribal governments, or about land management, or about horses . . . But in fact they knew a great deal about all of these. The man most responsible for the initiatives that led to the restoration of tribal government and the land conservation and stock reduction programs was John Collier himself, the Commissioner of Indian Affairs during the 1930s. He was an eloquent social activist who had taught at the People's Institute in New York, lived among the Pueblo, and was deeply committed to self-determination for native peoples and respect for the diversity of their cultures. But he ended up saying to the Navajo something like: "govern yourselves—but do it my way. And get rid of your horses." It was a mistake.

Indeed, one of the most perceptive of Collier's officials, Reeseman Fryer, who was his specially appointed Indian agent with the Navajo Service during this period, concluded: "One could continue to list significant 'hallmark' achievements during the period of the Navajo Service that made lasting contributions to tribal history and the quality of tribal life, but I should like instead to conclude this memoir with an admission of what I consider to have been the most significant of our errors, an error that made it nearly impossible for even the ablest of interpreters to dispel the confusion and fear it aroused: it was our use of the term 'sheep unit'."[35]

Language has often been a dangerous and deadly part of the frontier, and helped underwrite the concept of Manifest Destiny throughout the Americas. It continues to perplex both courts and parliaments in Canada when faced with treaty and other constitutional claims affecting aboriginal people. Thus, when the Gitksan and Wet'suwet'en peoples of what is now British Columbia went to court to confirm jurisdiction over their territory in what has become known as the DelgamUukw case, they told the history of their people in the stories and songs that represent their past. The judge, in response, said that since their ancestors had "no horses, no wheeled vehicles, no written literature," they were "unorganized societies roaming from place to place like beasts of the field."

That was in 1991. Although his judgment was later rejected by the Supreme Court, even that court was unable to find a much better way of characterizing the oral traditions that constitute the history and philosophy and literature of aboriginal peoples than by saying they are not "steeped in the same notions of social progress and evolution" as written traditions. In other words, they are backward.[36]

As cognitive psychologist Gerry Altmann put it more recently, "The advent of the written word must surely rank, together with fire and the wheel, as one of mankind's greatest achievements . . .the only other time that evolution came up with a system for storing and transmitting information was when it came up with the genetic code." "Science and technology would hardly have progressed beyond the Dark Ages," he continues, "were it not for the written word."[37]

For millennia, the absence of written traditions has been a defining part of the convenient European (and sometimes Asian) classification of peoples into primitive "them" and civilized "us." The stereotypes that have accompanied these classifications are fairly well chronicled. But there remains a persistent habit of reducing oral texts to the status of secondary documents and of discrediting the oral traditions of aboriginal peoples. More than that, orality has often been considered according to a model that presumes literacy to be a step further along the evolutionary scale: an assumption at best questionable.[38]

Clearly, we are not so far away from all this, and from the fatalism it represents. Michel Foucault, one of the church fathers of our contemporary understanding of how we live in the world, insists in *Les Mots et Les Choses* (1966) that only in the seventeenth century did language and other sign systems come to be seen as representations. Since knowledge of representation *is* knowledge for Foucault, this puts aboriginal peoples right where Altmann and others place them, without the cognitive and cultural enlightenment brought about by writing and (in the European Renaissance) by printing . . . the latter, in Marshall McLuhan's words, preventing "a return to the Africa within us."[39] A return to the heart of darkness.

It is an old story line. "The history of nearly every race that has advanced from barbarism to civilization has been through the stages of the hunter, the herdsman, the agriculturalist, and finally reaching those of commerce, mechanics and the higher arts," said U.S. Colonel Nelson Miles in 1879, a few years before he accepted surrender from Chief Joseph and the Nez Perce and sent them off to school to learn to read and write.

Notes

1. I am indebted to Lewis Hyde's book *Trickster Makes This World: Mischief, Myth and Art* (Edinburgh: Canongate, 1998) for the image of the hinge, though not for its association with the frontier.

2. I might just add my frustration at the use of the word "settlers" to describe migrating peoples. It's an issue I have taken up elsewhere (in *If This Is Your Land, Where Are Your Stories?* [2003]), but I feel it is especially important here because it has to do with language and terminology, the carriers of ideology and powerful agents of Manifest Destiny. Like many of us, I continue to use the word. Do I thereby continue to support the concept of manifest destiny, with its preference for civilized agricultural settlement over nomadic hunting and herding?

3. D. C. Scott, quoted in Frederick Abbott, *The Administration of Indian Affairs in Canada* (Washington, 1915).

4. See Henry E. Fritz, *The Movement for Indian Assimilation, 1860–1890* (Philadelphia: University of Pennsylvania Press, 1963), 43–44, 78–108, 206–208; and R. W. Mardock, *The Reformers and the American Indian* (Columbia: University of Missouri Press, 1971), 57–59, 129–31.

5. "Indian Affairs, 1763–1841," Vol. 4, 695–725; "Indian Affairs, 1840–1867," Vol. 5, 331–62; "Indian Affairs, 1867–1912," Vol. 7, 593–626.

6. "Indian Affairs, 1763–1841," *Canada and Its Provinces,* Vol. 4, 697.

7. "Indian Affairs, 1840–1867," *Canada and Its Provinces,* Vol. 5, 339.

8. "Indian Affairs, 1763–1841," *Canada and Its Provinces,* Vol. 4, 697.

9. Ibid., 695–96.

10. Canada. Parliament. *Journals of the Legislative Assembly of Canada,* Appendix 21 (Victoria, 1858), Report Part III.

11. T. R. L. MacInnes, "The History and Policies of Indian Administration in Canada," *The North American Indian Today: University of Toronto-Yale University Seminar Conference,* ed. C. T. Loram and T. F. McIlwraith (Toronto: University of Toronto Press, 1943), 157.

12. Canada. Parliament. *House of Commons Debates,* 1950, Vol. IV, 3946: Indian Act, 21 June 1950.

13. Canada. Parliament. *Minutes of the Proceedings and Evidence of the Special Joint Committee of the Senate and the House of Commons appointed to examine and consider the Indian Act* (Ottawa: King's Printer, 1946), 376–77.

14. Ibid., 478.

15. *The North American Indian Today,* 163.

16. Ibid., 4–5.

17. See Kenneth R. Philp, *John Collier's Crusade for Indian Reform 1920–1954* (Tucson: University of Arizona Press, 1977), 161–162; Graham D. Taylor, *The New Deal and American Indian Tribalism. The Administration of the Indian Reorganization Act 1934–1945* (Lincoln: University of Nebraska Press, 1980), 37; Brian W. Dippie, *The Vanishing American: White Attitudes and United States Indian Policy* (Middletown, Conn.: Wesleyan University Press, 1982), 327–332.

18. Foreword to Felix S. Cohen, *Handbook of Federal Indian Law* (Washington, D.C., 1942), v–vi; Author's Acknowledgements, ibid., xviii. Quoted in Brian Dippie, *The Vanishing American,* 332.

19. Jenness's detailed commentary was published in a five-part comparative study of *Eskimo Administration in Alaska, Canada, Labrador and Greenland,* with a concluding volume of *Analysis and Reflections,* published as a series of Technical Papers by the Arctic Institute of North America between 1962 and 1968.

20. Lewis Meriam, Technical Director, *The Problem of Indian Administration: report of a Survey made at the request of the Honorable Hubert Work Secretary of the Interior, and submitted to him February 21, 1928* (Baltimore, MD: Johns Hopkins Press, 1928), 784ff.

21. "Indian Wardship: The Twilight of a Myth" (1953), in *The Legal Conscience: Selected Papers of Felix S. Cohen,* ed. Lucy Kramer Cohen (New Haven: Yale University Press, 1960), 332–33.

22. "Policies and Problems in the United States," *The North American Indian Today,* 141–44.

23. "Indian Land Problems in Canada," *The North American Indian Today,* 186–87.

24. Quoted in Lawrence C. Kelly, *The Assault on Assimilation; John Collier and the Origins of Indian Policy Reform* (Albuquerque: University of New Mexico Press, 1983), 153.

25. Ibid., 183.

26. "Indian Land Problems in Canada," *The North American Indian Today,* 186–87.

27. "The Final Act: The First Inter-American Conference on Indian Life, Patzcuaro," *Mexico,* April 14–24, 1940 (Washington, Office of Indian Affairs, 1940). Kenneth R. Philp, *John Collier's Crusade for Indian Reform 1920–1954,* 206–07.

28. "Canada's Indian Administration," *America Indígena,* 6(4) (Oct. 1946): 229, 311, 313.

29. The text of Woody Guthrie's song, along with his description of the places where he sang, are from a script composed of his writings and lyrics titled

From California to the New York Island and published by the Guthrie Children's Trust Fund in New York in 1960.

30. Vattel was the author of *The Law of Nations; or Principles of the Law of Nature, Applied to the Conduct and Affairs of Nations and Sovereigns* (1760).

31. Letter written on September 7, 1783, from Washington to a Congressional Committee chaired by James Duane. Quoted in Reginald Horsman, *Expansion and American Indian Policy, 1783–1812* (East Lansing: Michigan State University Press, 1966), 9.

32. See *Documents Relating to the Constitutional History of Canada, 1759–1791*, eds. Adam Shortt and Arthur E. Doughty (Ottawa, 1907), 119–23; and *Constitutional Documents*, ed. Shortt, vol. I, Sessional Papers, no. 18, 199–200.

33. From a letter to Rufus King, June 1, 1785. Quoted in Horsman, p. 100. Pickering was later Secretary of War, with responsibility for Indian Affairs.

34. Irene Welch Grissom, "Clearing Sagebrush," *Verse of the New West* (Caldwell: Caxton, 1931), p. 3. Reprinted in *Idaho's Poetry: A Centennial Anthology*, ed. Ronald E. McFarland and William Studebaker (Moscow, Idaho: University of Idaho Press, 1988), 71.

35. Reeseman Fryer's description of the trauma of sheep units is from his unpublished monograph, "Erosion, Poverty and Dependency: Memoir of My Time in Navajo Service, 1933–1942" (1986), kindly made available to me by his daughter, Ann Van Fossen.

36. Judge Allan McEachern's comments here and later in the essay are recorded in the transcripts of the DelkgamUukw trial (1987–1991), finally decided (in favor of the plaintiffs) by the Supreme Court of Canada on December 11, 1997, from whose judgment the last quotation is taken). The journal *BC Studies* devoted a special issue to the trial and judgment. A book of excerpts, cartoons and commentary from the trial, compiled by Don Monet and Skanu'u (Ardythe Wilson), *Colonialism on Trial: Indigenous Land Claims and the Gitksan and Wet'suwet'en Sovereignty Case*, was published in 1992. Leslie Pinder wrote a powerful monograph titled *The Carriers of No: After the Land Claims Trial* (1991); and Dara Culhane has a scholarly study, *The Pleasure of the Crown: Anthropology, Law and First Nations* (1998).

37. Gerry Altmann, *The Ascent of Babel: An Exploration of Language, Mind and Understanding* (Oxford: Oxford University Press, 1997), 160.

38. After all, some of the worst wars in human history, as well as the genocidal acts of the Nazis, were prosecuted by literate, organized, "advanced" societies.

39. Marshall McLuhan, *The Gutenberg Galaxy* (Toronto: University of Toronto Press, 1962), 45.

8

The American West and American Empire

Richard White

Seventy years ago, in a book simply entitled *Manifest Destiny*, Albert Weinberg phrased the ideological issue of expansion in terms of the international morality of nationalism. He presented international morality as a mirror inversion of personal morality, which presumes that virtue involves self-sacrifice. But, Weinberg wrote, in "international morality these premises ordinarily go the wrong way: they lead not to the conclusion of self-sacrifice but to the conclusion of self-aggrandizement . . . the altruism of international morality leads to an aggrandizement which usually requires the contraction of some other party."[1] It is a view particularly apt for the United States. The classic morality of North American republicanism— the appeal to the virtue of its citizenry—involved the subordination of the citizen's self-interest to a larger public interest. Proponents of American expansionism usually framed expansion as altruism: the extension of what Jefferson called the Empire of Liberty. The result was an inversion. National altruism was an exercise in self-aggrandizement, and it has often remained so.[2]

Weinberg's *Manifest Destiny* remains a key text about the ideology of expansion, an astute study of the contradictions and ultimate incoherence of the ideology that has influenced other studies that have followed, but it is dated. It is dated, first of all, in its antique intellectual history, which spends little time on the social and political context of expansionist ideas.[3] What to Weinberg seemed a reflection of American confidence, Thomas Hietala more convincingly reads as American anxiety: a "domestic malaise that found expression in American aggrandizement."[4] Second, Weinberg saw expansionism as a product of American innocence and believed that it yielded little tragedy. When he thought about who had suffered, he mentioned Haitians and Filipinos, but otherwise "the story . . . is perhaps the most cheerful record of such perilous ambitions that one can find."[5]

Indian peoples are barely present in Weinberg's account, but if there was any group that had to contract as the United States expanded, it was Indian peoples.[6]

Over the last thirty or forty years, historians have removed the veil of innocence that Weinberg draped over the continental expansion of the United States. The Indian peoples who were largely invisible in Weinberg's account have become visible, but they have become visible as more than simple victims. They were and are complicated peoples as enmeshed in the modern world as their conquerors. The conflicts between the United States and Indian peoples were not simply clashes between an American modernity and an Indian traditionalism or between an expanding United States and a set of static tribal entities. Many of the tribes Americans displaced were as much modern creations as was the United States. Some, such as the Lakota, Cheyenne, and Navajo, were expanding peoples themselves. Some formed confederations and allied themselves with bordering European empires. Others had organized themselves into small republics with institutions paralleling those of the United States, within which they were recognized as domestic, dependent nations.[7]

In part, this literature about Indians has become central to the historical scholarship about empire and the early national expansion of the United States. Particularly before the defeat of Tecumseh's confederation in the War of 1812, Indians in alliance with European empires posed a real obstacle to American expansion. And in the modern scholarship on both Texas and the Mexican War, Indian peoples have become an integral part of the story.[8]

When dealing with the period following the Civil War, however, the new scholarship on Indian peoples has a more mixed relation with the literature on American expansionism. On the one hand, it has created a much more nuanced and complicated version of the conquest of the continent by exploring the reasons some Indians resisted Euro-Americans and others allied with them. It has created a fuller view of the societies the United States subordinated, and, above all, it has punctured Euro-American pretensions of innocence by demonstrating the calamities that followed conquest. On the other hand, it has had relatively little to say about the larger contours of United States expansionism. Scholars working on the West and Indian policy have written much about the motivations for policies toward Indians and their domestic context, but relatively little on what this relentless erosion of Indian land teaches us about the United States in a larger international context. Unlike Indian resistance in North America before the War of 1812, which had, in combination with European empires, a real possibility of containing the United States, the outcome of the wars following the Civil War seemed overdetermined.

And so, like the larger literature on Manifest Destiny, the scholarship on Euro-Americans and Indian peoples divides the nineteenth-century story into two parts. There is the expansionist story, which is largely the acquisition of what is now the western United States from Indian confederations, European empires, and Mexico. This ends just before the Civil War. The story briefly mentions the acquisition of Alaska and the failed annexation of the Dominican Republic, and then picks up again with Hawaii and the Spanish American War. In between the Civil War and the Spanish American War is a second Indian story, which is largely a domestic story of the relations between Indians and the federal government and the evolution of federal Indian policy.[9]

Implicit in this story is that expansionism ends not so much when territory is incorporated into the United States, but when other empires and nation states cede their claims to sovereignty to the United States. And so even though much of the land west of the Missouri was at the end of the Civil War claimed but hardly controlled by the United States, its occupation falls outside the usual studies of expansionism and Manifest Destiny. The incorporation of western Indians into the United States, however, clearly has connections with antebellum expansionism. These connections are ideological. Providential thinking, racism, and the assertion of racial hierarchies are ideological and so too are claims to widen the realms for freedom, a pervasive sense of uplift with its heavy Christian overtones, and the identification of American national interest with the progress of civilization. And these connections are also tactical: the techniques of filibustering.

Historians of the expansion and foreign policy of the United States, such as Walter Lafeber, do see intimate connections between the domestic policies and imperialism, but they include the West only as the source of agricultural surpluses that needed a market, and they do not include Indians. In Lafeber's *New Empire*, for example, the West gets passing mention and only in hackneyed frontier terms, and Indians are hardly noticed.[10] To the best of my knowledge, only Thomas Bender, in his new book *A Nation among Nations,* and Nathan Citino have integrated western expansion and Indian policy in the post-Civil War period with a larger story of imperialism. As Citino and Bender point out, many of the elements present in the expansion of the United States in the trans-Missouri West reappear in its expansion beyond the continent.[11]

The trans-Missouri history of relations between Euro-American and Indian peoples reintegrates the curious period between the 1850s and

1890s, during which the United States gained full control of the land within its continental boundaries, back into the larger imperial story. The ideological elements that Weinberg and Stephanson have identified as central to providential justifications of American national expansion also justified the acquisition of lands from western Indians, but this expansion also incubated new elements of what would be the hallmarks of later American imperialism: its exploitation of internal rivalries and reliance on indigenous allies; not only Christian justifications for expansion but the integration of Christian churches into the bureaucracy of expansion; and the identification of American national interests with corporate interests.[12] These latter elements involved what might be called the privatization of empire, and they came to fruition in the trans-Missouri West in the late nineteenth century. The story is full of the equivalent of what would now be called NGOs—the various organizations of the so-called Friends of the Indians, the churches, particularly Protestant churches, and private organizations such as the Boomers who followed David Payne in Oklahoma. It is also full of corporations, particularly railroad corporations.

Looked at in this way, the existing history of Indians and Indian policy and the American West in general has been, albeit accidentally, in the vanguard of showing the complexities, the multiple actors, and the prominence of non-state entities in American expansionism. There are strong parallels between nineteenth-century American incorporation of the West and twentieth-century foreign policy as described by the corporatist school of foreign policy.[13] Historians have given considerable attention to churches and the Friends of the Indians, but I want to concentrate here largely on corporations, particularly railroad corporations, and their tangled relation to the American state. Paul Wallace Gates and H. Craig Miner and a few others emphasized these relations thirty to forty years ago, but since then they have received considerably less notice.[14]

The first transcontinental railroads were chartered and subsidized quite consciously as agents of state purposes rather than as purely business enterprises. When they were denounced in Congress as commercially hopeless and economically reckless, Timothy Phelps of California answered that the immediate necessity was not commercial but military. It was necessary to hold California in the Union.[15] By the time the first transcontinental was completed, however, the Union had been saved and had stayed intact for four years. This altered rather than removed military and national justification for the railroad. Because the transcontinentals often failed as business enterprises, they reinvented and flouted their role as agents of the state. They took the credit for conquering Indians. "Experience proves," Grenville

Dodge, a leading figure in the Union Pacific and Texas Pacific, wrote, "the Railroad line through Indian Territory [is] a Fortress as well as a highway."[16] Or as Charles Francis Adams, president of the Union Pacific, put it, "the Pacific railroads have settled the Indian question."[17] Railroads provided the federal government with the ability to concentrate troops quickly and effectively. Railroads took away the great advantage of mounted warriors on the Plains who previously could disperse before Euro-Americans could concentrate troops and then regroup out of reach from slower infantry and cavalry columns. Railroads were a means of national and racial conquest. As W. Milnor Roberts, eventually chief engineer of the Northern Pacific, wrote in regard to that road, it "will forever settle the question of white supremacy over an area of country covering at least 450,000 square miles."[18]

Railroads served the state; they adopted the same kind of providential thinking and natural determinism typical of American expansionism, and in doing so they took on part of the civilizing function earlier reserved for the state. L.U. Reavis, a promoter and railroad publicist, informed the readers of the *Inland Monthly* of the "important fact" that the Atlantic and Pacific Railway had "for its axis the January isothermal line of forty-one degrees." All the great men of Europe and Asia had supposedly appeared within a few degrees of this line, which was the "path of empire." The Atlantic and Pacific was thus "in harmony with nature herself" in accomplishing the "destiny or mission of our people on the North American continent."[19] Reavis became something of an expert in discerning the congruence between railway lines, nature, and American or Saxon destiny. He later performed the same service for the Mexican International, no more deterred by the Mexican boundaries than he had been by tribal boundaries. "Let our second coming into the Mexican nation be like unto a divine mission, to regulate and reinvigorate old customs, old ideas and old institutions, and herald the progress and prosperity, the faith and mental illuminations of our race now dawning upon the western hemisphere which is destined to wrap the world in the new liberty given to mankind by this nation."[20]

This railroad rhetoric was both an echo of Manifest Destiny and a modification of it. Just as Manifest Destiny made the expansion of the United States synonymous with the expansion of republican freedom, Christianity, and civilization itself, so the railroads made their expansion an expansion of civilization. But in doing so they could render an expansion of American boundaries unnecessary—or inevitable. It depended. George Church mocked Mexican fears that the extension of the American railroad network into Mexico was a tool of Manifest Destiny. "They do not understand the problem of the age—the United States does not want them nor their territory, but civilization more powerful than the United States will sooner or later force upon them it inexorable Dictatorship—they will bend to it and perhaps break under it."[21] In Mexico American railroad promoters like Edward Plumb and William Rosecrans were willing to put off annexation in favor of commercial relations.[22] Once railroads secured American control over Mexican trade and development, "we need not hasten the greater event," by which he meant annexation.[23]

Railroads were, however, more than agents of the state. They were protean, and they stood in multiple relations to national states. Even as they became legally persons under the Fourteenth Amendment, they could also think of themselves as proto-states. Railroad men shared with the railroads' enemies a set of metaphors that portrayed corporate leaders as nobility—barons, kings, and princes—ruling over petty states. In Texas, Alexander Terrell denounced "a new breed of men in America, called 'railroad kings,' who dominate the great thoroughfares of trade, the public highways of the people, and who transmit their orders from New York, over telegraph wires, also owned by them, to their emissaries at National and State capitals, and have thus far defied control."[24] Charles Francis Adams once described the behavior of Charles Perkins of the Burlington as that of a "typical head of a small independent state."[25] Fannie Villard, in the brief and giddy days before her husband Henry lost control of the Northern Pacific, took to addressing him as "my dearest Railroad King." There was more than domestic silliness here. There was deep and revealing delusion. "The influence of such work as yours upon the general tone and improved morality of the people, whom you may half be said to govern," she wrote Villard in 1883, "can only be dimly imagined."[26]

Railroad leaders framed their activities in terms of war and diplomacy. Railroads had territories and subject populations. They defended and attacked. They went to war and made peace. They made and broke treaties. The men who ran them had aristocratic virtues and aristocratic emotions—honor, revenge, manliness, anger—that a democratic and capitalist society, for better or worse, had supposedly outgrown. Much of this railroad imperialism played out as middle-aged boys with maps, but then so did much actual imperialism. Leland Stanford was a man who should never have been left alone in a room with a map and time on his hands. He sent to his associate, Collis P. Huntington, a map early in 1881 detailing a route from the Southern Pacific into eastern Washington and Oregon in order to draw the business of the Columbian Plateau to the Gulf of Mexico. Huntington, either mocking or unsuccessfully attempting to be kind, replied that he did not have "so much faith" in the route and did not "suppose you have the data by which you can give the mileage or anything like it." An actual railroad would be "much longer than the one you have laid down on the map."[27]

Yet railroads, seemingly so powerful that they could co-opt the civilizing mission of the state and rhetorically regard themselves as states, could, in other situations, find themselves stymied by Indians and renew their demands for state aid without which their civilizing mission must fail. When Indians remained stubbornly athwart the line of empire, defying the isothermal, the Atlantic and Pacific howled. Its spokesmen created a literary parody of the actual Indian Territory inhabited by the Cherokees and other southern tribes. The Indian Territory was in fact dotted with farms and ranches, towns and schools. It had newspapers and legislatures and courts, all run by Indians, but for C. J. Hillyer, a lawyer for the Atlantic and Pacific, Indian Territory was a wilderness, and "[a] railroad and a wilderness are incompatible things, and cannot long co-exist. Either the wilderness will be subdued or the railroad will die of starvation." Indians were too few and too barbaric, he argued, to support a railroad or a modern society. "We might as well for all business purposes, build a road for three hundred miles through a tunnel or a desert, as through the fertile Indian country in its present condition."[28] Hillyer referred to what John Benson, a Cherokee, called the chief mistake of legislators and the American public about Indian Territory: "that the Indians of this territory are but savages, and that their country can be monopolized by railroad speculators and governed by the appointees of the president of the United States instead of those of their own selection." Benson favored connections with the larger economy, and he favored development. He just wanted development to take place under the governments of Indian nations and under Indian control.[29] This was certainly not part of the Atlantic and Pacific's plan nor, apparently, the divine plan.

The railroads' claim to serve and insure American expansion was rhetorical, but not merely rhetorical. In the service of expansion, the Indian policy of the United States and railroad corporate policy became intimately and messily intertwined. Western railroads and the federal government became enmeshed on such a variety of levels that it was sometimes hard to distinguish if particular people were acting in their capacity of government officials or because of their connections to the railroads.

During the Civil War, Samuel Pomeroy of Kansas had written the railroad purchase clause in the Kickapoo Treaty of 1862. It provided for the sale at $1.25 an acre of surplus Kickapoo lands (those left after allotments to tribal members) to the Atchison & Pike's Peak Railroad, which, it so happened, was controlled by Pomeroy. Senator Pomeroy then steered the treaty through the ratification process in the United States Senate. The Kickapoos protested that the agent and interpreter had been bribed, that the treaty clauses had not been properly interpreted, and that the agent had removed tribal leaders who objected to the treaty. Only one recognized tribal leader had signed the document. There were embarrassing investigations but, with the country in the midst of the Civil War, no action. Mark Twain used Pomeroy as the model for his fictional Senator Dilworthy in the *Gilded Age*—the 1873 novel that gave the era its name—and doomed him to become a man who ever after was less famous than his own parody.[30]

Pomeroy's device of giving Indian lands directly to railroads at bargain prices had only one flaw: settlers wanted those lands without having to pay the railroads a premium for them. The settlers had a case; they had played a crucial role in obtaining the Kickapoo cession. The expansionist tradition of filibustering survived in the trans-Missouri West. By treaty and American law, the Indians should have been safe in their occupancy. Forced across the Missouri by earlier treaties, the tribes had been promised their new lands in perpetuity. Their legal status as domestic dependent nations guaranteed them the guardianship and protection of the United States. In practice, however, this meant that to force Indian land cessions in Kansas, the government did not have to *act* to coerce Indians. It could coerce them through *inaction*. All it had to do was fail to protect the tribes from United States citizens. If the United States failed to remove squatters, failed to protect Indian timber from theft, failed to protect Indian livestock from American citizens, then Indians might become convinced that land cessions were their best option. By squatting on Indian lands, settlers had stolen them "fair and square" and resented being deprived of their prize at the last moment. The simple failure of the government to stop them had brought tribal negotiators to the table.[31]

The squatters assumed that the lands would pass in the usual manner from the Indians to the government to the public domain to the squatters, who were now preemptors; they had not counted on the railroads. In the wake of the Civil War the railroad man most adept at elbowing his way to the table was James Joy, the president of the Chicago, Burlington and Quincy, who managed to obtain the Neutral Tract of the Cherokee Nation in Kansas for $1 an acre. The Supreme Court would validate the sale in 1872, and settlers would pay average prices that ranged from $9.15 an acre in the mid-1870s to $5.45 for the less choice lands at the end.[32] "King Joy" was hardly done. He used treaty negotiations to arrange an even bigger transaction with the Osage: a sale of over 8 million acres for twenty cents an acre, nothing down. It was this treaty that came before Congress amidst huge public uproar in 1871. And when this treaty went down to defeat, it took the whole treaty system with it.[33] The Constitution reserved to the Senate the power to advise and consent on treaties, and the House had long resented being shut out of the treaty system. Since the House had to appropriate money for Indian Affairs and land purchases, it used its power of the purse to tack an amendment on to an appropriations bill in 1871 declaring that there would be no new treaties, although tribes would retain their status as semi-sovereign nations and existing treaties would be honored.[34]

The demise of the treaty system demonstrated the frictions that were very much part of an expansionism that combined corporate interests, state purposes, and a popular expectation of benefit, but the end of the treaty system did not mean an end of corporate/state partnership in expansion. William Windom of Minnesota was both a senator and a member of the Northern Pacific Railroad Board of Directors. A Gilded Age congressman routinely suffered a crisis of conscience in going on railroad payrolls that would be easier to take seriously if its outcome were not so predictable. It was a ritual of sorts. Moral concerns were raised; the relationship was clarified; the moral rectitude of the official was validated by the very people who had tempted him, and the official became a friend of the railroad. Windom was concerned with the appearance of conflicts of interest in his dual role, but Jay Cooke, the banker in charge of financing the road and a man who was not predisposed to irony, had assured him there was no impropriety in Windom's serving as a director of the road, investing in it, and borrowing the money for that investment from Cooke. "[W]e take it for granted," Cooke assured Windom, "that you are an honest man, and will do nothing that is not right strictly, especially when the subject of the Northern Pacific comes before Congress, which is the only possible complication."[35] One of the things that came before Congress in 1871 was the matter of the Wahpeton-Sisseton Sioux. The Northern Pacific needed their land. It was Windom's chance to demonstrate his honesty.

Cooke and Windom initially argued that if the treaty system was dead, then Congress had the right to abrogate Indian titles unilaterally. Cooke had a bill introduced to strip the Wahpeton-Sisseton of their land with Congress determining the price. The bill failed.[36] The treaty system was not as much dead, it turned out, as in hiding. The House didn't end negotiations; it merely demanded a say in them. The agreements enacted after 1871 looked like treaties, walked like treaties, and even quacked like treaties, but they weren't treaties. They were agreements approved by Indians, the Senate, and the House. The Wahpeton-Sisseton negotiations showed how they worked. To get negotiations moving, Cooke authorized payments to Assistant Secretary of the Interior, B. R. Cowen. Whether Cowen was actually paid is uncertain, but negotiations moved forward and Congress authorized a three-man commission to negotiate with the Wahpeton-Sisseton. One of the commissioners was James Smith, Jr., an official of a subsidiary of the Northern Pacific. He, in turn, recommended to Cooke that ex-Indian Agent Benjamin Thompson be put on retainer by the railroad to secure Indian approval. Thompson would get $5,000 when the Indians signed; $5,000 more when the treaty was ratified. Cooke, Smith, and Thompson were acting, or so Cooke persuaded himself, not just for the good of the railroad and the good of the nation, but for the good of the Indians.[37]

Things did not go smoothly. They rarely did for the Northern Pacific, a road never very lucky in its employees. Thompson didn't do it much good, but once hired he was retained because the company feared he could do harm if angered. Still the Indians, under enormous pressure, agreed to a cession. The agreement was submitted to Congress, which substantially altered it. It went back to the Indians for approval when it was, in 1873, caught up in two quarrels. The first was between stalwart Republicans and Mugwumps over the hard feelings left by the 1872 presidential election. This one Cooke, a prominent Republican, managed to finesse. The second was a quarrel between the agent, Moses Adams, also one of the commissioners, and Gabriel Renville and other polygamous tribal leaders.

The quarrel was revealing of other tensions in an imperialism that delegated tasks to private entities. Adams was an agent under the peace policy, which gave control over many reservations to officials appointed by the churches. It was an early faith-based initiative. Adams refused to give tribal leaders either rations or their annual payments due them under treaties until they banished their extra wives. They, in turn, refused to sign the revised agreement. In nineteenth-century American politics monogamy beat polygamy hands down, but it did not necessarily beat the railroads. Cooke, who was himself a devout Evangelical, wrote his brother Harry that the "Secy. of the Interior should order this gentleman, whoever he may be, to treat all the Indians alike (no matter how many wives they have.)"[38] Harry talked to Windom; Windom talked to Secretary Delano, and Secretary Delano wrote Agent Adams. Adams rearranged his priorities. With the ratification of the altered agreement, the Northern Pacific obtained, Cooke claimed, "at once over 5 million acres between the Red

River and the Missouri intact, not an acre of it lost. This of itself is worth a good deal more than the cost of the road on both coasts [and] all the expenditures up to this date to say nothing of our other larger grant on the Pacific and in Minnesota & the completed railroad." It may have been the only good thing that happened to the Northern Pacific in 1873. It was only one on a long list of bad things that happened to Indians.[39]

Still, the end of the treaty system weakened the Indians hand, and Congress decided unilaterally in 1882 to alter the conditions for a Frisco railroad route through the Choctaw nation. The bill actually increased the compensation granted the Indians, but that was not the point. This was simply a unilateral assertion of the power of the United States. There was no treaty authorizing the route. Government claims of eminent domain and not agreements with Indian nations would now determine where railroads ran and where they did not.[40] The United States had never hesitated to coerce Indians, but now it had the legal option of simply ignoring them. The majority of Congress defended the move, sometimes explicitly in the name of expansionism. As a Texas senator proclaimed, "We will not be penned up; we will not be hindered."[41]

The railroads had donned the mantle of American sovereignty and the right of expansion; they had created political conflicts that ultimately undercut the treaty system and increased the leverage of the government vis-a-vis Indian tribes; and all of this makes the story complicated enough, but there is more to it. The story is also about a struggle between corporations, which, depending upon the circumstances, could grind Indians between them or give Indians a chance to play them, and other corporations, off against each other.

Railroad corporations wanted to break Indian power over Indian Territory, but each corporation wanted to do so in ways that would help it and hurt their rivals. There was an inwardness, to use the expressive nineteenth-century term, to these struggles. All was not as it appeared on the surface. Precisely because multiple groups had a stake and a say in expansionism, the issues could not be reduced to the efforts of sovereign state—the United States—to infringe on the rights and territory of semi-sovereign states, the Indian nations. The state was the ultimate arbiter, but the state was subject to conflicting pressures from different railroads, settlers, cattle corporations, and Indians themselves.

Indians were the ultimate losers, but they were not helpless or without allies. The decision in 1882 of the federal government to allow the Frisco to build through Indian Territory on terms other than those negotiated with the Choctaws was a catastrophe for tribal government. Others would follow until the final abolition of the Indian Territory in 1907, but what can be lost in the ultimate tally of defeat was how long it took.[42] In Indian Territory, the Cherokees, Choctaws, Creeks, Seminoles, and Chickasaws were for more than a generation successful in attempts to prevent the railroads from turning Indian Territory into a conventional American Territory and forcing the cession of Indian land to the railroads.

In Indian Territory, the government had potentially given the railroads a vast bonanza, but it was contingent on Indians surrendering their land. The Missouri, Kansas, and Texas Railway, for example, regularly claimed in its annual report that Congress had granted the road a 100-ft. right of way and 4,121,600 acres of land. It even sold bonds whose security was that land. The asterisk in the report noted that this land was "subject to temporary Indian occupancy, under Treaty stipulations." Translated, this meant the land remained Indian land until the Indians ceded it, which no tribe proved willing to do. The railroad, in fact, had no land beyond its right of way except for what the Indian nations, or their citizens, would provide them through lease or other rights of occupancy, or until this land was restored to the public domain by laws that ended Indian rule and made their land part of a standard U.S. territory. Dozens of territorial bills would come before Congress in the 1870s and the 1880s to accomplish this end. The corporations would take an active role in writing some of them.[43]

This land issue made for a complicated politics of expansion. On the surface the interests of the railroads in land grants stood opposed not only to the interests of Indians but also to those of settlers, who preferred an abrogation of Indian rights that restored Indian land to the public domain rather than handing it over to railroads. In fact, the politics of expansion were such that some railroads played a complicated hand. At times the railroads controlled by Jay Gould, which were the first to run across Indian Territory, preferred to protect Indian Territory, even at the expense of their land grants, in order to prevent other roads from breaking their monopoly on north Texas. At other times, when the tide seemed to be running strongly against the Indians, they were ready to abandon the tribes. Settler organizations did at times denounce the railroads as monopolists, but they also forged alliances with the railroads and accepted their funding. The mutual interest of settlers and the non-Gould railroads was in breaking up Indian Territory even if it diverged after that goal was accomplished. The Atlantic and Pacific, the Frisco, and the KATY all had connections with David Payne or other boomers who demanded the opening of Indian Territory to white settlement.[44]

Finally, the tribes were themselves not a united front. Factions within them welcomed the development American railroads would bring no matter what the costs to the Indian nation as a whole. Indian peoples remained remarkably diverse in the late nineteenth century. Many had long experience in dealing with the United States and considerable differences as to the best policy to pursue. There were Indians willing to ally themselves with the railroads and the abolition of Indian Territory.

Elias C. Boudinot was one of those hopelessly flamboyant figures who seem to be utterly of a particular nineteenth-century moment. He was a striking man; people did not forget him. He looked like Wild Bill Hickock, who looked like Buffalo Bill, who looked like George Armstrong Custer: the same handsome face, the same shoulder-length hair, the drooping mustache, the same impassive stare, not at the camera, but slightly away. Except that his hair was not blonde. Boudinot had a New England mother, but he was still a Cherokee Indian. If the competition were not so stiff, he might be ranked among the great scoundrels of the Gilded Age. It was fitting that a Cherokee scoundrel should bear a resemblance to the variety of white scoundrels and showmen who came to personify the West in popular culture.[45]

Boudinot was the son of Elias Boudinot, the editor of the *Cherokee Phoenix*, murdered for his role in the Treaty of New Echota, which had led inexorably to the Trail of Tears. He was the nephew of Stand Watie, the Cherokee who was the last Confederate General to surrender during the Civil War, and he was himself, despite his New England mother and a New England education, a delegate to the Confederate Congress.[46] He came out of the Civil War with a need to recoup his fortune, and he blended business and politics in a familiar Gilded Age manner.

Boudinot argued for the abolition of Indian Territory, treaties, and the special legal status of tribes, and quite characteristically made himself exhibit A. He had once trusted in treaties, he claimed. He had relied on the exemption from U.S. tax laws in Indian Territory provided by the Cherokee Treaty of 1866, but Congress had passed laws in violation of the treaty, the courts had upheld them, and Boudinot had lost his property for back taxes. This had taught him, so he claimed, that treaties were a charade. Sovereignty could not stand against either the U.S. government or the corporations, and the Indians' only hope was the end of Indian governance in Indian Territory, division of their land in severalty, title in fee simple, and citizenship. This was, his opponents countered, a recipe for disaster, and time would prove them right, but Boudinot always claimed that he was acting in the best interests of the Cherokees and other Indian peoples.[47]

Elias C. Boudinot, so much a man of his moment, would also become a familiar type in later American imperial adventures. A man with only a limited following at home, he haunted Washington D.C., sought to hitch himself to American power, and saw in American-induced changes in his homeland a route to both personal wealth and power and, he claimed, the progress of his nation.

Boudinot was charming, well spoken, garrulous, courtly, mendacious, and violent. His tribal opponents, and this included the vast majority of Cherokees, labeled him a traitor and an opportunist, but this did not stop his lobbying for territorial government, railroad grants, and the division of Indian lands in their name. He claimed his life was in danger, and it probably was.[48] Boudinot denied that he was an agent of the railroads, but he had close ties to corporations whose land grants depended on either Indian cessions or the dissolution of Indian Territory.[49] He was involved with the Atlantic and Pacific in the development of Vinita in Indian Territory, about 34 miles from the Missouri border.[50]

Boudinot built a hotel in Vinita, where he felt acutely uncomfortable as people often do when they think their enemies want to kill them. He rented the hotel to a white man. The Cherokees ruled this to be illegal and finally tore the hotel down in 1879. Boudinot sued; Boudinot continued to lobby Congress to turn Indian Territory into a standard American territory with territorial government; Boudinot frequented Washington high society; Boudinot caned Cherokee representatives who denounced him. Being a familiar figure in D.C., he provided railroads with a Cherokee willing to argue against Cherokee attempts to maintain their sovereignty.[51]

The tide was running toward Boudinot in the 1880s and against Indian sovereignty. The various rights-of-way bills in Indian Territory stripped the so-called Five Civilized Tribes as well as the other Indian inhabitants of the territory of the right to decide whether and on what terms the railroads would proceed. The building of the railroads opened the region up to still more corporate activity.[52]

Nineteenth-century railroad corporations remained a mighty engine for smashing apart Indian country and fragmenting it into parcels suitable for white settlement. When Indians faced railroads with a virtual monopoly on transportation through their lands, they could not play them off against other railroads. The Northern Pacific did not want large reservations such as the Great Sioux Reserve, nor did it want small reservations in inconvenient places such as the Puyallup reservation adjoining Tacoma, its terminus. The Union Pacific wanted Indian lands near Fort Hall.[53] The Great Northern wanted land promised to the Umatillas in Washington. In these cases and many more, they used their power and influence to dispossess Indians.

Railroad intellectuals claimed that the new technology was a revolutionary force to which Indians along with everyone else would have to bow. Railroads supposedly carried a new industrial civilization. Charles Nimmo thought "the railroad with its vast possibilities for the advancement of the commercial, industrial, and social interests of the world, ran directly counter to the pre-existing order of things."[54] Theophilus French thought them "the great civilizer of modern times."[55] All peoples would have to yield to railroads, and this may, in a sense, have been true, but this claim to a universal subjection neglected a key issue: Americans owned, built, and operated the trains. They decided where they would go and how they would get there.

As they would overseas, the agents of American expansionism in the western half of North America demanded the breakup of existing social systems that stood in the way of progress, by which most meant market expansion, the spread of Christianity, a movement toward republican government, and a domesticity that replicated the gender roles and behavior that had evolved in the northeastern United States. The existing inhabitants of the lands needed for "progress" could not be left as they were. Americans claimed to act not only for the good of the United States—which they conflated with the good of the human race—but for the particular good of the peoples being stripped of their lands and whose way of life was deemed no longer appropriate for the modern world. These peoples became the objects of uplift. When all the elements of the larger project were aligned, Indians found themselves badly overmatched. But they were not always aligned.

Because railroad corporations in North America formed only one segment of state expansion, tensions between it and other segments gave Indians limited, but real, opportunities to deflect and mitigate American demands. In Arizona and New Mexico, the Zuni, Hopi, and Navajo reservations grew rather than shrank, incorporating lands within railroad land grants that had not yet been surveyed and patented. The railroads were hardly dispossessed; they got valuable lieu lands in return, but Indians were not at their mercy.[56] In actual practice the state was fragmented; the corporations were jealous of each other, the Indian nations were divided, and settler organizations were suspicious of arrangements that delivered land to the railroads as middlemen rather than directly to the settlers.

The cause that aligned corporations, the friends of the Indians, bureaucrats, settler organizations, Congress, and even some Indians most reliably

was the distribution of Indian lands in severalty, or, as it was called, allotment. The government would divide common lands into individual farms,
give title to Indian families, and open up the majority of the remaining
lands to non-Indian settlement. At one sweep, it would widen the reach of
the market, turn Indians to agriculture, increase the traffic and revenue of
railroads, push Indians toward nuclear families, and surround them with
whites whom, supposedly, they would emulate. The market, agriculture,
and nuclear families would, in turn, help in the conversion of Indians to
Christianity.

The man most responsible for making the allotment policy a reality was
Henry Dawes, a leading friend of the Indians, a long-time friend of the
railroads, and the architect of two bills that did more to open up the remnants of Indian country to market penetration, white settlement, corporate exploitation, and programs of "uplift" than the actions of any other
individual. Henry Dawes had many reasons for pushing for the allotment
of Indian reservations, but it is notable that he was a friend of the railroads
who was implicated in the Credit Mobilier scandal and, as a Massachusetts
senator, maintained close ties with railroad and other industrial interests.
Dawes was never just a tool of the railroads in pushing through first the
Dawes Severalty Act of 1887, which provided for the division of reservations in severalty and the selling of most "excess" land after the breakup of
communal holdings. He was a convinced social reformer and a Friend of
the Indian, as such reformers styled themselves. The result of his initiative,
he believed, would be the creation of small farms, but most Indian allotments passed relatively quickly into white hands and the creation, on those
reservations where it was implemented, of impoverished Indian communities living on small remnants of their previous holdings. He was also the
head of the Dawes Commission, which provided for the allotment of the
lands of the Five Civilized Tribes and the end, albeit temporary, of their
tribal governments.[57] The policy of allotment in severalty was as dracon-
ian a case of social reform forced on an outside group—most Indians were
not yet citizens—and with as disastrous consequences as anything in
American history. It was done in the name of capitalist progress, democracy, Christianity and what would now be called family values.[58] In its
moral certainty and its disastrous results, it would resemble later policies
in other parts of the world that people other than Indians would have
cause to regret.

In the larger context of American expansionism and its place in world
affairs, the expansion across the western United States and the subordination of Indian peoples is not a parochial story. Western expansion was

about empire, as much as the American people and many historians would like to treat it as a purely domestic development. As Thomas Bender argues, the creation of an overseas empire in 1898 was not "unthinking or accidental." It had precedents in continental expansion, which was just as conscious.[59] Bender is right to emphasize how much expansion into the West was a state activity and "not wholly the work of private actors." My emphasis here on the role of private actors is meant as an interpretation of the nature of this expansion as a complicated hybrid of government, private, and corporate agents.[60]

Notes

1. Albert K. Weinberg, *Manifest Destiny: A Study of Nationalist Expansionism in American History* (Chicago: Quadrangle Books, 1963, originally published 1935), 6–7.

2. The terminology used by historians of the United States involves a linguistic nationalism that is immediately apparent when the audience for their writing is hemispheric rather than national. Citizens of the United States, to the irritation of other inhabitants of the Americas, claim for themselves the title of Americans. The term is so common in writings by citizens of the United States that it is hard to escape. To use terms such as "citizens of the United States" is awkward, but to use "Americans" to refer to only a portion of the inhabitants of the Americas is deceptive. The issue is even more complicated since native peoples were the group originally termed Americans and now, in colloquial usage, they are distinguished from Americans. They do not become "Americans" until they are conquered and absorbed into the United States. In this article, I will try to avoid using American when I can do so without making the prose jarring and distracting. I will also try to distinguish between Euro-Americans, a term which at times is inaccurate since the actual peoples involved could be of African descent, and native peoples or Native Americans, also referred to as Indians, a time-perpetuated error. My major goal is clarity rather than consistency.

3. See for example, Anders Stephanson, *Manifest Destiny: American Expansion and the Empire of Right* (New York: Hill and Wang, 1995).

4. Thomas R. Hietala, *Manifest Design: Anxious Aggrandizement in Late Jacksonian America* (Ithaca: Cornell University Press, 1985), 270.

5. Weinberg, *Manifest Destiny*, 8.

6. Hietala does devote considerable attention to Indians, but given the focus of his book on the Jacksonian period, his concern is with the antebellum period.

7. Examples of this are numerous. Richard White, *The Middle Ground: Indians, Empires, and Republics in the Great Lakes Region, 1650–1815* (New York: Cambridge University Press, 1991); Alexandra Harmon, *Indians in the Making: Ethnic Relations and Indian Identities around Puget Sound* (Berkeley: University of

California Press, 1998), William McLoughlin, *Cherokee Renascence in the New Republic* (Princeton, N.J.: Princeton University Press, 1986), Theda Perdue, *Slavery and the Evolution of Cherokee Society, 1540–1866* (Knoxville: University of Tennessee Press, 1979), Michael Green, *The Politics of Indian Removal: Creek Government and Society in Crisis* (Lincoln: University of Nebraska Press, 1982), James Brooks, *Captives & Cousins: Slavery, Kinship, and Community in the Southwest Borderlands* (Chapel Hill: University of North Carolina Press, 2002).

8. Gary Anderson, *The Conquest of Texas: Ethnic Cleansing in the Promised Land, 1820–1875* (Norman: University of Oklahoma Press, 2005), Andres Resendez, *Changing National Identities at the Frontier: Texas and New Mexico, 1800–1850* (New York: Cambridge University Press, 2005), Gregory Dowd, *Spirited Resistance: The North American Indian Struggle for Unity, 1745–1815* (Baltimore, MD.: Johns Hopkins University Press, 1992), and Gregory Dowd, *War under Heaven: Pontiac, the Indian Nations, & the British Empire* (Baltimore, MD.: Johns Hopkins University Press, 2002).

9. This is true not only of Weinberg, *Manifest Destiny,* but Stephanson, *Manifest Destiny*; Hietala, *Manifest Design,* and Norman Graebner, *Empire on the Pacific; a Study in American Continental Expansion* (New York: Ronald Press Co., 1955).

10. Walter Lafeber, *The New Empire: An Interpretation of American Expansion* (Ithaca: Cornell University Press, 1963), 11.

11. Nathan J. Citinio, "Turner, Bemis, and the Western Roots of American Empire," unpublished paper. Thomas Bender, *A Nation among Nations: America's Place in World History* (New York: Hill and Wang, 2006).

12. Citino, "Roots of American Empire," 2–3.

13. See "The Global Frontier: Comparative History and the Frontier-Borderlands Approach," in *Explaining the History of American Foreign Relations,* ed. Michael J. Hogan and Thomas Paterson, 2nd ed. (New York: Cambridge University Press, 2004), 194–211.

14. Citino, "Roots of American Empire," 3. H. Craig Miner and William E. Unrau, *The End of Indian Kansas* (Lawrence: The Regents Press of Kansas, 1978); H. Craig Miner, *The Corporation and the Indian* (Columbia, Mo.: University of Missouri Press, 1976); Paul Wallace Gates, *Fifty Million Acres: Conflicts over Kansas Land Policy, 1854–90* (Ithaca: Cornell University Press, 1954), 137–39.

15. Arthur M. Johnson and Barry E. Supple, *Boston Capitalists and Western Railroads: A Study in the Nineteenth Century Railroad Investment Process* (Cambridge: Harvard University Press, 1967), 197. For other accounts of Congressional action see Maury Klein, *Union Pacific: Birth of a Railroad, 1862–93* (Garden City, New York: Doubleday, 1987), 13–16; David Howard Bain, *Empire Express: Building the First Transcontinental Railroad* (New York: Viking, 1999), 115, 141–43.

16. For policies during the Civil War, Heather Cox Richardson, *The Greatest Nation of the Earth: Republican Economic Policies During the Civil War* (Cambridge: Harvard University Press, 1997), 170–72, 175, 178–180. Dodge to Scott, Jan. 12, 1874, Letterbooks, Texas Pacific Railroad, Box 160, Grenville M. Dodge Papers, MS 98, State Historical Society of Iowa, 72–73, 77.

17. Adams to Moorfield Storey, Feb. 2, 1885, Pres. Office, Outgoing Correspondence, v. 27, series 2, r. 23, Union Pacific Railroad, Nebraska State Historical Society.

18. For policies during the Civil War, Heather Cox Richardson, *The Greatest Nation of the Earth: Republican Economic Policies During the Civil War* (Cambridge: Harvard University Press, 1997), 170–72, 175, 178–180. Dodge to Scott, Jan. 12, 1874, Letterbooks, Texas Pacific Railroad, Box 160, Grenville M. Dodge Papers, MS 98, State Historical Society of Iowa, 72–73, 77. Ellis P. Oberholtzer, *Jay Cooke: Financier of the Civil War,* 2 vols. (Philadelphia: George W. Jacobs, 1907), 156.

19. *Report, Directors of the Missouri, Kansas, & Texas Railway Co., Late Union Pacific Railway Company Southern Branch, 1872–73* (sic) (New York, 1872), 19, 24; Miner, *Corporation and the Indian,* 44–47; L.U. Reavis, "The Atlantic and Pacific Railway," *The Inland Monthly* (November 1872), 568.

20. L.U. Reavis, "An International Railway to the City of Mexico, An Address by L.U. Reavis" (St. Louis, Mo.: Printed by Woodward, Tiernan & Hale, 1879) *Pamphlets Pertaining to the Railroads of Mexico,* v. 2, no. 10, American Philosophical Society, Philadelphia.

21. George Earl Church to Plumb, June 11, 1872, Box 2, f. 21, Edward L. Plumb Papers, M 149, Stanford University Archives.

22. David Pletcher, *Rails, Mines, and Progress: Seven American Promoters in Mexico, 1867–1911* (Ithaca: Cornell University Press, 1958), 48. Plumb to George E. Church, Jan. 27, 1872, Box 2, f. 20, Edward L. Plumb Papers, M 149. Copia para el Sov. Ministro de Hacienda de las Bases presentadas informalmente al Ministro de Fomento de la República de México, por Don Eduardo Lee Plumb en representación de la "Compañía de Ferrocarril Ynternacional de Texas" . . . Abril de 1872. Edward L. Plumb Papers, Box 2 f. 20, M 149.

23. Pletcher, *Rails, Mines, and Progress,* 80.

24. Terrell, Alexander Watkins, "The Cormorant, the Commune and Labor, Speech of Alexander W. Terrell at the Opera House in Austin Texas, April 8, 188?" (Austin: Warner & Draughon, Steam Print.), 8; James F. Hudson, *The Railways and the Republic* (New York: Harper & Brothers, 1886), 10. James A. Ward, "Image and Reality: The Railway Corporate-State Metaphor," *The Business History Review,* 55, No. 4 (Winter 1981), 491–516.

25. Larson, *Bonds of Enterprise,* 173.

26. Alexandra Villard de Borchgrave and John Cullen, *Villard: The Life and Times of an American Titan* (New York: Doubleday, 2001), 326.

27. Huntington to Stanford, Feb. 11, 1881, *Collis P. Collis P. Huntington Papers, 1856–1901,* Outgoing correspondence (microfilm, 115 reels, Microfilming Corporation of America, 1978–1979), vol. 28, reel 6, series 2.

28. C. J. Hillyer, "Atlantic and Pacific and Indian Territory" (Washington, D.C.: McGill & Witherow, 1871), 5–6, copy bound with *Atlantic and Pacific R.R.'s Reports,* Stanford University Library.

29. John Benston, "To the American Public," Fort Gibson, I.T., Jan. 12, 1874, Graff 234, Newberry Library.

30. Miner and Unrau, *The End of Indian Kansas,* 47–48; Gates, *Fifty Million Acres,* 137–39.

31. Miner and Unrau, *The End of Indian Kansas,* 27–34.

32. Gates, *Fifty Million Acres,* 153–193, and Miner and Unrau, *The End of Indian Kansas,* 116–19, quote, 116.

33. Miner and Unrau, *The End of Indian Kansas,* 121–132; Gates, *Fifty Million Acres,* 194–229.

34. Francis Paul Prucha, *The Great Father: The United States Government and the American Indians,* 2 vols. (Lincoln: University of Nebraska Press, 1984), 1: 527–33.

35. Cooke to Windom, July 20, 1871, Northern Pacific, Letters No. 1 (Letterbook) Jan. 19, 1870 Sept. 27, 1871, Private Letters Jay Cooke, Jay Cooke Collection, Historical Society of Pennsylvania.

36. Duane Swanson, "The Northern Pacific Railroad and the Sisseton-Wahpeton Sioux: A Case in Land Acquisition," M.A. Thesis, University of Delaware, 1972, 24, 27, 29, 31, 33–36.

37. Swanson, "Northern Pacific and Sisseton-Wahpeton," 41, 43–44, 48–54; George Becker and James Smith, Jr. to Cooke, Sept. 5, 1872, Jay Cooke Collection, Correspondence, September 1872; Jay Cooke to Brother Harry, May 24, 1872, Cooke Collection, #148, May 1872; Cooke to Cass, March 17, 1873, Cooke to B.F. Wade, March 22, 1873; Cooke to Major Benj. Thompson, March 22, 1873; Letterbooks, Jay Cooke Papers, HSP.

38. Swanson, "The Northern Pacific Railroad," 61–64. Cooke to Professor Carey (?), March 10, 1873, Cooke to Bro. Harry, March 14, 1873, Letterbooks, Jay Cooke Papers, HSP 148.

39. Cooke to Wetmore, May 23, 1873, Letterbooks, Jay Cooke Papers, HSP.

40. Miner, *The Corporation and the Indian,* 101, 105.

41. Ibid., 108.

42. For aftermath, ibid., 110–111.

43. Speech of Elias Boudinot of the Cherokee Nation, Delivered at Vinita, Indian Territory, August 29, 1874 (St. Louis, MO.: Barns & Beynon, 1874), 1; Argument of Col. E.C. Boudinot Before the Committee on Territories, Jan. 29,

1878 (Alexandria, VA: G.H. Ramey & Son, 1878), 1–3. For land grant, Report, *Directors of the Missouri, Kansas, & Texas Railway Co, Late Union Pacific Railway Company-Southern Branch, 1872–73* (sic) (New York, 1872), 19.

44. Miner, *The Corporation and the Indian*, 97, 106, 114–15.

45. There is a picture of Boudinot in *In Memoriam: Elias Cornelious Boudinot* (Chicago: Rand McNally & Co., c. 1890), frontispiece. The best biography of him is James W. Parins, *Elias Cornelius Boudinot: A Life on the Cherokee Border* (Lincoln: University of Nebraska Press). Parins has done by far the most research and tries, in a limited fashion, to rehabilitate Boudinot by contextualizing him, 1–2.

46. Dewey Whitsett Hodges, "Colonel E.C. Boudinot and His Influence on Oklahoma History," M.A. Thesis, University of Oklahoma, 1929, 5–8, 18.

47. Boudinot outlined his position in, Speech of Elias Boudinot of the Cherokee Nation, Delivered at Vinita, Indian Territory, August 29, 1874 (St. Louis, MO.: Barns & Beynon, 1874), Elias C. Boudinot, The Memorial of Elias C. Boudinot to the Congress of the United States (Washington, 1877), Speech of Elias C. Boudinot, A Cherokee Indian, Delivered Before the House Committee on Territories, Feb. 7, 1872 in Behalf of a Territorial Government for the Indian Territory, in Reply to Wm. P. Ross . . . (Washington: McGill & Witherow, 1872). Parins, *Boudinot*, 85–205.

48. Miner, *The Corporation and the Indian*, 46. "Speech of Elias C. Boudinot . . . at Vinita," 1. Argument of Col. E. C. Boudinot Before the Committee on Territories, Jan. 29, 1878, 1–3, Parins, *Boudinot*, 109–152.

49. "Speech of Elias C. Boudinot . . . at Vinita," 1. Argument of Col. E. C. Boudinot Before the Committee on Territories, Jan. 29, 1878, 1–3; Miner, *The Corporation and the Indian*, 20–29, 42.

50. Miner, *The Corporation and the Indian*, 44–46; Boudinot, "Speech of Elias C. Boudinot . . . at Vinita," 13.

51. For a summary of Boudinot's life that certainly paints a brighter picture of him, see Hodges, "Colonel E. C. Boudinot and His Influence on Oklahoma History." For lobbying, Argument of Col. E. C. Boudinot before the Committee on Territories, Jan. 29, 1878. For Boudinot, railroads, and attempt to organize the territory, Tom Holm, "Indian Lobbyists: Cherokee Opposition to the Allotment of Tribal Lands," *American Indian Quarterly* 5 (May 1979), 116–18. Parins, *Boudinot*, 153–174.

52. Miner, *The Corporation and the Indian*, 115.

53. See C. F. Woerishoffer to Villard, June 1 ?, 1881, Mss. 8893, v. 719, b. 38, f. 267. Henry Villard Papers, 1862–1928, Baker Library, Harvard University. Gregory Smoak, *Ghost Dances and Identity: Prophetic Religion and American Indian Ethnogenesis in the Nineteenth Century* (Berkeley: University of California Press, 2006), 161–62.

54. Joseph Nimmo, Jr., *Railroad Federations and the Relation of the Railroads to Commerce* (Washington, D.C.: GPO, 1885), 8.

55. *Report of the Auditor of Railroad Accounts,* House Ex. Doc. 1, 46th Congress, 2nd Session, 1911, 17–18.

56. For the complicated politics of such exchanges, see William S. Greever, *Arid Domain, the Santa Fe Railway and Its Western Land Grant* (Stanford: Stanford University Press, 1954), 80–102.

57. For Dawes, corporations, and Credit Mobilier, see George Ward, Lewiston Mills, to H. L. Dawes, Nov. 28, 1866; Dawes to Ward, Nov. 29, 1866 (two letters), Receipt $195.33, Feb. 10, 1868, Dawes to My Ever Dear Wife, June 11, 1868, receipt. June 11, 1868, Ames to Dawes, Oct. 30, 1871, Dawes to Ames, Nov. 19, 1872, Ames to Dawes, Oct. 18, 1872, James Garfield to Dawes, March 23, 1873, Henry L. Dawes Papers, Box 37, Credit Mobilier, Manuscript Division, Library of Congress. For Dawes Severalty Act, see Prucha, *Great Father,* 2: 666–671.

58. Bender, *A Nation Among Nations,* 213, 217. Lafeber, *The New Empire.*

59. Bender, *A Nation Among Nations,* 183, 190, 219.

60. Ibid., 191, 220.

9

Afterword

Biorn Maybury-Lewis

My father and co-editor of this book, the social anthropologist David H. P. Maybury-Lewis, concluded his 44-year career at Harvard in 2004, retiring to deal with the increasingly strong symptoms of the illness that was debilitating him. Shortly after becoming *emeritus*, during 2005, he successfully worked to bring together in Cambridge the scholars who have contributed the chapters included in this volume. At that time, I happened to be serving as Executive Director of Harvard's David Rockefeller Center for Latin American Studies (DRCLAS) under whose auspices, two years before my arrival at DRCLAS, the original conference proposal on which this book is based was approved and came into being.

David had planned to hold the conference in Santiago, Chile, at DRCLAS's facilities there, but his increasing physical problems precluded lengthy air travel. Instead, he and the contributors to this volume gathered together in Cambridge, Massachusetts, for an extraordinarily lively two-day conference in early 2006. Energized, we returned home from Harvard to write our chapters in late 2006 and early 2007.

This effort to organize the conference leading to this edited volume was unfortunately David's last project as a professional scholar. Following the conference and after a brave battle with the illness, my father died in December of 2007. The conference was the culmination of his life-long effort to address the theoretical and historical questions that permeate this book. For years he grappled with the meaning of what he termed, since the 1970s, "the Second Conquest": the penetration, by the descendants of the original European conquerors, "of the rest of the hinterlands of the Americas" during the nineteenth and into early twentieth centuries; that is, those territories not overrun during the first phases of colonization in the Americas. How did this process come about? What prompted the Europeans to move further into various interiors, eliminating or subjugating indigenous peoples, their territories, and their ways of life? What were the justifying ideologies underpinning these usually bloody and devastating (to the Indians) processes? What was the range of responses of the indigenous peoples? What did these processes have in common, and what were their specificities? Could we group them accurately under the rubric of the Second Conquest, or as products of an ideology of Manifest Destiny, or were they too different to group together in one analytical construct?

Upon conclusion of the works contained here, David and I were meant to write this afterword in an effort to assess these questions in light of the research our colleagues have offered in this volume and his years of reflection. But now it falls to me to prepare "our" afterword. I have chosen, under the circumstances, to put aside the critique and instead write the afterword as both a short memoir and an explanation for why David dedicated himself for many years to the themes of this book. This concluding essay revolves, then, around four vignettes illustrative of my father's life and his life-long intellectual passions and preoccupations. I hope they will add a dimension of meaning to this book that our readers will both understand and find useful as the context of this book's creation.

Vignette 1. *The Old World: Racism, culturalism, elitism, colonialism, globalization*

On May 5, 1929, David Henry Peter Maybury-Lewis was born in Hyderabad, Sindh, under the British Raj in what was then British India. The area is now in contemporary Pakistan. His father, Sydney Alan Maybury-Lewis, known as Maybury to his friends and family, was a formidable civil engineer who led teams of engineers and workers to build what the English call "barrages" and the Americans "dams" in the Sindhi desert. They rendered that dry countryside into farmland. Our family attic contains extraordinary pictures, dating from the 1920s, of Maybury and my grandmother, Constance (Connie), his demure wife, surrounded by their Pathan tribal body guards, armed to the teeth, camels at their sides, somewhere out in the desert, while doing work for the British civil administration. Connie too was a daughter of the British Empire, born to the family of a soldier who had traveled the world on campaigns defending the interests of England. Connie, on one occasion in my childhood, told me hair-raising stories of when she and her family, during the Boxer Rebellion in China, were surrounded for weeks by Chinese intent on either killing them or throwing them out of the country! Father himself was born in the midst of another upheaval, on the eve of the Great Depression.

A distinguished engineer, my grandfather Maybury would rise to the position of chief British functionary in charge of all steel allocation in the Indian subcontinent during World War II. The British army gave him the

military rank of general. David always wondered why the British bureaucracy, cold-hearted and bloody-minded though it often was, was not more
corrupt in those years. Maybury too, playing a part in this civil service,
apparently never accepted any bribes from the numerous moneyed interests and maharajahs needing steel in wartime India. David often remi-
nisced about this experience, asking himself and me what it was that kept
the British bureaucratic imperative relatively "clean" and efficient; the
norm in many developing areas, after all, was something different.

The puzzle of Maybury's (and his colleagues') professional attitude was
particularly acute given the notable racism which he and his family suffered. Maybury, you see, was the son of an Indian mother and British
father. "Port Out Starboard Home: POSH"—a word that has entered the
English language—was the shorthand for the preferred cabins, on the
shady side of the vessel, on the ocean ride to and from India, the British
Crown jewel. Civil servants in the British Raj, like Maybury, were at regular intervals given round-trip ocean passages to England for themselves
and their families to visit home on extended holidays. But because of
grandfather's mixed heritage, this privilege was not part of his benefits. He
paid out of pocket for his and his family's costly trips home to England, as
well as tuition for the English boarding schools of his three daughters and
his only son and youngest child, David.

My father went to England to begin boarding school at the age of eight,
his sisters even younger, in order to become proper English citizens. The
sacrifice of these children, months away from their parents, trying to
become essentially a part of England's upwardly mobile professional
classes, was a cause of some quiet suffering to the whole family. "Stiff
upper lips" come to mind. Meanwhile, they were obliged to manage, in
countless ways, the racist and culturalist snubs endemic to the British
bureaucracy and society at large. Fortunately for Maybury and Connie's
children, they were all reasonably intelligent and good-looking, though "a
little colonial-looking" for mid-twentieth century English sensibilities.

David distinguished himself as an English public school student and
athlete at King's College in Canterbury. By his late teens, he had become a
European class quarter-miler in track and field, as well as a keen rugby
player.[1] He went to Cambridge University on a full scholarship, where he
concentrated in modern languages as an undergraduate. By the time he
was through studying languages in the late 1950s, he dominated, quite flu-
ently, English, French, German, Danish, Spanish, Portuguese, Russian,
Shavante, and Sherente. He probably knew Hindi and Urdu as a small
child also but never made much of this.

On one of his earliest trips to Brazil, David earned a master's degree in São Paulo. He went on to Oxford to take his D.Phil. in Social Anthropology in the late 1950s. He was curious about the classic anthropological/philosophical problematic of "Us" versus "the Other": complementary opposites. He became fascinated with developing areas and, while living in the midst of the Cold War, harbored a longing for adventure and the exotic. He himself *was* an exotic, though trained thoroughly, for better and for worse, as a Britisher. This is why he decided to head off to Brazil to face an extremely challenging South American research project.

Vignette 2. *The New World: Racism, culturalism, elitism, colonialism, modernization, globalization, dictatorship, the Cold War*

David's first encounters with the Americas were not in the United States, where he would make his permanent home, but in Brazil. He first went to São Paulo with his young Danish wife, my mother Elsebet (or "Pia"), at a moment when Brazil still remained under the sway of the great leader Getúlio Vargas. Vargas was, remarkably, elected president of Brazil (1951–1954) in a fair election *after* the collapse of his Estado Novo dictatorship (1938–1945), only to die by his own hand, apparently overwhelmingly frustrated by the contradictory national and international pressures on the direction of the Brazilian political economy.[2] I remember father telling me of the great growing roar of the crowd that he heard outside of my parents' modest apartment, in São Paulo, on the day that Getúlio committed suicide. With the dramatic figure of Vargas gone, a new era began in Brazil, eventually dominated by the quintessential modernizer, President Juscelino Kubitschek.

Kubitschek vowed to achieve "50 years of development in 5" during his presidency (1956–1961), which featured prominently the construction of the city of Brasília. Brasília would become Brazil's new capital in 1960 and, equally important, open Brazil's interior, pulling the country's energy and what critical observers term "developmentalism" inland from its traditional pattern of hugging the Atlantic coast. The consequences for Brazil's indigenous peoples would be dire.

It was during this time, in the mid 1950s, that my parents came to Brazil to obtain authorization from the Brazilian authorities to study Gê tribal societies in almost inaccessible Central Brazil, in Mato Grosso, Goiás, and western Maranhão. They encountered enormously time-consuming bureaucratic problems with the Brazilian government as they sought permits to achieve their prime research goal: to enter the interior and visit the

Shavante Indians whose language was of the Gê linguistic family. The Shavante had been "pacified" by the Brazilian authorities in the mid 1940s,
after almost two centuries of running battles with frontier outposts of
Brazilian civilization. The Brazilian government, perhaps understandably,
has always been leery of potential foreign meddling among the indigenous
minorities of the nation, and my parents were no exception to this bureaucratic stance. They encountered innumerable roadblocks in their petitions
to the federal authorities to go and live with the Indians to conduct fieldwork. Eventually, they succeeded, obtaining permission to visit with the
relatively acculturated Sherente Indians, whose culture and language were
close to those of the Shavante, having, in the previous century, been one
and the same people before the Shavante had separated from the Sherente
when they moved westward across the Araguaia River.

David picked up the Sherente language during this first phase and
steeled himself, along with Pia, for the daunting task of going on to visit
the Shavante who, they were told, were much more *brabo*: naked
hunter/gatherers with a reputation for lethal truculence. The Shavante
lived mainly along the banks of a Mato Grosso river know as the Rio das
Mortes, the river of the dead, a macabre name given because of the missionaries who had gone up to convert the Indians only to be murdered and
thrown in the das Mortes' clear, cool waters to float back to where they
came from.

It was at that time that a baby came into the picture: yours truly, born in
March of 1957. Father and mother took a calculated risk: taking a baby to
a faraway interior of Central Brazil posed risks to their child. Yet any human
society can understand that a man who comes with a woman and a baby is
so vulnerable that he is unlikely to present much of a threat. As in all
research projects involving humans—who are quite normally "researching
the researcher" to gauge his/her intentions—David and Pia decided that the
three of us would more likely disarm the tough Shavante than father alone.
So we headed off to Central Brazil in 1958, where father and mother would
work for 18 months with the Indians and with me in tow: literally hunting
and gathering with them, going on trek, inhabiting their mobile hunting
camps, and "going Indian" temporarily, as David gathered his D.Phil. material for Oxford's Department of Social Anthropology.[3]

When David and Pia were finally able to secure the proper permits to go
into the interior to conduct research on Brazil's frontier, they would travel
by boat, on foot, on horseback, and on what the Brazilians call *teco-tecos*:
mono-propeller aircraft, sometimes private and sometimes of the Forças
Aéreas Brasileiras, the Brazilian Air Force. Many years later my parents

commented that the Brazilian Air Force officers who flew these regular, small aircraft flights to Central Brazil were some of the nicest and most competent people that they had the pleasure of working with. The officers knew the interior, they loved their country, they had a mission of service to Brazil's remote outposts, they took pride in helping foreign researchers like David and Pia on their crazy but somehow important endeavor, and they felt a part of the project to develop Brazil properly. The officers were, on the whole, respected by the Indians and the frontiersmen whom they served.

Similarly, when we returned to Brazil's interior in 1963, this time able to travel overland in a four-wheel drive vehicle to revisit the Sherente Indians, I remember another telling incident directly relevant to the military. We had stopped, inevitably, near the new Brazilian capital of Brasília, where my father, once again, was out dealing with a bureaucratic matter. My mother and I sat in the car awaiting his return, when we saw an irate man with a rolled up newspaper in hand, yelling at a military policeman, "I want to talk to the President!" he exclaimed repeatedly. He refused to leave, waved his arm and paper around, and made a scene. The military policeman—armed with an automatic rifle, clad in a spiffy uniform, and following him around—obviously did not know what to do. He let the man rant until he finally lost his momentum and wandered off. My mother remarked, still in the spirit of the 1950s, that "this is a country that still has hope since the police won't use force in a situation like this!"

Times, of course, changed with the intensification of the Cold War, the conflagration in Vietnam, the unfolding Cuban Revolution, the pending U.S. invasion of the Dominican Republic (1965), and the installation of military rule in Brazil in 1964: a dictatorship that would last until 1985. Brazil's almost euphoric "can do" civic spirit of the 1950s crumbled, ushering in an era of top-down authoritarian developmentalism of the military and its civilian elite and United States allies. This in turn was the political context of the anti-government guerrilla campaigns, emerging in the mid 1960s, and the military government-sponsored human rights abuses of the late 1960s, 1970s, and 1980s that repressed the opposition.

By 1968, David had secured his position and tenure at Harvard's Social Anthropology department and was engaged in leading two major projects: the Harvard Central Brazil project in which soon-to-be distinguished Brazilian and American graduate students and professors worked on a comparative study of all of the Gê language group cultures of Central Brazil, and a Ford Foundation-supported effort to establish U.S.-style graduate programs, first at the Federal University of Rio de Janeiro and second, late in the 1960s and early in the 1970s, at the Federal University of Pernambuco in Brazil's northeast. While he was working on the Rio project, we lived in an apartment in Copacabana for a year.

Copacabana, in the late 1960s, was a sun-splashed oceanside area with none of the crime and much less of the pollution that now besets it and, indeed, the entire city. When we were not in school, mother would walk with my brother Anthony and me to gather sea shells on the beach in the days before completion of the landfill that extended Avenida Atlântica, the oceanside highway going up and down Copacabana beach. We and everyone else swam in remarkably clean ocean waves in those days. I remember even paddling within feet of penguins, swept northward by South Atlantic storms from Patagonia.

This idyll was punctured for me, as an 11-year-old in 1968, when I returned with mother and brother, late one morning, to our home near the beach on a sweltering summer day to discover my father, in swim trunks, on his home office floor poring over a large stack of books. I asked him what he was doing. He looked really concerned and showed me the books. They were by Marx, Marxists, and about Marxist theory. Father was not a Marxist, but throughout his career, of course, he had carefully addressed himself and his students to the Marxist literature, particularly in the 1960s and 1970s. These volumes were part of his pedagogy at the National Museum where he was teaching at the Federal University of Rio de Janeiro's graduate anthropology program. He had co-founded this program with his life-long friend and colleague, Professor Roberto Cardoso de Oliveira.[4] But the world and Brazil had changed. Police, secret police, and thugs related to the government were regularly attacking scholars and students whom they suspected of being with the clandestine underground movements to liberate Brazil from the U.S.-backed military dictatorship.

My father, feeling understandably vulnerable as graduate programs around Brazil were being watched, with students and faculty occasionally "disappearing," was spending a Saturday afternoon agonizing over whether or not he should find a hiding place for his books. He eventually decided, I think correctly, that it would be wiser to have the "red books" out in the open rather than hidden should the military police decide to pay us an unexpected "visit." At that time, in the late 1960s, they were less likely than they had been when we first visited the new capital in 1963 "to not know what to do." The hopes and optimism of the 1950s were long gone, and the late-century paranoia and low-intensity warfare had set in, with severe consequences for all. As for the Indians, the developmentalism of the 1950s was a pattern of rural policy-making that the military embraced wholeheartedly, making the Indians suffer even more.

This developmentalist policy-making that runs historically rough shod over peasantries and indigenous peoples in Brazil is a constant in contemporary Brazilian history. Starting with Kubitschek in the late 1950s, through the military regime from 1964–1985, and on through the relatively conservative presidencies of the civilian New Republic beginning in 1985, this pattern of unthinking developmentalism is now ironically also embraced by the Workers Party and the presidency of Luis Inácio Lula da Silva. All regimes, from the political right to the political left, agree, through their actions at least, that Indians and peasantries are to be "inevitably" shoved aside in favor of policies favoring elite economic interests and militarist imperatives.[5]

Vignette 3. *The Changing New World: Globalization, capitalism, culturalism, developmentalism, the end of "tradition"*

Diachronic comparative history is only interesting in the span of relatively short human lives because of the lightning-fast change in Brazilian and Latin American studies. Unfortunately, change has had dramatically negative consequences for previous social formations, particularly those of indigenous and peasant peoples in the Central and South American hinterlands. But the manifestations of the assaults on traditional cultural patterns are by no means exclusive to the rural areas. Two key cultural phenomena in urban Rio de Janeiro, and my father's reaction to them, are examples of this point. They reveal his attitude to what in the social sciences is generally known as "the passing of tradition." I submit that this is one of the most important reasons why David organized this book. To be sure, David was not anti-modern. After all, his life and that of his family had ridden waves of modernization from China, to India, to the Americas. However, what has been passing for modernization in late-century Latin America is more often than not a pastiche of imported cultural patterns coupled with the breakdown of public order as a function of rampant drug trafficking and violence: a norm in much of the region following years of repression and dictatorship followed by weak, often deeply indebted democratic regimes unable, or unwilling, to attenuate Latin America's inequalities.[6]

In 1968, while we were living in Rio de Janeiro, we had time to enjoy the unique culture of Brazil, particularly as it manifested itself in public spaces in that now truly tragic city. New Year's Eve, *Ano Bom*, for example, is a traditional celebration of the Afro-religious goddess, Iemanjá: the goddess of the sea. All along the six kilometers of Copacabana's white sandy beach, literally millions of New Year's Eve revelers, for the most part dressed all in white, the traditional garb for paying respects to Iemanjá, would arrive with bouquets of flowers in hand to sacrifice in the breakers while awaiting the midnight fireworks. Meanwhile, in candle-lit circles up and down the length of Copacabana, Afro-Brazilian Candomblé rituals were taking place.

As a child, I remember the fascination I felt walking around these Candomblé spectacles, on New Year's Eve, with my mother and father. Hundreds of candles would illuminate the swirling dancers. A leader, normally a man, known as a Pai de Santo, would be at the center of each circle, surrounded by white-clad men and women, mostly Afro-Brazilian. But there were also others from Brazil's racial rainbow, singing, clapping, swaying and chanting rhythmically with the drums. We would watch the leader, smoking a cigar, with many bead necklaces around his neck, wander around the center of the gathering until one of his fellows, man or woman, would become, as they say, possessed by one of the spirits: *quando baixa o santo*. The leader would then ceremoniously go to the one possessed and place a cigar in the possessed one's mouth as he or she convulsed, sobbed, yelped, or moved about wildly, with hair and arms going in every direction, propped up and supported by one or two fellows, manifesting the presence of one of the gods. It was mysterious and moving. Adding to the drama was the fact that there were countless circles of Candomblé all up and down the beach engaged in similar celebratory rites. The beach's focus was theirs. We all were mesmerized, believers or not.

Twenty years later, in the late 1980s, I was conducting research for my own Ph.D. dissertation on rural labor in Brazil. My immediate family and I lived once again in Copacabana, for a little over two years. It was a kind of homecoming for me, using Rio as a base to travel all over Brazil by bus, car, and airplane. David and Pia came to Rio to visit on one of the New Year's and Christmas holidays. Of course, they went to the beach with us to celebrate what we thought would be the rite of Iemanjá, the one that we had grown to know and respect. What we found would shock us all profoundly.

The Candomblé circles were still there, all right, but the beach and the focus of the celebration was no longer theirs. Instead, Brazil's omnipresent Rede Globo television network, with its quarter-century long hand-in-glove relationship with the military dictatorship, and with its *modernizing* ideological ethos and slavish devotion to all things North American, had now won the rights "to produce" the New Year's celebration on Copacabana beach before the midnight fireworks. Instead of allowing everyone to focus on the traditional Candomblé, Rede Globo had installed sequentially a series of mammoth mountains of loudspeakers along the beach through which the network piped in deafening popular music. And, following its now well known impulse, most of the music was North American—in the midst of the celebration of Iemanjá!

I remember David walking along the beach with a pained smile on his face, nonplussed at the music and syrupy DJ's voice booming, as if he no longer knew this country which he had been studying, by then, for over thirty-five years. When a recorded hit of the great Tina Turner, of Ike and Tina fame, came across the loudspeakers right after midnight to celebrate the apotheosis of the New Year's celebration, he asked me, "Can we go back to your place now?" as if to say to me, it is now definitively over . . . We were witnessing a triumph that, of course, had nothing to do with poor Tina Turner and her struggles and triumphs, but the ushering in of a dictatorial un-Brazilian ideology along with the quashing of something important and profoundly Brazilian. Technological fascism, dictatorship, neocolonial cultural domination: the change was unmistakable.

In a similar pattern, in 1968 my parents had dragged me along, as a sleepy child, to witness the famous Rio de Janeiro samba schools as they danced through the night, 4,000 members strong each, floats, drum corps and all, down Avenida Presidente Getúlio Vargas in Rio de Janeiro's center. I remember three telling details. Although the lead singer's amplified voice, attached to a primitive truck-borne loud speaker system, warbled noticeably, you could actually hear the dancers' voices sing each samba school's thematic song. Mysteriously, you could also hear all of the participants' dancing shoes "shush, shush, shush" along in time with the samba rhythm; a wave of sound I shall never forget. One felt a profound human element, as the people went by, because one could hear their voices and see and hear their dancing. The bad sound system was a trivial detail, particularly when the world-class drum corps—typically 400 strong—came by. At about five o'clock in the morning, mother, father, brother, and I emerged from the grand stands along the Avenida into the streets of Rio, to be swallowed up by a sea of street revelers all too dancing in rhythm. David swayed into the crowd and was enveloped by people of every color, as he and we danced our way home, safe in the immense solidarity of Rio's street Carnaval of the late 1960s, leaving me with an indelible memory of something unique.

Pia and David returned to Rio in 1988 to find the Carnaval celebration recently transferred from Avenida Presidente Vargas to the Sambódromo, a modernist half-mile long venue especially prepared for the annual samba school celebrations. In many ways and from a modernizing perspective, the Sambadrome represented an upgrade over the grandstands, electronic sound problems, and amateurism of the samba celebration on Avenida Getúlio Vargas that had preceded it. But the new venue lent itself, first and foremost, to Rede Globo and the other television production teams. The dancers, their voices, and quite personal participation were relegated to a secondary plane as the overwhelming new sound system, the production values of the designers, the TV cameras' zoom-in possibilities for stars and beauties, and the show for TV all took over the primacy of the occasion in a pattern similar to what had happened to the Afro-Brazilian ritual at Copacabana Beach at New Year's. Carnaval, twenty years later, was also no longer a street celebration outside of the samba school spectacle. With the excesses of violence and accompanying fear, the street party into which David and our family had been swept up in 1968 was over. Perhaps forever.

Sound systems, production values, and TV had won the culture war against the cultural patterns of a gentler recent past, while Rio's authority had degenerated from being the leadership center of Brazil.[7] The city's public authorities, as is widely known now, effectively divided municipal power with drug gangs on every street and hillside. Fear, violence, and modernity, in all their perverse interactive glory, had taken hold. And David, though by no means a reactionary or traditionalist, was a pained observer of this "passing of tradition" insofar as what replaced it was a narrower and paler reflection of imported culture. Meanwhile the Indians were under assault, it seemed, everywhere.

Vignette 4. *The Changing New and Old Worlds, Cultural Survival, passing the baton, the Indians*

Pia and David returned to Cambridge from Brazil in the early 1970s, completing what would turn out to be their last extended stay overseas. But they continued to worry about the developmentalism going on in Brazil's interiors and its devastating impact on the Indians. Father and his colleagues sought ways through which they might influence those in a position to make positive change. He went to Washington, for example, to speak with the senators charged with funding the World Bank as the Bank was going about financing the Polonoroeste Project in the southwestern Amazonian Brazilian state of Rondônia. He argued that sooner or later the Bank would be saddled with the negative publicity of devastated indigenous communities and forests razed to the ground if it did not take into consideration their land, cultural, and human rights as well as the environmental impact of Bank policies. Though the Polonoroeste Project was partially blocked for a time, the Brazilian government and the Bank went ahead anyway, with the negative results occurring exactly as David had warned.

He and Pia, along with colleagues at Harvard and other universities, felt that a more constant pressure could and should be applied for defending against the perversities of development. They decided to found a non-government organization called Cultural Survival in 1972. Ever since, Cultural Survival has defended the cause of indigenous peoples and ethnic minorities, not only in Latin America but around the world. It has served as a clearinghouse for information and scholarly analysis as well as an underwriter of a number of projects designed to help indigenous peoples defend themselves and their rights.

Cultural Survival is now one of the longest running NGOs in the Boston area and, indeed, in the political area of defending the rights of indigenous peoples and ethnic minorities. It has gone through a number of incarnations. For example, it dabbled, with mixed success, in the area of fair trade through Cultural Survival Enterprises, working with the likes of Ben and Jerry's ice cream and Anita Roddick and the Body Shop in 1980s.[8] Dame Anita Roddick would eventually underwrite father's ten-part Millennium television series, which was shown on Public Television and is still shown in many classrooms around the world.

Meanwhile, I decided to become a political scientist in my own right, pursuing a Ph.D. at Columbia University in New York City, beginning in 1984. I took on a project to discover how the Brazilian rural workers' trade union movement managed to not only become one of the very largest labor movements in Latin America, but also one of the more progressive ones in the middle of the anti-popular military dictatorship.[9] To investigate this paradox, my research design called for long trips into Brazil's interiors. I had wanted it this way. It required that I take a page from my parents' and the anthropologists' book of methods, particularly those known as *participant observation*.

On one of these trips, my then wife, our young son David (named after his grandfather), and I traveled from Rio de Janeiro, in our small Volkswagen, all the way up to the north of what is now the state of Tocantíns (then the north of the state of Goiás). There I spent three weeks studying the history of a labor union in one of the land conflict zones in the municipality of Porto Nacional. After concluding the research on which I wrote a chapter for my book, I realized that my family was then about 250 kilometers away from one of the Sherente Indian villages my parents had taken me to about thirty-five years before, in 1963. We decided to go and visit them!

As we bounced along hundreds of kilometers of dusty dirt roads toward them through Brazil's backlands, I wondered if the Sherente would remember my family and me. I was, during the last visit in the summer of 1963, only 6 years old. I remember playing with the girls and boys of the village in a sort of childish bliss: swimming in crystalline waters with them, learning to hunt with bows and arrows, skewering hapless lizards with spears, roasting cashew nuts on makeshift fires, teasing the girls who made a point of teasing back! The Tocantíns River—mighty, fast moving, beaches exposed midstream, elegant in the dry-season countryside—was the backdrop to everything.

I wondered, would they remember David and Pia and the small boy (me), as we drove deeper into the bush; whether they would recall those strange days before any of the highways to Central Brazil were built with asphalt, when the Indians and their culture were able to more or less continue as they gradually acculturated with the surrounding Brazilian civilization encroaching upon them. I was a bit scared too.

What if they were now going to be hostile? After all, what might they know of my family's lobbying efforts, Cultural Survival, and efforts to create coalitions of pro-Indian allies around the world? These efforts—representing my parents' life work—though admirable, had all too plainly fallen short insofar as so many indigenous peoples' lands were no longer theirs, their villages were broken, their cultures destroyed. Why should they sympathize with us and our research into our and their past?

Misgivings, on my part, heightened when we spotted our first Sherente Indian, a youth who wanted to hitch a ride with us. He seemed agitated and quite nervous, but we decided to risk picking him up because at that point, although we were not invited, we were committed to entering Indian country. As we rumbled along over the rutted road, the youth told us of "white men who wanted to kill him and the Sherente." His Portuguese was minimal so I could not really understand what he was afraid of or what was bothering him. But he rode with us further and showed us the way to the nearest Indian village.

We passed a large sign pertaining to the National Foundation of the Indian (FUNAI), the Brazilian tutelary agency responsible for administering the federal government's Indian policies. It said, unmistakably, that nobody was allowed into the Sherente Indian Reserve without written permits from the Brazilian government. Flashes of memory came to me of my father going from office to office in the then capital, Rio de Janeiro, on his months' long quixotic quest for permits to go to the interior. This time, we had done nothing of the sort. I looked at the Sherente Indian in my car and he looked at me and waved me on. I made my calculus. Between the Brazilians and Brazilian law and the Sherente and Sherente ways, inside of Indian Territory, I would go with the Sherente.

And then we saw the village up ahead of us. My apprehension peaked. How would they respond to our technically illegal incursion? Would they be unfriendly or worse? Would they understand me? Would I be encountering people who spoke Portuguese well? How was I to behave? Should I touch them physically and effusively as is the normal Brazilian custom, or should I be more reserved? How might I expect them to behave? Was I crazy to have taken this uncertain path?

As in most back-country encounters, men and women gathered in the village center to see who was coming. They wore plain Brazilian-style clothes, long ago having eschewed the virtually naked habit of their ancestors. They strained to examine us from afar, as we bounced up to them through the dust. They noted that we had a Sherente youth with us which certainly helped to break the ice. I stopped the car and got out and asked who might be the chief. A slight, mature-looking Sherente woman came forward and, with a serious expression, asked me in heavily accented Portuguese who I was. I explained that I was a foreigner from the United States, that I had been here many years before, and that my parents were David and Pia Maybury-Lewis, anthropologists who had lived with the Sherente and then had gone to live with the Shavante, their "cousins."

To my immense surprise and relief, the ice melted completely! She smiled. And then she gently tugged on my arm and brought me to greet the others. She said: "Of course we remember you and your parents! You were small then, but big now! How is David? How is Pia? Will they come to see us? We miss them and you!" And then, the painful question, "Perhaps you can help us, because it has not been at all easy here . . ." I looked at them and then into my heart with both happiness and relief, and then shame at knowing that my efforts and even the efforts of my parents and of all those who have written this book and the many others who have worked on behalf of the "indigenous cause" really have not even blunted the onslaught of development, much less shielded the Indians from it. But now here these people welcomed me, for the second time in my life, into their midst, sharing with me their hopes and anxieties, treating me like a long-lost cousin who has come back from the war. I was humbled and elated.

My wife and I learned that they would be performing a special and rare name-giving ceremony for the young men who would be changing their names to ones more appropriate for warriors. They asked me if I would care to participate. I said I could hardly play the role, and besides, which moiety would I end up belonging to in the Sherente's binary social organization? The chiefs insisted that I participate, but they agreed that I had raised an important point. After a lengthy consultation, they decided that

I would join their infrequently performed forest ritual and would end up representing both of the moieties; an unusual compromise. Once again, the Sherente expressed their traditional flair for all things political! I would spend a day and a night in the forest, eating nothing until the climax of the ritual. They would paint me from head to toe and would initiate me in mock indigenous combat maneuvers. After our retreat from the village, we were to "attack" it in a stylized raid. The elders insisted to us young initiates that we were under no circumstances to break into a smile or laugh. This was serious business and to be performed as such. So we geared ourselves up, darkened the war paint on our bodies, crouched low, and, upon a signal from the chief, dashed into the village with our clubs, spears, and bows and arrows. Impressed, the villagers not participating directly stood by and observed us as we circled the entire village and then concentrated into a circular, rhythmic dance at the climax of the name-giving ceremony.

The women, meanwhile, had been baking meat for hours in an underground oven covered with palm leaves. When we finally broke our fast, one woman came over to me and gave me a slab of roast meat weighing, I estimated, four pounds! We gorged and the ceremony was over.

In 2005, Hipa Shavante, the very first Shavante Indian to graduate from the University of São Paulo, made his way to Cambridge to visit Cultural Survival and my father. The Shavante, of course, also remember well who David was.

———

In 2006, one weekday morning, I was walking to work in Cambridge, in springtime, and I noticed a fabulous garden at a house belonging to Harvard University. I went over to the professional gardener who was working there to compliment him on the state of his flower beds. I sized him up and began speaking with him in Spanish. He said he did not understand Spanish. Surprised, I asked him where he was from. He smiled and said he was Brazilian. Now, doubly intrigued, I asked him, in Portuguese, from where in Brazil? And he said, "Sou de Mato Grosso do Sul!" He apparently had made his way, most likely as a clandestine immigrant, from the same region in which the Shavante had made their final stand to face the onslaught of civilization.

I walked on strangely happy, knowing that now ordinary people, from ordinary backgrounds, in the deepest interiors of Brazil, can find their way to the United States to attempt to make a new life for themselves, right in the gardens of the University where David taught for forty-four years. The memory of my parents' huge difficulties in getting to that far away back-country in the 1950s and 60s—by ocean liner, *teco-teco*, horse, and on foot—was becoming a distant, somewhat ironic, and nostalgic memory.

That man from Mato Grosso, as the Brazilians would say, "*me deu saudades.*"

Notes

1. In addition, throughout his adult life he was very good at a sport played at Harvard but dominated internationally by the Pakistanis: squash.

2. The classic text on the period is Thomas E. Skidmore's *Politics in Brazil 1930–1964: An Experiment in Democracy* (New York: Oxford University Press, 1967).

3. Incidentally, the episode almost cost me my life. Infants are subject to dehydration when struggling with gastric distress in hunting camps in Central Brazil or anywhere else. At a certain point, I was so sick that my mother was obliged to leave the field, make the long journey back to São Paulo, and seek a doctor for me. I apparently just barely escaped with my life. Astrid Sternberg, a Jewish lady from Berlin who had herself just escaped the Holocaust and was a close friend of ours, scolded Pia severely for her and David's recklessness and then paid for a good São Paulo doctor, whom my parents (poor graduate students) could not afford, to hydrate me again and make me whole.

4. Roberto Cardoso de Oliveira, among my father's very closest friends in Brazil, passed away in 2006 and is greatly missed by us all.

5. Recent research presented by a variety of scholars working on contemporary Brazil, at the 2007 Latin American Studies Association conference in Montreal, concurs on this crucial point.

6. Though Latin America is, in the aggregate, not the poorest region in the world, it is very much the most unequal in terms of income and asset distribution: something that persists across political regime changes.

7. Brazil's capital, after all, had been moved from Rio to Brasilia in 1960.

8. At that time, in the late 1980s, much to my surprise, I received a phone call from Dame Anita Roddick at my Rio apartment, out of the blue, asking if I was free to take her to the Amazon to, among other things, go to the gathering of the Cayapó Indians who were protesting a major dam project on the Xingú River in the Amazon. I was to accompany Anita on what turned out to be her first trip to the Amazon region. She went on to do a great deal of business there with indigenous peoples, a project that sometimes landed her in heated controversy. Her Body Shop franchise company would become one of the most successful "green" companies in the world. Dame Anita Roddick passed away in August 2007.

9. I eventually completely rewrote and edited this dissertation. See Biorn Maybury-Lewis, *The Politics of the Possible: The Brazilian Rural Workers' Trade Union Movement, 1964–1985* (Philadelphia: Temple University Press, 1994).

Acknowledgments

We are grateful to the David Rockefeller Center for Latin American Studies (DRCLAS) at Harvard University for the generous funding that made possible the initial conference. The directors, John Coatsworth and, more recently, Merilee Grindle, maintained the continued personal interest essential for transforming a set of preliminary ideas into a conference and then a book. DRCLAS staff was, as usual, enormously helpful and enthusiastic. Edwin Ortiz provided all of the logistical support and budgetary discipline needed for the conference. Steve Reifenberg, Director, and Daniela Merino, Intern, at the DRCLAS-Chile office provided the research and imaging for the cover. David Rockefeller Center Publications Director June Erlick and copyeditor Anna Safran were, again as usual, professionally rigorous, personally interested, and pleasures to work with.

Translation of chapters from Spanish and Portuguese was done by Richard Dodge (Bengoa chapter), Pilar Pérez (Briones and Delrio chapter) and Thaddeus Gregory Blanchette (Pacheco chapter).

INDEX